CE

Britain's Economic Prospects Reconsidered

Britain's Economic Prospects

Edited by Richard E. Caves
Richard N. Cooper, Edward F. Denison, John H. Kareken,
Lawrence B. Krause, Richard A. and Peggy B. Musgrave,
Merton J. Peck, William G. Shepherd, David C. Smith,
Lloyd Ulman

The Brookings Institution

Britain's Economic Prospects Reconsidered

Edited by
Sir Alec Cairncross

London · George Allen & Unwin Ltd
Ruskin House   Museum Street

Printed in Great Britain
in 10 on 11 point Times New Roman type
by Billing & Sons Limited,
Guildford and London

Contents

Preface

by the Provost of Ditchley

This book is a sequel to *Britain's Economic Prospects*, the report
issued in 1968 by the Brookings Institution[1] and universally accepted
as the most thorough and comprehensive study of the British
economy to have appeared. Two years later, just after the British
General Election, six of the American economists who prepared the
Brookings Report met with a number of other leading experts from
Britain and the United States at a week-end conference at Ditchley
Park to review the findings of the Report. Papers submitted to the
conference by four of the British economists covered the same ground
as the Brookings Report – the role of demand management, trade
and balance of payments problems, labour policies and industrial
policies. The conference also had before it a fifth paper on fiscal
policy and stabilization, by Mr G. D. N. Worswick, which took
issue with some of the views expressed in the Brookings Report.

These papers form the core of this book, which also contains an
account of the conference discussions and concluding reflections by
its Chairman, Sir Alec Cairncross, formerly Head of the Government Economic Service; to these, the editor of the Brookings Report,
Professor Caves, has added a brief reconsideration of its conclusions.

Britains Economic Prospects Reconsidered is neither a detailed
critique of the Brookings Report nor a rejoinder to it, but rather an
attempt to reassess British performance and policies in the light of
experience since devaluation. Its central concern is the question
why economic growth in Britain since the Second World War has
been slower than in other countries.

The Ditchley Foundation is very happy to have been concerned
with the initiation and organization of the conference, to have been
host to its meetings, and to be associated with this book. The enterprise fell squarely within its continuing purpose of the study of
matters of common concern to the peoples of Britain and America,
and of education in such matters. I would like to offer comprehensive thanks to all those who took part, at every stage, mentioning
particularly among them Mr Gordon Richardson, through whose
good offices Messrs Schroder Wagg & Co. generously provided the
necessary finance, and Sir Alec Cairncross, who, besides his contribu-

[1] Washington, Brookings Institution; London, George Allen & Unwin Ltd.

tions to this book, organized the contributed papers, chaired the conference, edited the proceedings and was, throughout, the indispensable and indefatigable leader and consultant.

H. V. HODSON

Introduction

by Sir Alec Cairncross

When the Brookings Report appeared it was greeted in Britain with respect and envy as a *tour de force* and there were many wry comments on the failure of British economists to do the job themselves. Unfortunately, although the Report became a kind of bible it was never submitted to a really thorough analysis except perhaps in some comparatively brief reviews in the learned journals, including those contributed by the authors of papers in this volume. Yet the appropriate response would surely have been to organize a debate on the Report among British economists. Proposals for such a debate were made from time to time and arrangements for a Conference at Sunningdale were well advanced when I left the Treasury at the beginning of 1969. Nothing came of the idea at that time; but, thanks to pressure from a number of people (including Professor Harry Johnson, Kermit Gordon, and Peter Jay), the idea was revived and extended to make provision for the inclusion of American as well as British economists. The Provost of Ditchley took the initiative in calling a conference and in offering the unique facilities available at Ditchley. Through Mr Gordon Richardson, the merchant banking house of Schroder Wagg and Co. generously agreed to meet the cost of the conference. The Brookings Institution and the National Institute of Economic and Social Research acted as joint sponsors.

The participation of several of the authors of the Brookings Report was not designed to produce a confrontation. What was aimed at was a joint enquiry without any line-up by nationality. The conference was an effort to revive interest in the fundamental questions about the British economy that were apt to be neglected in the middle of an election campaign. Put briefly, the terms of reference of the conference were to discuss what makes the British economy tick, with all the overtones in that expression of heavy debt and an imminent explosion.

The purpose of the conference was also to bring the Brookings Report back on stage by issuing in a new volume the conference papers and an account of the main lines of discussion. The papers were intended as an attempt to draw out the issues as they appeared two years after the publication of the Report rather than as a critique of its findings.

11

Although the conference was attended by several ex-government economists, and one or two government economists, it was essentially an academic occasion. Government departments had no hand in the preparation of any of the main papers; of their authors only one, Michael Posner, had served in government in the recent past, dividing his time between the Treasury and the University of Cambridge.

Broadly speaking, the first paper deals with the subject-matter of Chapter 1 of the Brookings Report, and to a lesser extent of Chapter 2 (monetary policy had been the subject of a conference elsewhere), the second with Chapters 4 and 5, and the third with Chapters 3 and 8. The fourth gallantly takes on all the others, i.e. Chapters 6, 7, 9 and 10. The first two papers are on the macro-economic aspects and the second two on the micro-economic aspects of the British economy. In addition, two other papers were circulated. One of them, by David Worswick, is included in this volume and should be taken in conjunction with Professor Matthews' paper as a comment on British demand management. The second, the White Paper on the cost of joining the EEC, is not included here but epitomizes many of the underlying issues of the conference.

The digest of the conference discussion, which follows these papers, was prepared by Conrad Blyth. It does not attempt to do more than provide an indication of the main points that were raised without seeking to recapitulate the whole discussion.

A commentary on the discussion is also included, based on my own summing-up at the last session of the conference. This should be treated merely as the reflections of the Chairman listening to the successive sessions of the conference and not as an attempt to set out any conclusions that might have won general agreement.

Finally, Professor Caves was kind enough to respond to an invitation shortly before this volume went to press to let us have his own reflections on the Report two years after its appearance. The reader will, I hope, be encouraged to go back to the Report and find more food for thought in it after looking at it through the eyes of all the contributors to this volume.

1 The Role of Demand Management

by R. C. O. Matthews

The Brookings Report's conclusions on demand management may be roughly summarized as follows:

1. There is no clear case for believing that the average level of demand in the British economy in the post-war period was either too high or too low.
2. The authorities did not make a very good job of stabilizing demand around this average. The resulting stop-go cycles had harmful effects, especially on investment.
3. The instruments used for demand management had undesirable side-effects. More use should have been made of fiscal measures and less of monetary measures.
4. These faults in demand management, however, were not the main reason for the poor productivity performance of the UK relative to other countries. The main reasons for this lie at the micro level, that is to say in more general inefficiencies pervading the economy.

I shall not attempt in this chapter a detailed critique of the Brookings appraisal of the successes and failures of demand management as such and of its various instruments. The problems relating to individual instruments of fiscal and monetary policy do not lend themselves to discussion in a single chapter; and the monetary aspects have been the subject of a recent conference.[1] Section I of this chapter discusses the general aims of demand management in the British economy and its place in government economic policy. This follows up the points raised by David Worswick in his chapter on 'Fiscal Policy and Stabilization in Britain'.[2] Sections II and III deal with the effects of demand behaviour on the long-run real performance of the economy.

I. DEMAND MANAGEMENT: AIMS AND PROSPECTS

There would now be fairly general agreement that post-war fluctua-

[1] D. R. Croome and H. G. Johnson (eds.), *Money in Britain 1959–69* (1970).
[2] Originally published in *Money Credit and Banking* (1969). See pp. 36–60 below.

tions in the British economy are not to be regarded as simply due to the authorities' lack of technical skill in demand management. Mistakes of a technical kind have undoubtedly been made from time to time. In addition to certain well-known specific occasions, the Brookings authors attach importance – perhaps rather more than most British economists would do – to persistent tardiness in action due to failure to allow for the lag between demand changes and unemployment changes. But the chief reason why steps were sometimes taken that had a destabilizing character was that *stabilization* of the level of activity was not as such the objective. For most of the post-war period, a better summary description of the objective would be achievement of as high a level of activity as was compatible with the state of the balance of payments. Pursuit of this objective meant that courses were changed as changes occurred in the balance of payments and in the authorities' expectations about it.

The above description of the objective is, of course, an over-simplification. In particular, it does not take account of the scope for choice that existed about the amount of direct protection that should be given to the foreign balance by restrictions on trade and payments. But, as over-simplifications go, it is a better description of the objective than stabilization.

This being so, the answer to the question whether the net effect of government intervention on the level of activity was stabilizing or destabilizing does not provide a measure of the technical success or failure of the authorities in making demand behave as intended. The question remains, of course, one of interest in itself, particularly in connection with the sources of the fluctuations in the economy. Dow, in a well-known passage, held that government action was in net destabilizing and a main source of the fluctuations that occurred.[1] This is supported, with some qualifications, by the Brookings authors. The present writer has argued that although the authorities' actions were destabilizing on some occasions, more importance should be attached to endogenous sources of fluctuations than is done by Dow.[2] Worswick, in his paper (Chapter 2 of this book), has pointed out the difficulty of resolving the issue and the objections to measures proposed by the Musgraves in the Brookings Report and by others.

In principle the question could be answered properly only by a

[1] J. C. R. Dow, *The Management of the British Economy, 1945–60*, (1965), p. 384.
[2] R. C. O. Matthews, 'Postwar Business Cycles in the United Kingdom', in M. Bronfenbrenner (ed.), *Is the Business Cycle Obsolete?* (1969), pp. 99–135.

simulation exercise in a full-scale econometric model. This would compare what actually happened with what results when 'neutral' values of all government decision variables are substituted for actuals over a substantial period of time. Full allowance would thus be made for lagged and indirect effects of government action. Even supposing we had a model that we trusted sufficiently for such a refined purpose, there would remain a difficulty in defining 'neutral' policy in an economy where government, including nationalized industries, plays such a large part. The interest of such an exercise, if it could be carried out, would be in connection with the stability or instability properties of the economy rather than with the *ex post* award of marks to the government.

Demand management could achieve both stabilization and accommodation to the state of the balance of payments if changes in the level of domestic demand were the only source of disturbance in the balance of payments. But the latter condition is never likely to be fulfilled, so the two objectives conflict. This very general and elementary point holds whether the fundamental balance-of-payments position is strong or weak. The British authorities during most of the post-war period were confronted by the more specific problem that the balance of payments has been in fundamental disequilibrium – and getting worse – in the sense that it was all right only when either the level of activity was lower than desired or trade and payments restrictions were more severe than desired.

It is obvious that in these circumstances the task of demand management is an impossible one, as Worswick convincingly argues; it cannot achieve both a satisfactory level of demand and a satisfactory balance of payments. What is *not* so obvious *a priori*, however, is why the attempt to square the circle should lead to *cyclical* movements. If it is a correct interpretation of post-war British cycles that it did, or at least that it strengthened other cyclical tendencies, this may be taken to indicate the tendency for economic behaviour patterns, including here not least the behaviour patterns of governments, to translate non-oscillatory stimuli into oscillatory results.

The foregoing relates to the period up to 1967. Since devaluation, there have been some significant changes in demand management and in its environment. First, devaluation seems to have rectified the fundamental balance-of-payments disequilibrium. Secondly, the authorities have become acutely conscious of the danger that an upswing, once stimulated, is liable to develop unexpected momentum: failure to appreciate this was one of the more strictly technical faults of earlier demand-management policy. Thirdly, the authorities

15

appear to have been converted to the Paishite view that the economy is best run with rather more slack than in the past (more than in the *average* of post-war years, not merely more than in post-war cyclical peaks). This last change has had far less adverse political repercussions than would have been expected some years ago. The public appears gradually to have adjusted its expectations to a combination of perpetual squeeze and perpetual inflation.

If the strengthening of the balance-of-payments position turns out to have been fundamental, the context of demand management will certainly be very different from the past. However, it is unlikely that even so demand management will become separated from the balance of payments. It has certainly not done so yet. The Chancellor's 1970 Budget speech retains the tone of the company chairman announcing what dividends (growth) can be afforded in the light of the year's profits (balance-of-payments surplus). This is still the frame of mind that is liable to generate stop–go. No one can judge with any confidence whether the state of the balance of payments at any point of time is transitory or permanent, and, once the objective of stabilization has been compromised by balance-of-payments considerations, there is a strong tendency for the Chancellor's decision on the appropriate 'dividends' to be guided by vagaries of optimism and pessimism, not to say political expediency. All this is distressing to the economist steeped in Keynesian–Meadean principles, who recognizes that the state of the balance of payments *may* provide a guide to whether the economy is overheated or the reverse, but denies that it necessarily does so.

Experience has shown that countries with basically strong balance-of-payments positions, like Italy and Japan, while not immune from this kind of trouble, suffer less from it than the UK has done. This is the respect in which devaluation has altered the broad prospects, although it remains uncertain whether devaluation has corrected the tendency apparent in the 1960s for the balance-of-payments position to deteriorate over time (as distinct from the tendency for it to be bad absolutely).

Given the absence of fundamental disequilibrium in the balance of payments, it is not difficult to state what the ideal policy should be: demand management should steer a straight course, aiming to maintain the level of demand that is considered to be the best from the point of view of long-run output maximization. Fluctuations in the foreign balance originating from fluctuations in domestic demand would not then arise; and fluctuations in the foreign balance due to other causes would not be allowed to affect demand but would be dealt with by drawing on reserves or other compensatory short-term capital movements.

A basically strong balance-of-payments position goes some way towards permitting such a policy. It strengthens a country's international credit standing, and so makes temporary borrowing easier; of course it also helps it to build up reserves.

Despite the apparent improvement in our fundamental position, there are several reasons, some good, some bad, why it is unlikely that demand-management policy will in the near future be independent of balance-of-payments considerations. In the first place, excess domestic demand may indeed sometimes be manifested by an adverse foreign balance earlier or more clearly than it is manifested by domestic indicators; so it may be quite consistent with a policy of steering demand on a straight course to apply restrictions when the balance of payments deteriorates. In the second place, we are still far from being in a position when we have enough reserves or a sufficiently well-established international credit standing to be able to shrug off a temporary adverse balance. In the third place the balance-of-payments obsession has bitten so deep after all these years that the country's economic performance is largely judged by its balance of payments, and any sizeable deterioration in it is bound to appear as a failure of policy. In the fourth place, not many people really believe that the present (May 1970) low level of demand is the ideal one from the domestic point of view. There is bound to be pressure to allow it to rise if the foreign balance remains favourable. Indeed some rise is envisaged in current official policy. We have here the uncertainty of aims already several times referred to. The deeply ingrained habit of treating the balance of payments as the main object of policy is still preventing us from squarely facing the question what balance between supply and demand we *do* consider best from the domestic point of view.

In these circumstances the Brookings authors are probably right in believing that balance-of-payments considerations are likely to continue to play a large part in British demand management, regrettable though this may be. It is no doubt against this background that one should view their recommendation (p. 489) that consumption should take the brunt of short-term adjustments in demand and that investment should be kept on a steady path. From the point of view of welfare theory, this is a paradoxical prescription. One of the motives for saving is to even out the flow of consumption over time, in face of a diminishing marginal utility of consumption schedule. To cut down on provision for the future in a period of temporary

B   17 stringency is therefore a rational policy. It is an interesting and debatable question how far this principle continues to apply when what is at issue is reduction in the rate of growth of consumption rather than absolute reduction.

The prescription of stabilizing investment is based, of course, on the supposed advantage of smooth planning of investment programmes. But it is still rather a puzzling recommendation if one is thinking solely of *stabilizing* demand. If investment *is* kept on a steady path, what is it that the short-term adjustments in consumption are intended to offset? Surely not stockbuilding, which is too volatile to be easily offset in this way; or public authorities' current expenditure, which has not been a source of much cyclical disturbance. And surely the idea is not that consumption should be stimulated when exports are bad and restrained when exports are good – a rational policy, indeed, from the Keynesian point of view, as was argued above, but one requiring a degree of disregard of the balance of payments which is hardly in prospect. No doubt they were thinking the opposite, and thus not really about stabilization at all: that when the *balance of payments* calls for restrictions, they should fall on consumption rather than investment; and, as an additional point, that they should fall on consumption generally rather than on the parts of consumption affected by hire-purchase regulation.

Apart from this last qualification the recommendation is not so different from the policy actually adopted. Efforts have been made to stabilize at least certain priority classes of investment, especially manufacturing. They have not, however, been very successful, though perhaps more so in the last few years than formerly. If substantial fluctuations in other items in GDP persist, the stabilization of investment is likely to be a difficult task.

It is not difficult to establish that demand-management policies have not rated an 'A' as far as stabilization is concerned, and that it was hardly possible for them to do so, given the constraints. It is also obvious that things will be easier in the future if the underlying weakness in the balance of payments turns out to have been corrected. The more interesting and important question, however, is how much difference the failures and successes of demand management have made to the long-run performance of the economy; and hence how much difference will be made by any future improvement (or deterioration) in this regard. The Brookings view on this, as already mentioned, is that they made some difference, but were not at the root of the trouble.

This question will now be considered. The effects of the *average*

18

level of demand attained will be considered in Section II; those of *fluctuations around the average* in Section III. This distinction is to some extent artificial, but it provides a convenient framework. What follows is concerned with the effects of the levels and fluctuations in level of demand that have been actually experienced. It thereby sidesteps the question how far the observed behaviour of demand was determined by government policy and how far it was determined by other influences. Because of the difficulty of answering this question, it is more helpful to focus attention on the effects of demand behaviour rather than on the effects of demand management.

II. WAS THE AVERAGE LEVEL OF DEMAND ABOUT RIGHT?

The affirmative answer given by Brookings to this question represents agnosticism about the net balance of offsetting considerations rather than a firmly held conviction. However, as will be seen, it has some quite important implications.

Perfect success in avoiding fluctuations has in principle a simple criterion, that there should be no fluctuations at all. No such simple criterion is available of an ideal average level of demand. Nor are differences between possible alternative levels negligible. Even within the context of the general high employment of the post-war world, there have been significant differences between countries. If unemployment is taken as the indicator, the average pressure of demand has, of course, been higher in the UK than in North America; but at least in the 1960s it has been lower in the UK than in most of the other major industrial countries with which our general economic performance is unfavourably compared.

Estimated average unemployment percentage, adjusted to US definitions, 1959–66 (1961–6 for Sweden)

Canada	5·5
United States	5·4
Italy	4·1
United Kingdom	2·6
France	2·3
Japan	1·6
Sweden	1·5
West Germany	0·6

Source: A. F. Neef and R. A. Holland, 'Comparative Unemployment Rates, 1964–6', *Monthly Labor Review*, April 1967, pp. 18–20.

Most of these countries, incidentally, have regional disparities pulling up average unemployment no less than we do.[1] So it will not do to say demand was obviously higher than in the past and high enough for unemployment not to be a social problem, so there was not much scope for it to be lower: there *was* scope for it to be lower, as well as higher. There have, moreover, been differences over time as well as between countries; apart from cyclical fluctuations, there has been a trend towards less tightness in the labour market in the UK in the course of the post-war period.

As a preliminary to asking whether the average level of demand was right, we have to specify: right for what purpose? The level of demand affects not only the level (and possibly the rate of growth) of production, but also the balance of payments and the rate of price and wage inflation. Clearly if equilibrium in the balance of payments and the avoidance of inflation are regarded as the only objectives, and other policy variables, such as the exchange rate, are taken as given, the average level of demand that has prevailed must be held to have been too high. But these objections had to be weighed against the desirability of high production and the social ills of unemployment. Now, while such a trade-off between conflicting aims may be necessary in practice in deciding what the best level of demand is, it is important that the actual effect of demand on each of the objectives should be properly assessed. Such an assessment should not be corrupted by the thought that a compromise in the interests of one of the other objectives is likely to be called for in the end. Otherwise we do not know what the terms of the trade-off are. So the question now under consideration, what is the effect of the average level of demand on the level and growth rate of production, is important, even if policy-makers were not free to be guided by it alone.

The Brookings authors incline to the view that, at least within the practically relevant range, the well-known advantages of high demand for productivity growth – high inducement to invest, reduction in the restrictive practices that result from fear of unemployment, and so on – are just about balanced by the equally well-known disadvantages in the form of absence of competition and general slackness. (Labour hoarding is also mentioned as a source of waste resulting from high demand, but the treatment here is a little confusing: the statement in the introduction [p. 17] that labour hoarding has probably hampered the long-run reallocation of labour between industries is not

---

[1] A. J. Brown, 'Surveys of Applied Economics: Regional Economics, with special reference to the United Kingdom', *Economic Journal*, December 1969, p. 762.

really supported by the main discussion of the subject elsewhere in the book [pp. 329–31], which is concerned with the quite different phenomenon of short-run labour hoarding in cyclical recessions.) The Brookings authors are not impressed by the 'virtuous circle' hypothesis that prevailed in certain quarters in the early 1960s – the hypothesis of self-sustaining fast growth procured by going full steam ahead. In this they are following the swing of opinion among British economists in the last few years.[1]

The 'virtuous circle' hypothesis was, perhaps, never very convincing. On the other hand the swing of opinion away from it can hardly be said to be the result of new evidence accruing. The apparent failure of the expansionist policy in 1964–5 was a failure on the balance-of-payments side. It does not by itself refute the hypotheses that full-steam ahead *would* be good for productivity growth (and possibly even for the balance of payments in the long run). It may be suspected that the change of opinion on this point partly reflects the corruption of judgment referred to above, where the assessment of the effect of X on A is coloured by what is thought about the effect of X on B. However, the burden of proof remains with the expansionists, and Brookings is probably right to treat the 'virtuous circle' hypothesis in its extreme form as wishful thinking.

It is unlikely that a slightly higher average level of demand, or a slightly lower one for that matter, would have brought about a transformation in the British growth rate. It remains an open question whether it would have affected the growth rate to *some* degree. This has not really been the subject of systematic research, by Brookings or anyone else. On the face of it this is a serious gap in our knowledge. But it is at least arguable that to attempt more systematic research would not be very useful. Not only are there effects pulling in opposite directions; in addition, the effects are indirect. The level of demand affects the growth rate through its effects on a number of variables, such as the inducement to invest and innovate, competitiveness, flexibility, and motivation, each of which is affected also, and probably to a greater extent, by a multitude of other forces. The result also depends on where the demand impinges, and when. There is therefore no presumption that the relationship is at all stable. Comparison of different countries and periods does not suggest any

[1] An interesting commentary on the change in opinion, as reflected in the differences in emphasis between Samuel Brittan's *The Treasury under the Tories, 1951–64*, published in 1964, and its revised edition published in 1969 under the title *Steering the Economy*, is contained in A. Shepherd (pseudonym), 'The Treasury after Five Years', *The Banker*, January 1970, pp. 99–105.

clear relation between the growth rate and the pressure of demand, at least within the broad 'full employment' range. The agnosticism of the Brookings authors therefore commands sympathy. This is not to deny that deficient demand on the inter-war scale is bad for productivity growth, as well as for the level of production. This is a very important matter for comparisons over time, but less for the international comparison here mainly at issue.

All this relates to the *rate of growth* of productivity. Similar considerations relate to the *level* of productivity. It, too, is liable to be affected by competitiveness, restrictive practices and so on, and hence by the level of demand in so far as it affects them. But here there is a direct loss of output at any time by running the economy below capacity – a consideration which does not apply in connection with growth. It is therefore a stronger proposition to say that a higher average level of demand would not have led to a higher average level of output than it is to say that it would not have led to faster growth; it implies that the apparent slack due to the (average) below-full utilization of resources was an illusion, because an attempt to take it up would have created offsetting inefficiencies.

The amount of this apparent slack was not enormous but also not negligible – between 2 and 4 cent per according to how it is calculated. About 2 per cent is the figure obtained by averaging the shortfall below the peak-to-peak trend in *annual* data. Professor Paish reaches a figure of 4 per cent by taking as the standard of full productive potential a trend line passing through the *quarterly* peak with the highest level of activity in the whole period (1955 IV).[1] In saying that the level of demand was probably about right, the Brookings authors were presumably having regard both to the level of output and to its growth rate, or to some mixture of the two, such as the sum of income over the entire period. While sharing their agnosticism about the effect on the growth rate, one finds it more difficult to believe that a higher level of demand would not have meant a higher sum of output over the period as a whole.

The experience of the last few years leaves this issue unresolved. Since 1965 demand had been kept at a lower average level than previously. From the beginning of 1965 until the third quarter of 1967 output was in a downswing phase (relatively to trend) which was unusually protracted by past standards, though not unusually acute. After the third quarter of 1967 there was recovery, especially in industrial production, but the rate of growth of output remained below its trend level and unemployment remained comparatively high.

[1] F. W. Paish and J. Hennessy, *Policy for Incomes?* (1967), pp. 34–42.

In the downswing phase, 1965–7, productivity per man grew significantly faster than in previous downswings, and the performance in respect of productivity per man hour was still better. In 1968–70 the ground previously gained was not lost, but it is not so clear that the growth rate of productivity continued to exceed previous standards. It is not possible to be categorical about this, because productivity growth from one year to the next is much affected by the phase of the cycle, and there is no past period that in the least resembles 1968–70 from the cyclical point of view.[1] Fine calculations of productivity growth rates are also hampered by suspicion of increasing unreliability of the employment data as a result of switches from employee status to self-employed status. And of course other causes besides slack demand may have been responsible for any acceleration in productivity growth.

It is usually held, and no doubt rightly, that a 'shake-out' of surplus labour took place, especially in 1966–7; that this accounted for the good productivity performance; and that it owed a good deal to the prolongation and expected further prolongation of conditions of relatively slack demand. It remains to be seen, however, exactly what this shake-out consisted of. It could represent a decision by employers to practise less labour-hoarding of the cyclical kind; in other words it could represent an increase in the short-run output-elasticity of employment. If that is the case, it does not carry with it any permanent upward shift in productive potential: it merely makes it possible for unemployment to be relatively high without output falling as much below productive potential as previous relationships would have led us to expect. On the other hand the shake-out may have involved a permanent elimination of certain forms of over-manning and thereby made possible a permanent increase in productive potential. In so far as this happened, it constitutes an argument for having *periodical* spells of slack demand. It cannot, of course, be built into an argument for having permanently slack demand, because there is no point in shaking out surplus labour if it is not subsequently put to good use. It may be concluded that the evidence of the last few years has given some degree of support to the view that reducing the pressure of demand can have a good effect on the level of productivity; but not to the point where it can be asserted that a lower pressure of demand involves no sacrifice of output at all. For the reasons indicated, it is not yet possible to say anything definite on the potentially more

[1] Differences from past cyclical patterns are discussed in *National Institute Economic Review*, February 1970, pp. 33–5.

23

important question of its effects on the rate of growth of productivity.

Let us for the sake of argument accept the hypothesis that demand *was* on average about right *from the production point of view*. Two quite strong implications then follow.

1. Criticism of policies making for stop–go must be confined strictly to the ill-effects of the variations of demand about the mean. We are debarred from the most obvious sort of criticism, the one that comes from pointing to the unused resources in the stop phases. For although an ideal policy would, on this assumption, have prevented the degree of under-utilization being as great as it was during the stops, it would also have involved foregoing some of the output produced during the go-years. The two cancel out, except in so far as the instability of stop–go was deleterious. (This implies that 'demand' is identified with 'output relative to trend'. If demand is identified with some other concept to which output stands in a non-linear relation, e.g. absorption, the same average level of 'demand' would in the absence of fluctuations have been compatible with an average level of output somewhat higher than that actually attained.)

2. We are debarred from saying that the balance of payments was protected by having undesirable recourse to deflation; for there was on average no more deflation than would have been desirable on other grounds. In fact, demand management on this reckoning was probably harmful to the balance of payments, because peaks stimulated imports more than troughs discouraged them. In other words, our fundamental balance of payments position was, if anything, better than would be supposed by just looking at the actual upshot, and the stop–go policy, dictated by balance-of-payments considerations, did not actually help the balance of payments at all.

Another apparent implication is that if the average level of demand over the whole period was about right, the average in the last few years must have been too low. However, this could perhaps be answered by saying that the structural changes resulting from devaluation made it necessary to have a greater amount of slack during the transitional period.

It may be that in interpreting Brookings as having said that the average level of demand was about right, I am reading too much into statements that are neither very categorical nor very precise (pp. 17, 488). Perhaps what they meant was rather that the right level of demand is the average, not of all years, but of all years excluding the worst cyclical troughs. If so, it makes a considerable difference to the argument, and the above implications do not then follow. But what exactly the Brookings authors meant is not the most important question, as the doctrine in its stricter form is widely held.

If the optimum level of demand from the point of view of production was rather above the actual average, then there was a loss from foregoing potential output. But whether this was so or not, it is still important to distinguish any such loss from the losses due to the fact that the level of demand fluctuated about its average. This is the subject of the next section.

III. How Much Harm Was Done by Fluctuations?

'We have not been able to measure the costs imposed by periodic demand constraint, but we believe them to have been substantial' (p. 488). In what do such costs consist, and how important are they? This question, like the question about the net effect of government action on stability, ideally calls for an econometric model of a higher degree of refinement and reliability than we are likely to have in the foreseeable future. We may approach it in the light partly of *a priori* considerations and partly of the complaints about stop–go made by observers and by interested parties.

A. The most specific point relates to capital-capacity. Given that capital-capacity has to be sufficient to provide for peak output, the average capital-output ratio for any given technique of production will be higher, the more widely output fluctuates; average total factor productivity tends to be lower as a result. Moreover, the higher the capital-output ratio, the slower will be the rate of growth of the capital stock at any given saving-output ratio. In other words, the country's savings are wastefully used because of the large margin of spare capacity that exists for most of the cycle. If output rose smoothly along a trend line instead of averaging about 98 per cent of its peak-to-peak trend, as it has actually done, the reduction in the capital-output ratio would allow an increase in the annual percentage growth rate of the capital stock on this reckoning by the same proportion, that is to say by about 0·06 of a percentage point (2 per cent of the actual growth rate of the capital stock). Allowance for disaggregation would probably raise this figure somewhat, but hardly to the point of making it very impressive. Disaggregation would raise the figure in so far as (a) fluctuations are not synchronized between indust-

25

ries, so that the average shortfall of output in each industry below its peak-to-peak trend is greater than the average shortfall of GDP below its peak-to-peak trend, or (b) the industries most affected by fluctuations have an above average capital-intensity. It is doubtful if (b) would make much difference, because although manufacturing is more capital-intensive than services and has wider fluctuations, the most capital-intensive elements in GDP (utilities and occupation of dwellings) have a low cyclical amplitude, and moreover the construction industry. which has low capital-intensity, is one of those most subject to fluctuations.

B. To the individual firm, the foregoing effect of fluctuations appears as something tending to depress the rate of return on capital. It may therefore be induced to choose techniques of low capital-intensity, so as to avoid fixed costs being too large a proportion of total costs. This will avoid or mitigate the tendency to a high capital-output ratio referred to under *A*, but at the cost of using methods of production that have a relatively low labour-productivity. This has usually been mentioned as a threat of what might happen, rather than as something that has actually happened. The large fluctuations undergone by the motor industry have not, for example, prevented it carrying out an investment programme that has increased the proportion of fixed to total costs to a marked degree.[1] A similar possibility is that expectation of fluctuating output may have induced firms to prefer *flexible* methods of production, involving the use of batch production rather than flow production, again at the cost of productivity. Here too it is difficult to produce specific instances, although of course it is possible that such considerations have been present in the choice of production techniques, notwithstanding that the point has not been made explicitly a subject of comment or complaint.

C. A point similar to *A* may apply to labour, in so far as it is treated as an overhead. If the size of the labour force is determined by the needs of peak production, labour will be under-utilized for the rest of the cycle. If instead employment *is* reduced in recession, other sorts of costs will be experienced, e.g. through labour-training costs; firms will strike a balance between the different kinds of cost in deciding what to do. Thus the source of

[1] NEDO, Economic Development Committee for the Motor Manufacturing Industry, *The Effect of Government Economic Policy on the Motor Industry* (1968), pp. 18–20.

waste is in the demand fluctuations themselves, rather than in the decision not to allow employment to fluctuate in line with them. If fluctuations were avoided, average labour productivity would be higher. Output could therefore be maintained at a higher average level than that actually achieved, without raising the average level of employment; some transfer of labour from the more unstable to the less unstable industries could occur in the process. The magnitude of the observed fluctuations in total output and employment is such as to suggest that the absence of fluctuations would have permitted output on average to be slightly over 1 per cent higher than it actually was without requiring any higher employment on the average. This is subject to deduction, as is the corresponding estimate under A, in so far as firms have to keep some margin of spare labour and capital capacity anyway to meet seasonal and other non-cyclical movements and draw on it at cyclical peaks, thus permitting productivity at peaks to be higher than would be maintainable as a permanency.

The point raised in the last paragraph, unlike the corresponding point about capital (A above) does not directly affect growth rates; this is because labour, unlike capital, is not a produced means of production. Its significance is that if employment had been kept steady at its average actual level, output could have been rather higher than *its* average actual level.

D. A very general argument may be put forward about non-linearities. It is agreed that a high level of activity is favourable to efficiency in some ways (e.g. by helping to eliminate restrictive practices) and a low level of activity is favourable to efficiency in other ways (e.g. by increasing the sharpness of competition). If both kinds of effect are subject to some sort of diminishing returns, a middling position will be best, and alternating between extremes will be bad. In other words extremes are only moderately more favourable in the respects in which they are more favourable, and they are very unfavourable in the respects in which they are unfavourable: a very high level of activity is only a little better for eliminating restrictive practices than a moderately high level of activity and it is *very* bad for competitiveness. This is so general as to be extremely intangible, but there must be something in it if we accept the idea of there being a unique level of activity that is optimum from the point of view of efficiency.

It would be possible logically to sustain the opposite point of view and to conclude that fluctuations are actually beneficial.

27

Suppose that the relationships in question are not subject to diminishing returns but rather to increasing returns, at least within a certain range: e.g. that there needs to be a quite severe recession in order to drive out the less inefficient firms and on the other hand quite an acute labour shortage in order to induce firms to adopt new capital-intensive techniques. Suppose too that advances on both fronts are needed to sustain growth; and that advances once made are not lost, whatever happens to demand. Then the best thing will be for the economy to alternate from one state to the other – just as it is better to sleep at night and be awake during the day, rather than to be half-asleep all the time. Such a view about the potentially beneficial role of fluctuations, suggested in the past by Schumpeter and Robertson, is out of favour today. But it has just enough plausibility to arouse doubts about whether perfectly steady growth is necessarily best in all circumstances.

E. The foregoing wastes from fluctuations would all arise even if firms were able to foresee them accurately. In practice they cannot, and the uncertainty may cause further costs. Thus it has been argued that uncertainty about demand for household durables has led firms to adopt short pay-off periods for investment. More generally, it is held that uncertainty inhibits rational planning and causes decisions to be taken on a hand-to-mouth basis, not only in the private sector but also by nationalized industries, local authorities, and spending departures of the central government.

This is a kind of ill-effect from stop–go that is most difficult to assess. It *could* be important, and it is often alleged; but direct evidence of it is rather thin.

There is no reason to doubt that costs under some or all of these headings did result from stop–go. A serious objection to regarding them as a *major* source of Britain's poor performance compared with other countries is that the amplitude of fluctuations in the UK has not been large by international standards.[1] The standard deviation of the annual growth rate has been markedly lower than in most other countries. Amplitude of fluctuations is not an unambiguous concept, and alternative measures give somewhat different results;

[1] T. Wilson, 'Instability and the Rate of Growth', *Lloyds Bank Review*, July 1966; *idem*, 'Instability and Growth: An International Comparison, 1950–65', in D. H. Aldcroft and P. Fearon (eds.), *Economic Growth in 20th-Century Britain* (1969), pp. 184–95; E. Lundberg, *Instability and Economic Growth* (1968), Chapter 3 (see especially pp. 86 and 89).

but on any reckoning it cannot be held that deviations from the trend-line have been conspicuously larger in the UK than elsewhere. It is true that the rate of growth in recession phases in the UK has been brought down to a lower level than it has in recession phases in other countries; but this is to be debited to our slow average growth rate rather than to the magnitude of our cycles. It is true also that there are certain differences in the exact shape of cycles between countries. Ours have been unusually regular and rather short, and the relative durations of the downswing and upswing phases have tended to be more nearly equal than in most other countries. But it seems rather far-fetched to attach much significance to minor differences of this sort.

A more substantial point concerns the impact of fluctuations on individual industries. Although the UK ranks low among countries in the magnitude of fluctuations in GNP, it ranks nearly at the top in the magnitude of fluctuations in consumer durables.[1] This doubtless reflects the unusual degree of reliance placed by the British authorities on consumer credit control as an instrument of demand management. It gives some support to the complaints about stop–go that have come from producers of consumer durables (especially cars and washing machines). Investment in machinery and equipment, by contrast, has been very stable by international standards.

I suspect, however, that many of the complaints made about the effects of stop–go are not really about fluctuations. In part they are simply complaints about the average level of demand being kept too low; this applies notably to the complaints made by the motor industry. In part they are the result of false expectations, in the following sense.

It is certainly true that there have been periods when demand has been managed in such a way as to keep total output well below what was possible. However, the constraints that appeared to be the result of demand management, and which accordingly were felt as arbitrary and frustrating, to some extent merely reflected the underlying limitations of productive potential. Not all elements of expenditure reached cyclical peaks simultaneously – in particular peaks in consumer durables have tended to precede those in investment. Moreover, some classes of expenditure were never allowed to reach such high levels as it appeared that they would, because the brakes were imposed before the plans approved in the go-phases had been fully translated into action. People tend to feel that there is a certain 'natural' level and growth rate of their expenditure, namely that

[1] Wilson, 'Instability and the Rate of Growth', *op. cit.*

which would be possible if artificial brakes were not being imposed, i.e. if there were no balance-of-payments problem. If they all identify this with their own peaks, frustration is inevitable, because not all sectors can sustain their own actual or hoped for peak levels of spending simultaneously without outrunning the economy's potential. In this way the continual harping on the balance of payments as the key problem has tended to arouse false expectations about what would be possible once the economy had 'got round the corner'. But to what extent they have actually led to worse performance is much less clear.

The most important unsettled question is the effect on investment. As the Brookings authors give a good deal of prominence to the low level of investment, it will be useful now to consider it more specifically, looking not only at stop–go but also at other factors that may have served to keep it lower than it was in other countries.

There are two general types of explanation of why investment in Britain in the post-war period has been lower than in other countries.

The first is that it was no more than the natural concomitant of other more deep-seated causes of relatively slow growth, including here both unavoidable causes, such as the limited scope for transferring labour from agriculture, and also causes of a potentially avoidable kind, such as lack of enterprise or motivation. Given that causes of both these kinds were tending to make for a slow growth rate, a correspondingly limited scope for expansion of the capital stock was to be expected.

The second approach is in terms of influences tending to keep down investment as such. The suggestion here is that other more general causes of slow growth were not necessarily absent, but that any obstacles they placed in the way of investment were reinforced to a significant extent by forces specifically operating to keep down investment; and that the resulting low level of investment was an important contributory cause of the slow growth.

Various forces of this second kind have been suggested at one time or another as having tended to make for a quantitatively inadequate level of investment. They include the following: (a) stop–go, as creating uncertainty, short pay-off periods, and underutilization of capacity; (b) unscientific methods of investment appraisal, tending to produce or rationalize timidity and conservatism; (c) inadequate savings, both private and public (this is associated with the suggestion that too much use has been made of monetary as opposed to fiscal restraints on expenditure); (d) pre-emption of the resources of the investment-goods industries by armaments expenditure in the early

30

part of the post-war period; (e) sundry policies designed for social or other purposes but having an incidental adverse effect on investment; for example, withholding industrial development certificates for investment projects in the more prosperous regions of the country may in some cases have prevented investment altogether instead of having its intended effect of diverting it to the development areas.[1]

Each of the suggestions in the last paragraph has some plausibility, and others could be added. But any attempt to find the main explanation of our comparatively low investment in terms of purely quantitative obstacles to investment as such is open to a serious general objection. If this were right, we should expect to find macro-economic indicators of capital shortage. But we do not. If investment opportunities were being allowed to pile up because of lack of saving or lack of enterpreneurial confidence, we should expect to find a rise in the profit rate over time; those firms that *had* made large additions to their capital stock should be being richly rewarded in the environment of general capital shortage. In fact profit rates have tended to fall.

Admittedly profit rates may be affected by taxation and other extraneous factors, as well as being difficult to measure statistically, and so may not be a good indicator of capital shortage. But the same conclusion can be reached without reference to profit rates, by looking at the trend in the capital-output ratio. In the post-war period this has tended to rise slightly in Britain and to fall significantly in most other countries. This is the opposite of what would be expected if the trouble lay in overall discouragement to investment resulting in or from excessively high cut off-rates. If underlying investment opportunities were accumulating at much the same rate as in the other countries where investment and the rate of growth of the capital stock are higher, the British capital-output ratio should be tending to fall. A similar argument, with implicit reference to a model with wholly 'embodied' technical progress, has been put forward by those who have pointed to the high ICOR as an indication that a deficient *quantity* of investment has not been the main trouble.

This line of argument does not, of course, rule out the possibility that there may have been some forces tending to keep investment decisions at too low a level in relation to the real opportunities. But it seems to me a decisive objection to regarding such forces as

[1] The Hunt Committee considered this particular point and found some evidence that it had occurred, but did not believe it was quantitatively important. *The Intermediate Areas*, Cmnd. 3998, 1969, pp. 102–6.

31

the whole or chief reason for investment having been lower in this country than elsewhere. We therefore come back to the first of the two approaches referred to above, that which regards the low level of investment as part of a more general phenomenon and the result of investment opportunities, as seen by those making investment decisions, being low.

This argument is subject to some qualification in so far as investment has been misdirected as well as quantitatively inadequate. Some of the forces referred to above will tend to produce this effect. Misdirected investment will tend to earn a lower profit rate and to result in less addition to output than investment that is optimally allocated. In so far as misdirection of investment causes the capital stock to become *increasingly* ill-adjusted to needs, it will make for a falling profit rate and a rising capital-output ratio. This could in principle offset and conceal a tendency in the opposite direction resulting from increasing quantitative scarcity of capital. But this argument merges into the first approach in placing major emphasis on inefficiencies of some sort.

These inefficiencies, on which the first approach is based, could be more or less directly connected with the investment decision as such. For example, restrictive practices by labour may inhibit investment, among their other ill effects, but their causes and consequences are best viewed in broader terms. Reference may here be made to two hypothesis suggesting inefficiency of a kind particularly affecting investment. These hypotheses both receive some degree of support in the Brookings Report, although they are quite different and indeed on the face of it may appear inconsistent.

The first of these is the 'defensive investment' hypothesis of Lamfalussy. The idea is that because of early industrialization Britain started the post-war period with an unusually large stock of old capital, and that subsequent investment was too largely geared to complementing it, when it would have been better to scrap it and start afresh. The hypothesis was first put forward by Lamfalussy[1] with reference to excessive concentration of investment in declining *industries* such as coal and railways; as such it related to the early post-war period only and can hardly be sustained for the post-war period as a whole. In Lamfalussy's second book[2] the emphasis was shifted to an analogous but different point: the existence of a large stock of old capital in Britain was held to have created a tendency to do too much patching up and improvement of existing factories

---

[1] A. Lamfalussy, *Investment and Growth in Mature Economics* (1961).
[2] A. Lamfalussy, *The United Kingdom and the Six* (1963).

and not enough building of complete new factories. Evidence for this comes from the low ratio of buildings as opposed to equipment in British industrial investment.

This interesting hypothesis has often been discussed since it was proposed, but not much has been done to test it further. The evidence in its favour cited by Brookings (pp. 16 and 326) does not stand up to examination. The evidence is an inverse correlation found between initial capital-intensity and change in capital-intensity over time as given by Pyatt for twenty-eight industries over the period 1948–60. The rationale of this is that a high initial capital-intensity indicates the presence of 'an old, highly integrated and large stock of capital' which would serve to discourage investment in totally new facilities. The relevance of this test can be criticized on several grounds; but the most serious is that differences in capital-intensity between industries reflect basic technical characteristics of the industries (common to all countries) far more than peculiarities of the initial capital stock situation in the British case. The correlation found from the Pyatt data is dominated by the experience of two industries, water and electricity, which have capital-intensities many times greater than the mean for all industries. When comparison is confined to manufacturing industries, Pyatt's data show a slight *positive* correlation between initial capital-intensity and its change over time. But although this test does not support the hypothesis in the way claimed, it does not refute it either.

The second view is that which follows from Denison's estimates of the capital stock in the Brookings Report, based on his earlier findings in *Why Growth Rates Differ*.[1] These estimates suggest that already in 1950 (and hence presumably in 1939) the amount of capital per worker in Britain was lower than on the Continent, let alone in the United States. The rate of growth of the capital stock in the post-war period was only moderately lower in Britain than in the major Continental countries, apart from Germany, but our investment-income ratio was considerably lower. Essentially, therefore, the low rate of investment in the post-war period represented the continuation of a bad old tradition of low capital-intensity. The Continental countries increased their capital-labour ratios within the post-war period more than we did, but the comparison was already to our disadvantage before that.

There is a *prima facie* conflict between this view and the Lamfalussy hypothesis, according to which the UK economy at the outset of the post-war period had too much capital, not too little. However,

[1] Washington, Brookings Institution; London, George Allen & Unwin Ltd.

although the emphasis is considerably different, there is not an absolute inconsistency, because Denison's data relate to the net capital stock (that is to say, net of accumulated depreciation), whereas the Lamfalussy hypothesis rests on the existence of a great deal of old (and hence very largely depreciated) capital.

Some aspects of Denison's calculations are open to question. His estimate of the net capital stock in 1964 is derived from accumulating post-war investment, and therefore gives a zero weight to capital installed during or before the war; such old capital is likely to be more important in a slow-growing economy like the British than elsewhere, especially in the case of buildings, when the British post-war investment has been particularly low by international standards. But it is certainly true that the rate of industrial investment in the UK had been extraordinarily low in the first forty years of the twentieth century. It is therefore a reasonable conjecture that low-capital intensity and insufficiently frequent replacement of equipment were among the inefficient practices to which British management had become habituated. Put in this way the doctrine is not necessarily inconsistent with the view that there was also some tendency to devote too large a proportion of whatever investment was done to purposes complementary with the existing stock. Indeed an insufficient readiness to scrap and replace would naturally produce both results.

The foregoing discussion of investment has not gone much beyond the recital of alternative hypotheses and reference to a few macro statistics. The conclusions do not dispose of the hypothesis that stop–go had a major influence in retarding capital accumulation; indeed, such a hypothesis is in principle hard to dispose of, because of the difficulty of saying what would have happened to business and labour attitudes if growth had been perfectly steady – a contingency never experienced. Equally, however, our conclusions do not give the hypothesis much support.

IV. CONCLUSION

The Brookings Report performed a major service in directing discussion of the problems of the British economy away from short-run macro issues towards long-run micro ones. This helped to correct the tendency present in too much earlier discussion to exaggerate the importance and potential importance of demand-management policies, whether for good or ill. It is not difficult to understand why such a tendency should have been present. The balance of payments has been seen by the authorities (though not by the man in the street) as the country's chief economic problem, and demand management is closely connected with the balance of payments. Moreover, demand-management policies are something concrete, whereas the effectiveness of government action to improve the performance of the economy at the micro level is unclear.

Demand management may not have a major effect on the growth rate, but mistakes in this area lead to waste, just like mistakes in other areas of government economic policy. This is true even if we rule out the possibility of really catastrophic mistakes which *would* have a major effect on growth. In the future the improved balance-of-payments position may make things easier, but problems will remain. Not least among these is the place to be assigned to price stabilization in demand management. Traditionally the intellectual framework of demand-management policy has been the attainment of a certain level of demand measured at constant prices, with prospective price movements taken into account in so far as they affect this. More recently, the world acceleration in the rate of price increase, together with the influence of Chicagoan monetary thinking – itself, originally addressed, it may be noted, largely to the quite different problem of the optimum *long-run* monetary policy – has led to some swing towards regarding the GNP at current prices as the object of control. Here, as in the somewhat different environment of the previous twenty years' experience, clarification of aims is going to be at least as important as improvement of regulatory techniques.

2 Fiscal Policy and Stabilization in Britain*

by G. D. N. Worswick

I. INTRODUCTION

In his major work on the *Management of the British Economy*, published in 1964, which deals with the period up to 1960, Dow concluded that 'As far as internal conditions are concerned then, budgetary and monetary policy failed to be stabilizing, and must on the contrary be regarded as having been positively destabilizing' [3, p. 384].[1] Little pointed out that Dow's conclusion was open to misunderstanding [6, p. 983]. If all that was meant was that policy had contributed to the boom in 1953 and 1954 and that again the stimulation of the economy in 1959 was excessive, this could be accepted, but that was quite a different thing from claiming that monetary and fiscal policy from 1952 to 1960 was positively destabilizing in the sense that the actual fluctuations observed were greater than would have occurred under some 'neutral' policy held unchanged throughout the period. Little's comment was, and remains, fully justified. Nevertheless, Dow's conclusion has found its way into conventional wisdom and has lately been reinforced by Professor Prest in a lecture to the British Association in 1967 [7] and more recently by Richard and Peggy Musgrave in their chapter on fiscal policy in the Brookings study of *Britain's Economic Prospects* [2]. In the first part of this paper the arguments of Prest and the Musgraves are closely scrutinized, as well as an interesting counter-argument by Bristow [1]. The conclusion will be that the case was never made out in the first instance and has in no way been strengthened by the further work. The main thesis of the second part of the paper

* This paper was presented to the Sixth Conference of University Professors organized by the American Bankers Association and held at Ditchley Park in September 1968. It was published, with the other papers and proceedings of the conference, in a special issue of the *Journal of Money, Credit and Banking*, August 1969. Its subject bore directly upon some aspects of the Brookings study of the British economy, and so was included as a conference paper. We are grateful to the editors of the *Journal of Money, Credit and Banking* for permission to reproduce it here.

[1] NOTE: Numerals in square brackets relate to the References at the end of this Chapter.

is that stabilization as such was never in any case an objective of the authorities and a mistake is being made if we try to seek, with the benefit of hindsight, some ideal combination of fiscal and monetary policy which would have suceeded in preventing the emergence of major problems for the British economy. The argument will be that the fiscal and monetary policy instruments alone were insufficient for achieving a reasonably satisfactory performance with respect to all the various economic objectives which the British people and their governments were setting themselves.

II. WAS BRITISH POLICY 'DESTABILIZING'?

1. *Prest's argument*

In his 1967 Presidential address to section F of the British Association, Prest quotes, with approval, Dow's judgment referred to above and goes on to observe: 'the inability of the government machine to act in a co-ordinated fashion, in such wise that revenue and expenditure policies are reinforcing rather than pulling against one another' [7, p. 5]. In support of this contention, Prest provided a chart of two variables: (a) the percentage deviation from trend of public expenditure on goods and services, and (b) Professor Paish's index of the percentage margin of unused resources, both quarterly from 1955–1 to 1966–IV. The broad impression given by this chart is one of an inverse relationship and the correlation co-efficient between the two series is −0·603. 'Obviously', says Prest, 'no simple deduction about the perverse influence of government spending policy on the pattern of cycles in the last few years can be drawn from this picture; but at least one can hardly say, when the correlation coefficient is negative and not positive, that public expenditure has followed the pattern one might have expected on simple macro-economic grounds' [7, p. 5].

There is the obvious objection that one should not appraise the use of *one* of the possible instruments for regulating total demand (in this case public expenditure) in isolation from all the other instruments, e.g. changes in taxation, hire-purchase regulations, or changes in interest rates. Even if there were a high level of activity and an excessive pressure of demand, it could still be permissible to increase public expenditure while raising taxes at the same time to reduce private expenditure by rather more. It all depends what the government's objectives are.[1] But leaving this aside, let us con-

---

[1] The proposition that revenue and expenditure policies ought to reinforce one another is seemingly innocuous, just common sense. But so is it common

sider the case where the sole instrument for regulating aggregate demand is the variation of public expenditure on goods and services. Prest's argument from simple macro-economics must have gone something like this: 'If there is unemployment, you should raise public expenditure; if there is overheating, you should reduce it. Therefore, if you pursue a good stabilization policy, there should result a positive correlation between the level of unemployment and the level of public expenditure. If the correlation is negative, this is sufficient evidence that the policy must be bad, or perverse.'

Let us look a little more closely, in the context of the simplest possible case. We postulate zero trend in working population and productivity. There is a multiplier m which in the first instance operates without a lag. There is no leakage from this multiplier into imports nor is there any accelerator-type feedback from changes of income to investment. One could take into account strictly autonomous components of output, for example a housing programme, but the simple device is to make all the autonomous items zero. We now impose on this otherwise very static system a perfectly regular and wholly exogenous cycle of 'primary expenditure' generated, let us suppose, by exports. Before intervention, the system is defined by two variables only:

$$E \text{ (exports)} = \sin \lambda t$$

$$Y \text{ (output)} = m \sin \lambda t$$

Units need not detain us and for convenience we start from $E = Y = 0$. This economy is illustrated in Figure 1.

We now call in the government and ask it, by varying public expenditure on goods and services, P, which we also classify as primary expenditure, to try to stabilize the economy. We endow the government with perfect foresight concerning the future movement of E – in all respects except one, namely the amplitude of the fluctuations. Their view of the future movement of exports, that is to say, is: $E = a \sin \lambda t$, where a is not necessarily equal to 1. Not only do we postulate that our government correctly foresees the timing and

---

sense to say that, *ceteris paribus*, if we want more public expenditure, we must pay more taxes, so that expenditure and revenue policies should normally pull against one another. When the economy is running at a fairly high level of activity, common sense may become like the White Knight and ride off in all directions at once. This is the more so when we remember that other instruments to regulate consumption may be in use, e.g. hire-purchase regulations. However, my concern here is with Prest's interpretation of the correlation.

38

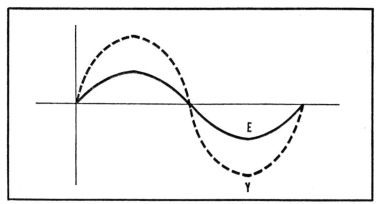

Figure 1. Cycle of output Y, generated by exogenous variable E (no lag).

direction of movement of E but we also postulate that it acts at once, with the object of eliminating the fluctuation of output. In this case, its correct public expenditure policy is simply defined as: $P = -a \sin \lambda t$.

Net primary expenditure in the system now becomes $(E+P)$ or $(1—a) \sin \lambda t$, and the movement of output becomes $Y' = m(1—a) \sin \lambda t$.

Figure 2 illustrates the case where $a<1$. We now have a number of possibilities:

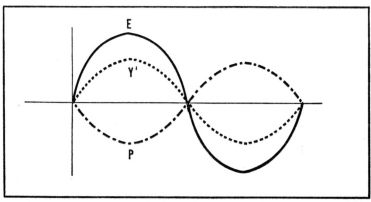

Figure 2. Cycle of exogenous variable E, partially offset by policy variable P, resulting in Y, (no lag).

Case 1: a<1. The system is more stable, i.e. the amplitude of *Y* is reduced by the intervention. The correlation between *P* and *Y'* is −1. If *U* is an index of the margin of unused resources which is exactly inversely related to *Y*, then the correlation between *P* and *U* is +1.

Case 2 : 1<a<2. The system is again more stable but this time the correlation between *P* and *Y'* is +1 or between *P* and *U* is −1. The authorities have overdone it and so have generated an opposite cycle but the amplitude of this cycle is still less than the original one.

Case 3 : a>2. In this case the government intervention not only generates an opposite cycle but it increases its amplitude as well, i.e. creates more instability.

Case 4 : a = 1. In this case *Y'* is constant (at zero) and the correlations between *P* and *Y'* or *P* and *U* are zero. Complete success requires neither positive nor negative correlation of *P* with *U* but zero correlation.

So far we have assumed instantaneous adjustment of output to primary expenditure, whether *E* or (*E*+*P*). Let us now examine briefly the consequences of a lagged multiplier. We start with an apparently extreme case where the lag is exactly half the length of the original cycle of *E*. Denote by *N*, the net primary expenditure (*E*+*P*). We further start with the case where we are 'underdoing' it, i.e. *a*<1, and the cycle of *N* is exactly in phase with that of the original *E*, only smaller in amplitude. The behaviour of consumption *C* is then also a sine curve, but lagged exactly a period behind

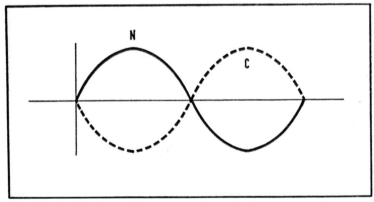

Figure 3. Cycle of net primary expenditure *N*, Generating cycle in consumption *C* (multiplier lag of half cycle).

N (Figure 3). Total output Y is the algebraic sum of $N+C$. Three cases arise, depending upon the size of the multiplier.

Case 1 : $m>2$. The amplitude of C will be greater than that of N. Consequently, the course of Y will be a sine curve, in phase with C, but 180° out of phase with N, Since this was the case of 'underdoing' it, N is in phase with E and out of phase with P. Therefore, P and Y are in phase and P and U out of phase. The correlation between P and U is -1.

Case 2 : $m<2$. The amplitude of C will be smaller than that of N, so that the cycles of Y and N will be in phase; of Y and P out of phase; and those of P and U in phase. The correlation of P and U is $+1$.

Case 3 : $m = 2$. The amplitude of C is now equal to that of N, so that the N and C curves are mirror images. Y is therefore constant, at zero. In this case Y is always constant, irrespective of the size of P (or more strictly the size of a). (The seeming oddity of this comes from the fact that in simple textbook cycle illustrations, we are usually looking at a multiplier-accelerator combination – whereas we have here cut out any accelerator response of investment.)

If, instead of starting with $a<1$, we were to overdo it, i.e. take $a>1$, the signs of the correlations reached in Cases 1 and 2 above would be reversed. Case 3 would be the same.

We summarize the results for r, the correlation of P and U, reached so far, as follows:

r = correlation of P and U

	No lag			Multiplier lag of half cycle		
	$a<1$	$a = 1$	$a>1$	$a<1$	$a = 1$	$a>1$
$m < 2$	$+1$	0	-1	$+1$	0	-1
$m = 2$	$+1$	0	-1	0	0	0
$m > 2$	$+1$	0	-1	-1	0	$+1$

In all of the above cases, so long as $a<2$, the amplitude of the cycle will be less than that which would have been generated by the original E cycle with no intervention. Moreover, in the lagged case, some of the resultant Y curves would have smaller amplitudes, even when $a>2$.

Because, so far, we have taken lags of either zero, or half a cycle, all our sine curves for the components of output are either in phase, or 180° out of phase, with one another. Consequently, all our correlations are either $+1$, -1 or zero. If we imagine a multiplier lag which

41

starts at zero and is gradually lengthened, the correlation coefficients will begin to become less than 1. P and Y will be going in the same direction part of the time and opposite to one another for the rest. Where r changes sign between the zero and half-cycle lag cases, there must therefore be further instances of a zero coefficient.

Sufficient has been said to indicate that even in the very simplest model, the sign of the correlation between P and U tells us nothing whatever about the success or otherwise of the stabilization. Ideally, the correlation ought to be zero. If we endow the authorities with perfect timing, then the issue is whether they underdo or overdo their intervention and, as we have seen, according as they do one or other systematically, the correlation will come out either positive or negative. But what is at stake, whether or not they have generated any opposite cycle, is whether, as a result of their intervention, the amplitude of output is less than it would have been without the intervention. Doubtless, statistical tests would show that most cakes baked are either slightly underdone or slightly overdone but most of us still prefer slightly underdone or slightly overdone cakes to consuming the raw ingredients. The model just illustrated is extremely over-simplified. In the real world, not only do we have lags of various kinds (and we have seen how lags can alter the signs of the correlation coefficients) but there are in fact feedbacks which need also to be allowed for and which make it increasingly inappropriate to put forward as testable hypotheses simple expectations based upon simple macro-economics. In short, Prest's diagram and correlation tell us nothing one way or the other about stabilization policy.

2. The Musgraves' argument

The quotable judgment – it was used by three well-known British economic journalists within a few weeks of publication – occurs in the 'Epilogue'. It is:

> 'The level of unemployment, which normally triggers changes in policies for demand management, lags about a year behind changes in the growth rate of actual gross domestic product, the variable to be controlled. Destabilizing changes in fiscal and monetary policy have resulted from the failure to heed this relation, so that restrictive policies have taken hold only after the growth of aggregate demand has slackened' [2, p. 489].

The Epilogue unfortunately does not give cross-references to the main body of the book. It is conceivable that the expression 'changes in growth rate' should read either 'the growth rate' or simply 'change in GDP'. Both Professor Cooper in his chapter on the balance of payments [2, p. 159] and Professor and Mrs Musgrave in their chapter on fiscal policy [2, p. 36], provided charts using annual data showing the troughs of unemployment lagging a year behind the peaks of a chart showing changes in GDP.[1] Professor Cooper's concern with this problem is only incidental. What I wish to discuss is the allegation concerning destabilization, and this I take to be derived from the fairly extensive analysis in the Musgraves' chapter.

The method by which this conclusion is reached is one of multiple regression. The central idea is that 'fiscal policy' can be crystallized in a single policy variable. Estimates are made of the 'leverage'[2] of the consolidated public sector and of the leverage of the central government alone. Expressed as ratios of GDP, these provide two candidate policy variables – Z_1, Z_2 – from which we can get two more candidates – V_1 and V_2 – by deriving the year to year changes in Z_1 and Z_2. A fifth candidate. Z_3 , is obtained by looking at the taxation side only and estimating the ratio of the changes in the discretionary yield of taxation to changes in GDP.

We now look for a number of candidates as 'independent' variables to explain the behaviour of the dependent policy variable.[3] The

---

[1] Assuming that my interpretation is correct and that the term 'change in growth rate,' which is the second order difference in output, should read 'growth rate', which is the first order difference in output, the evidence for the length of the lag of one year appears to be derived from this chart based on annual data. Professor Cooper added a footnote as follows: 'The lag is probably not as long as a year. Paish's chart on quarterly data suggests that in the late 1950s the lag may have been two quarters, somewhat longer than it was in the early 1950s. It is significant that when annual data are used, as here, the inverse correspondence is much closer for a lag of a full year than it is for no lag.' I would not wish for a moment to dispute the existence of this lag, which has been well known for many years. My own guess is that the authorities got hold of it around 1955–6, when unemployment failed to rise as quickly as might have been expected from the slowing down in the growth of output. The most recent Treasury work suggests that the lag may well be variable, partly depending on the level of employment itself [9]. The response of employment to output also changes when there is a major reduction in the normal working week, which has occurred twice in the past decade, on each occasion running through industry over a period of a year or more. The Brookings summary has unfortunately made the lag appear too definite, both as to length and constancy.

[2] Leverage is defined as the difference between the actual level of GDP and the hypothetical level which would result if public sector expenditures and receipts were withdrawn.

[3] In the mimeographed Appendix V, the Musgraves point out that there are two distinct questions, according as we look at the direction of causality. The

Musgraves put forward as candidates for the independent or target variables, the following:

	Level	Change
Growth rate of GDP	X_1	Y_1
Unemployment rate	X_2	Y_2
Cost of living index	M	Y_3
Gross exchange reserves as per cent of average	X_4	Y_4
Net exchange reserves	—	Y_5
Balance on current and long-term capital account	—	Y_6

They go on to say: 'The policy variables, with the exception of Z_3, are defined in terms of expansionary effect. Being the dependent variables, they should thus be related positively to the unemployment and balance of payments target variables and negatively to the growth rate and cost of living variables.' [2, mimeographed Appendix V.]

Accordingly, multiple regressions are worked out between the policy variables and the independent or target variables, correlating levels on levels and changes on changes. I some instances, lagged independent variables have been tried.[1]

Conclusions are then drawn from the regressions, according to the statistical significance and the sign of the regression coefficients, whether the policy response to the independent variables was 'correct' or 'perverse'. A number of questions may be asked and comments made about this procedure.

1. Is it possible to lay down, without qualification, what the policy response to a change in any particular independent variable ought

---

first question is: Given the behaviour of the independent variables, did the policy variable respond in the correct manner? The second question is: Given the change in the policy variable, e.g. reduction in leverage, did the target variables respond accordingly, e.g. did unemployment rise or output grow more slowly? All the regressions are in fact estimated with the target variables as independent and with the policy variables as dependent and it is with this line of causality that I am concerned here.

[1] The choice of some of the variables is questionable, in particular those representing foreign exchange reserves. Because of 'window dressing', the movement of published reserves signifies little. Reserves can change because of movements in the rest of the sterling area which do not necessarily call for any change in UK leverage or taxes. The use of annual data, when quarterly data are available, is a weakness admitted by the authors. However, our concern here is with methodology.

to be? Take the balance of payments on current and long-term capital account. According to the Musgraves, if this shows an improvement, then the leverage should be increased – for short, let us say 'we should expand.' But surely it depends on the objective? Suppose that last year we had full employment and equilibrium in the basic balance and this year we observe a spontaneous increase of exports, creating a balance of payments surplus. Then, say the Musgraves, the correct response is to expand. If we do expand, we will get a bit of inflation which will cut back exports and increase imports, thus pulling back the balance of payments. This might well be the right prescription for an ideal world in which all countries start in equilibrium and agree in the common interest to play the same game of expanding to eliminate surpluses rather than exclusively imposing contraction upon deficit countries. But what if we are in the real world and wish to keep the surplus, e.g. to accumulate reserves or to pay off debts? Then we should 'contract', so as to leave room for the maintenance of the higher surplus. Take another variable, the growth rate. The correct response to a rise in output must surely depend upon where we start from, i.e. from a low or high level of capacity utilization? The response to an acceleration of the growth of output would also depend on whether or not this is being accompanied by a corresponding change in capacity or productive potential. It is true that most measures of this concept tend to show smooth year-to-year movements but that is primarily because they are distilled out of fluctuating time series by econometric devices which have a built-in guarantee to give a smooth answer. There could be cases where there is reason to believe that there has been a step up or a step down in the capacity curve, in which case the correct policy response might be opposite from that which would be indicated when the output rise was purely conjunctural.

2. Quelling any doubts raised in the previous paragraph, let us assume that we have found a number of independent variables, X_1, X_2, etc. and accept that the correct policy response to these variables is unambiguous. Let us further suppose that the X's are completely independent of one another. How, then, should we interpret the results of a multiple regression of a policy variable Z on the Xs? To simplify matters, let us postulate perfect timing by the authorities. Let us also assume that our regression comes out with an r^2 of 0·99 and the regression coefficients are all highly significant. What should be the sign and the size of those co-

efficients? If the X is genuinely exogenous to the system, the sign of the regression coefficient will tell us whether the policy response was correct or perverse. But if, as with the growth rate, the X variable is endogenous, i.e. affected by the policy response itself, we are back with the trouble we found in analysing Prest's argument. In this case, perfect success, i.e. complete stabilizing of any of the endogenous variables, now entails that the corresponding regression coefficient should be zero. Even if it is non-zero, the sign of the coefficient alone will only tell us whether we have underdone or overdone it. It will not tell us whether we have so much overdone it as to lead to wider fluctuations than would otherwise have occurred. That is to say, our policy intervention might not have been ideal but merely damping; but damping is not the same thing as destabilizing.

3. The target variables, however, are not all independent of one another. We have every reason to expect to find relationships between output or its change, unemployment and prices. If we postulate an exact theoretical model, without lags, then the value of any one independent variable entails corresponding specific values for the other two, so that the government should simply choose one of the variables to operate on, knowing that any change brought about in it has exact consequences for the other two. If, however, there is only a stochastic relationship, we have to face the possibility of the independent variables issuing conflicting instructions to the policy variable. To which, then, should priority be given in deciding the correct response?

4. A more serious problem is where there are relationships between the independent variables but with lags. Once again, if we could establish exact lag relationships between, say, GDP, unemployment and prices, then, as in the previous paragraph, the government should pay attention to one only, e.g. GDP, since whatever it does with that entails exact consequences for the other variables later on. In real life, of course, such relationships may be suspected but not exactly known. But their presence will give rise to such situations as output rising fast and unemployment still rising. What is the correct policy response?

The Musgraves make considerable play with the lag between output and unemployment but there is another lag which they appear not to have noticed, for in describing the process of fluctuations, they write: 'When demand and output move up, prices rise' [2, p. 35].

46

This looks innocent enough. It needs, of course, something of a gloss in the post-war British case since prices and output have both been rising all the time, through Stops as well as through Goes. Their dictum, therefore, needs some such interpretation as: 'When demand and output rise above trend, prices will rise above trend,' or 'Large rises in demand and output are associated with large rises in prices: small ones with small ones.' But this is precisely what does not happen.

The chart on p. 48 shows the annual percentage changes of real GDP at factor cost and the annual percentage change of the GDP deflator and of the index of retail prices. It will be seen that there is a fairly marked inverse relationship between the output changes and the price changes; sharp increases in the former are associated with small increases in the latter and vice versa. Recent cycles, in terms of rates of change, have lasted roughly four years and the price cycle appears to be lagging two years behind or in advance of the output cycle, i.e. the lag is about half the total cycle. There is no lack of possible explanations for this inverse relationship between output and price changes but it is interesting to consider one possible lag-type explanation along the following lines. The above trend rise in GDP leads to a corresponding change in employment and unemployment some months later. The change in unemployment in turn reacts with a lag upon wage rates which then works through to prices. In the comments on Prest, it was pointed out that the sign of the correlation coefficient would be reversed when we had a lag of half a cycle, or become zero with a lag of a quarter of a cycle. Now the actual British cycles of recent years have been of the order of four years, yet here we have a situation where three of the important independent variables are separated from one another by lags of about a quarter of a cycle each, adding up to half a cycle in all. Given the difficulties which arose in the most simplified two variable case, I confess that I am quite incapable of working out from first principles what I ought to expect from the regressions, whether the coefficients should be significant or not, and where they are significant, what signs they should have, as a means of indicating whether the policy response of the authorities was correct or perverse.

In short, the methodology attempted in the Brookings study is not helpful in throwing light on the question whether the budgetary responses were destabilizing or not.

3. *Bristow's argument*

Both Prest and the Musgraves reached their conclusions by examin-

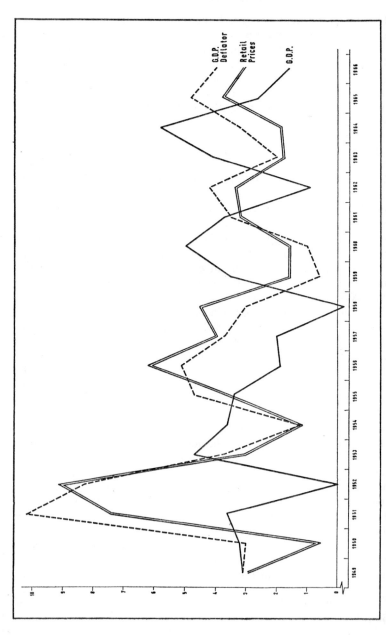

Annual percentage changes in real output (GDP) and prices (GDP deflator and index of retail prices), UK, 1949–66.

ing the *direction* of changes in the policy variables. But, if the charge of destabilization is to be made to stick, something more is needed. This is the starting point of an interesting recent article by Bristow [1]. A truly satisfactory test of Dow's conclusion with regard to destabilization would require a prediction of what would have happened if policy had been 'neutral'. 'However, it is doubtful whether even an econometric exercise of great sophistication could cope adequately with this sort of 'might have been' problem. Even if 'neutrality' can be suitably defined, not only would an extremely complex model be required to estimate the effects of the alternative policy, but even more important, certain crucial factors may be unquantifiable' [1, p. 299]. After all, if the neutral model were at some point to run the economy into a major balance of payments deficit, can we suppose that the authorities would have remained neutral, or would have got away with it if they had tried?

Bristow's exercise is confined to taxation and to asking what might have happened if taxation policy had been different in certain respects. The method he uses is an extension of one developed by two Treasury economists [4]. These authors had made estimates of the effects of changes in rates of different types of tax in their amount and in their timing on the principal components of national income in subsequent quarters. Implicit in their calculations was a fairly straightforward lagged multiplier-accelerator mechanism. Since their objective was in short-term national income forecasting, they stopped short three years after the original tax change. For Bristow's purposes, this will not do: in theory, any tax change sets up movements which will continue indefinitely. Although he does not give a mathematical formulation, he tells us that what he is postulating is that his multiplier-accelerator mechanism produces a very heavily damped fluctuation, i.e. a tax reduction leads to an expansion of the variables somewhat beyond equilibrium level and then a gradual decline to the equilibrium level, which is reached for all practical purposes at the end of the sixth year after the change. With this assumption, he builds up tables of the quarterly changes in four variables: GDP at factor cost Y; total final expenditure at market prices E; consumer expenditure at market prices C; and gross fixed-capital formation at market prices I; all at constant prices, which would follow from any of a number of specific tax changes.

Armed with these standard tables, Bristow starts off with the tax rates ruling after the Budget of 1954 and proceeds to undo each subsequent Budget in the period 1955–65. He thus finds a new time path for each of his four variables which represents what would have occurred if there had been no tax rate changes after 1954. To summarize the course of each of the variables, both before and after removal of the Budgets, he uses a simple device. To any variable, Y say, is fitted a logarithmic trend, i.e., $Y = a(1+g)^t$, and r^2 is estimated in each case.

His first result is that for each and all of his four variables, the value of g, the growth rate, is lower and of r^2 lower for the no-tax-change series than for the actual series. In fact, over the period as a whole, tax changes had an upward influence upon income growth. He concludes from the r^2 result that actual tax changes had a stabilizing effect.

Bristow tries a second exercise, this time advancing every tax change one year earlier than it actually occurred. This time the r^2 for three of the variables is raised, though for one, I, it is lowered. The conclusion is that stabilizing might have been better still if the changes had been made earlier. Bristow admits very frankly that his procedure has weaknesses. He was unable, he says, to discover a suitable statistical test for the significance of the differences in the values of r^2. His method of obtaining the growth rate postulates complete independence of that rate from fluctuations. No allowance is made for 'confidence' effects, which have in fact played a substantial role in recent years.

4. A review of the evidence

How much light do these three sets of arguments, described above, throw upon the stabilizing/destabilizing issue?

All three are, in various degrees, partial. Prest is concerned only with public expenditure, Bristow only with taxation. The Musgraves used three basic policy variables, i.e. total public sector leverage, leverage of central government only and discretionary tax changes. None incorporates monetary changes as well. This is not unimportant because, apart from the fact that substantial use was made of monetary instruments, e.g. interest rates, ceilings on bank advances, special deposits with the Bank of England and changes in hire purchase regulations (which have a substantial effect and were very frequent, sometimes twice in one year), it was clear that in the middle of the period, from 1955 to 1960, the government was showing a preference for monetary over fiscal controls, especially when it came to restriction. As to methodologies, various objections were raised to the correlation conclusions drawn by Prest and to the regression method of the Musgraves, which are, in my opinion, sufficient to rule their evidence out of court altogether. Bristow's method, on the other hand, is not objectionable on principle, although there are many detailed objections which can be raised, and most of which in fact Bristow himself does raise, when he comments upon the results of his calculations.

If one is seeking a formal and systematic procedure to find the answer to the stabilization question, it does seem that Bristow's line is the one which has to be developed. Nevertheless, even within its own terms, it must be doubted whether it can be expected to produce a conclusive answer. First, there is the thorny question of settling upon what is a neutral policy. There are no scientific principles for determining this although possibly one might get round the difficulty by putting up a range of possible neutral policies and examining what happened under each of them. For the examination itself, we require an articulated econometric model to tell us what the economy might be expected to do under different assumptions. Specifically, also, we need to be able to quantify precisely the effects to be expected from all of a variety of discretionary measures in expenditure and taxation and in credit policy, taking this last term to cover interest rates, controls on bank advances and hire purchase regulations. The practical difficulties here are enormous. The British authorities have had the habit of delivering 'packages' of measures, the contents of which have varied from one instance to another. Consequently, it is extremely difficult to separate the contribution of each item of the package to the subsequent movements of the relevant variables. Even if these difficulties could be overcome, there would still remain the question of the balance of payments. If, in any year, the model generated a deficit, should we ignore it, perhaps because the model will produce a surplus next year anyway, or might we not have to admit that had such a deficit emerged, corrective action would in fact have had to be taken, thus making the neutrality assumption irrelevant for comparative purposes? Finally, there is always the danger when using models of this type of forgetting about historical time. The amount of econometric work being done on various aspects of the British economy is very much greater than it was ten years ago. It needs an effort to remember that in fact quarterly estimates of national accounts are available only from 1955 and were in fact published for the first time only in 1957. There now exist runs of twelve years on a quarterly basis, which are the foundation of a good deal of current econometric work. But this sort of estimation simply could not be undertaken fifteen years ago

51

or ten years ago because the data did not exist or the series were too short. Yet, if we are to make judgments about policy, we ought to make some allowance for this. Judgment of a period as a whole is a kind of average. In some contexts this is acceptable but it is dubious when there is a strong reason to believe that there has been a trend of improvement or worsening within the period itself.

If judgment of policy has to be made, there does not seem therefore any substitute for a careful examination of each move made by the authorities in the light of the situation as it was seen at the time. This is in fact precisely the programme which Dow carried out for the period up to 1960. But in the nature of things, any generalizations emerging from such a programme are bound to be impressionist and there is ample scope for subjective valuations. The author, who made the detailed studies, reached the conclusion quoted at the beginning of this paper. Others who have read his 'case-studies', and including Little who had himself made a somewhat similar 'blow-by-blow' study of British fiscal policy [5], think that the evidence does not support the generalization concerning destabilizing. Not a very satisfactory state of affairs, perhaps, but there may be some consolation in the argument of the remaining section of this paper to the effect that the issue is not very important anyway.

III. WHAT REALLY WENT WRONG

The words stable, stability and stabilization are widely used in economics but while there is a penumbra of approbation about them, there is also considerable ambiguity.

What, for example, is meant by 'stable prices'? Firstly, I suppose, that there are no great fluctuations through time. Secondly, that the level does not alter much either way, i.e. the trend of movement is zero. In a changing world it is improbable that price relatives can remain unaltered so that if we refer to some general level of prices being stable, we recognize that this may well entail an upward trend of some components of some index number offset by a downward trend in others. A sensible use of stable, and stability, for prices, then, is the absence of severe fluctuations and zero trend. The same is true for unemployment when it is expressed as a ratio of the labour force and for the balance of payments. In all these cases, that is to say, stability is perhaps best taken to mean an absence of severe fluctuations around a constant level. On the other hand, for output, productivity and, in most cases, employment, while we retain the attribute of an absence of fluctuations, we nowadays associate stability with a steady upward trend and use some such word as stagnation to denote zero trend.

When we come to stabilization policy, there is no ambiguity as long as we confine our attention to one variable only, but ambiguity enters in the moment we have to deal with more than one. The most familiar example of this is in commodity stabilization schemes: is the object to keep the prices of the commodity constant or to stabilize the incomes of the producers? As a rule, one can do one or the other but not both at the same time. Similarly with the stabilization of an economy; if, for example, one studies the changes of British exports in the past fifteen years, one finds a pretty strong association with changes in the movement of world trade and a much weaker association with anything else that might be thought relevant, for example the pressure of demand in the British economy itself. In fact, the year-to-year fluctuations in British exports have been smaller than they were before the second war; nevertheless, they have continued. Thus, had we succeeded in securing stability (i.e. steady growth) in the output of the British economy, the presumption is that we could not have had stability in the balance of trade as well.

Two features of what I have just said about the determinants of British exports should be noted. In the first place, it is a summary statement concerning recent history and the kind of statement which can only be made at the end and not at the beginning of a period. Each time a 'stop' had been engineered, it was apparent that the authorities believed (or hoped) that after a sufficient lapse of time exports would somehow become more competitive than they had been, so that renewed expansion would not simply repeat the story which had preceded the original stop. The authorities may have subscribed to the toothpaste tube theory of exports – that when home demand is squeezed, exports are extruded. Or they may have hoped that the stop would lead to a permanent reduction in the trend rate of increase in money incomes and prices (at any given level or unemployment or capacity utilization) and that improved competitiveness would be achieved by this route. In retrospect, such hopes are seen to have been unjustified. Secondly, it happens that the exchange rate was unchanged throughout the period and we do not know what would have happened if it had been at a different level throughout or had been changed at some point. The presumption is, however, that if this was simply a question of a different level of exchange rate, the year-to-year fluctuations in exports would still have appeared.

The potential conflict between stabilizing an endogenous variable and one such as the balance of trade whose movements contain a large exogenous component, is straightforward enough. But is there also any possible conflict between stability of the endogenous variables? The answer is partly a question of semantics, a question of the precise distinction which is being made between exogenous and endogenous. Characteristically, some variables, consumption for example, are treated as wholly endogenous. That is to say, if output, or real disposable income, rises steadily, without fluctuations, we would expect consumption to rise steadily too. Investment is trickier. If output grew steadily, that, of itself, would be expected to have a stabilizing influence on investment, because the accelerator-type fluctuation was being cut off. But we would not be surprised to find bursts of innovatory investment and consequent echo cycles which were not in any obvious way induced by changes in output or consumption. In other words, in real life investment is partly endogenous and partly exogenous. Bearing this in mind we might say that if all our variables were strictly endogenous, there is no logical reason why we should not be able to eliminate fluctuations from all of them. We should not forget, however, that variables which we characteristically treat as endogenous are capable of strictly exogenous behaviour. Investment is the case in point: there could also be spontaneous jumps in consumer behaviour. But such exogenous behaviour may be less obvious and less frequent than for a variable like exports.

Thus, so far as the fluctuation aspect of stabilization is concerned, there need be no logical conflict between stabilizing output, say, and stabilizing employment. But if, as we suggested above, the stability notion nowadays implies also a steady rate of growth, the question of the particular rate of growth becomes important. It is conceivable that there could be a connection between the trend value of the growth rate of output and the level of unemployment. Some have argued that the way to increase output per man is to keep labour scarce – to have a high pressure of demand. Others have argued that this policy would generate bottlenecks which would be deleterious to growth and what is needed is a higher margin of unemployment than we have had on average since the war. It is easy to make up a formidable list of pros and cons concerning this relationship, but so far, at any rate, conclusive evidence has not been produced. Another potential conflict is between the level of unemployment and the rate of inflation. Here quite a lot of evidence has been produced of some sort of association between these two variables. This evidence, however, has been observed from a period in which the variables have both been fluctuating and is not conclusive as to what steady rate of inflation would be associated with any particular steady level of employment.

Let us suppose, however, that we did know what this relation was and also what the precise connection between growth and the unemployment level was. Then we would have an indefinite number of stabilisation solutions for the economy with different rates of growth of output, different rates of inflation and different levels of unemployment. The first task of economic policy would then be to decide which of these possible mixes was wanted. There would have to be set up some kind of economic policy function which incorporated relative valuations of faster growth versus faster inflation and so on. Once we knew what this policy function was, we could set about appraising how successful fiscal management had been in maximizing it.

There are three merits in formulating the economic policy objectives in this way. It brings out the point that the best economic policy – taken as a whole – may yield a solution in which the performance of any one variable is not as good as it might be if everything were put behind that variable to the neglect of consequences elsewhere. It makes it clear that if constraints are imposed on any one variable, for example, that unemployment must not exceed, say, 2 per cent, then this may severely reduce the range of possible solutions. Finally, it warns us that we cannot impose arbitrary constraints on as many variables as we like; if we try to we may find that the system yields no solution at all.

Given the procedures for the determination of wages and prices which have existed in Britain in the 1950s and early 1960s, the constraint of political acceptability imposed upon the unemployment level has entailed rising prices. Had we been a relatively closed economy that might not have mattered too much, but the economy is rather open and the price increases entailed by the unemployment constraint were not compatible with the policy of fixed exchange rates combined with the continuing removal of direct controls over trade and capital movements. This proposition is synthetic and not analytic. There could well occur actual circumstances in the rest of the world which would permit us to get away with the rate of inflation entailed by the unemployment constraint. The circumstances possibly existed in the early 1950s. The point is simply that they did not have to exist indefinitely and in fact they did not exist in the later part of the period.

There has, that is to say, been a major inconsistency in our economic policies during the past decade or more. We were attempting to achieve simultaneously a variety of objectives which were mutually incompatible. This was a mistake of economic policy.

There was also an equally important mistake concerning the potential role of fiscal and monetary policy. From the early 1950s onwards, it was widely believed that, given an economic policy objective, fiscal and monetary policy between them were, in principle, not merely necessary, but also sufficient instruments to push or pull the economy towards these objectives. Let me try to illustrate by reference to two of our policy objectives why I believe this view to be mistaken.

If faster growth is to be achieved, there must occur somewhere or other in the economy real changes which increase real output per unit of input. The variety of such possible changes is very great. Some consist of the removal of obstacles of various kinds, restrictive practices of labour or of management. Others, and in the long run these are the decisive ones, consist of speeding up the incorporation of new discoveries into industrial production, often requiring the installation of new types of equipment and the training of personnel in new skills to operate it. If there are 'schools' in these matters, I belong to the school which says you should concentrate your attention on the supply side. But improvements on the supply side could be frustrated if they are not matched by proper demand management. In this sense, correct fiscal policy is necessary for growth to ensure that the potential gains on the supply side are in fact taken up and do not inadvertently generate a higher level of unemployment. But this is not the same thing as saying that the correct fiscal policy will of itself cause growth. To take another aspect of this same problem; faster growth may not occur unless there is more of the right kinds of investment, and the tax system should certainly be arranged so as not to discourage such investment. On the other hand, fiscal stimuli alone may not bring about the right kinds of investment. Some, like J. R. Sargent [8], have argued that they may stimulate the wrong kinds. The views of the British authorities on this subject are, I believe, changing at this time, but certainly in the early 1960s there was a fairly prevalent belief that fiscal policy could be a powerful and active agent for growth, partly through the general stimulus given by demand expansion and partly through the stimulus to investment given by investment allowances.

Similarly with the balance of payments, if, when there is already full employment, there is a spontaneous improvement in the trade balance which it is desired to maintain, then there must be a corresponding reduction in home demand to accommodate this improvement, and to achieve this there is once more an appropriate fiscal policy. It does not follow, however, that merely to pursue that fiscal policy will cause the trade balance to improve.

Until recently, therefore, there have been two major errors in British economic policy. The first was the implicit and unquestioned assumption that the various objectives of policy – full employment, steady growth, stable prices and an absence of balance of payments troubles – were compatible with one another. The second was the belief that because correct fiscal and monetary policies are necessary to achieve various economic objectives, they are also sufficient. What the authorities have been trying to do has been to square the circle – with the added complication that it might not turn out to be a circle after all but a somewhat eccentric ellipse.

Given the intrinsic difficulties of this task, it might seem irrelevant to bother at all about their technical performance in the year-to-year management of demand. But if we set aside for the moment these fundamental incompatibilities of objective, some comment may be in order.

Taking the post-war period as a whole, and using rather broad historical and international standards of comparison, I would award the British Treasury high marks for their willingness to learn the Keynesian tricks, and other besides. I am aware that for an academic economist to say a thing like this comes near to betraying his profession. Harry Johnson will, I am sure, at once conclude that I have been offered some preferment, some minor office in the Royal Household at the very least. In extenuation, I can only plead that as an academic economist it is my duty to speak the truth.

It is, of course, difficult to distinguish the technical contribution of the Treasury officials and economic advisers from the contribution of ministers and a word about the attitudes of the Conservative and Labour governments may be in order. Neither party has shown any great concern for the balance of the budget as such. Both have been prepared to alter company taxation and indirect taxation in both directions. In the earlier part of its long period of office, the Conservative government was clearly prepared to reduce taxes when stimulus was needed but preferred as a rule to use monetary measures, including hire-purchase regulations, when restriction was called for. They did, however, become increasingly concerned about the apparent ineffectiveness of monetary measures and in 1957 set up the Radcliffe Committee to inquire into 'the working of the monetary system'. One conclusion of that committee, which duly reported in

1959, was that fiscal measures might well be stronger than monetary ones and the legislation to introduce the Regulator, which was in fact very quickly used in a restrictive way, was a logical outcome of the Radcliffe inquiry. What the Conservatives were not prepared to envisage was any increase in direct personal taxation and by 1959 this attitude had developed into something of a dogma. The present Labour government has found itself raising taxes more often than it cuts them and it raised income tax as soon as it came into office in 1964 as an offset to the increase in statutory pensions. But in his severe Budget of 1968, the Chancellor of the Exchequer put the greatest weight on indirect taxes and in his speech ventured the opinion that direct taxation could go no higher, though he did not produce any new evidence or reasoned argument in support of it.

What has just been said refers to broad political attitudes. Mention should also be made of two of the instances of 'bad management' most commonly noticed by economists who examine the period as a whole, namely the April Budget of 1955 and the Budget of 1959. The former was in the 'wrong direction' and the latter 'excessive'. The dominant consideration in both cases was a forthcoming general election and what was economically wrong might be judged politically right, according to one's point of view. It is after discounting as best I might these political factors, which undoubtedly exist, both of the broader kind and of the narrower electoral variety, that I reached my conclusion concerning the management competence of the Treasury. It is my contention that the Treasury has in general shown a good understanding of macro-economic theory and has developed skills in judging where the economy is at any time and in which direction it should be pushed according to the principles of macro-economics. Indeed, it is possible to argue that their concentration upon developing skills in judging the conjunctural aspects of the economy actually prevented them from appreciating sufficiently the point which I have been stressing, that macro-economic management in the orthodox Keynesian sense was not enough and that additional instruments were required, besides those of aggregative fiscal and monetary policy.

To look at stop–go in the period 1952–67 simply as a failure of stabilization policy, something which might not have occurred if the authorities had been more skilful in the timing or in the size of the fiscal changes which they made, is wrong: it is to perpetuate the very mistakes which the authorities made concerning the incompatibility of policy objectives and the limitations of fiscal policy.

It is as though we have been playing a game of musical chairs among our policy objectives of full employment, growth, stable prices, and so on; stop the music in any year you like from 1952 to 1967 and you will find one and sometimes two of the objectives without a chair. The mistake of the authorities was that instead of fetching more chairs, they simply started the music again, selecting a different tune. It is interesting that the Musgraves, in their Brookings study. lend some support, perhaps unconsciously, to this interpretation. At one point they talk of output as being 'the variable to be stabilized'. At another they speak of the 'level of unemployment which normally triggers changes in policy for demand management' but later still they say that 'the key to the problem' rested with the balance of payments position.

How many extra chairs would have been needed? One certainly was incomes policy. It is common ground that the rise in money incomes and prices can be moderated or accelerated by means of changes in aggregate demand engineered through fiscal or monetary policy. But what was needed was some instrument which moderated their increase at any given level of capacity utilization. There is now a major attempt being mounted in Britain to construct such an instrument. It is not the first attempt at this and there are still a great many people who are thinking in terms of temporary measures; for example, a halt for a year or so, after which we can somehow scrap the machinery and go on thereafter without inflation.[1] This is an illusion. That is to say, there is a need for a permanent incomes policy in the sense that a new instrument is required which will enable us to get at the level of money incomes and prices and their movement by means additional to the influence which can be exerted by fiscal and monetary policy of the traditional kind.

If our task were simply to re-live the past fifteen years or so, a second, additional, chair would have been needed. At each stage when the balance of payments was for the time being favourable, imports and capital movements were liberalized too soon and it was a mistake to dismantle so completely the machinery of control for operating directly upon the balance of payments and not only indirectly via the level of aggregate demand. This, rather strong, statement assumes, of course, that other aspects of policy remained unchanged. If, for example, overseas government expenditure had stayed at the low levels of 1952–3 instead of rising steadily there-

[1] See, for example, Royal Commission on Trade Unions and Employers Associations, 1965–8, HMSO, 1968, paragraph 52: 'incomes policy is concerned with the short run improvement of the country's economic position. . . .'

after, the balance of payments problem would have been considerably easier. What is a datum from one point of view is a policy option from another. It is possible that the 1967 devaluation will be so successful that for a while at any rate the balance of payments will cease to act as an overriding constraint upon our ability to achieve other objectives of policy. But this does not depend only on developments within the British economy itself. It also depends on the speed with which reform of international monetary arrangements and the co-ordination of national policies of demand management can be pushed forward. It is too soon, therefore, to say with any certainty whether an additional balance of payments chair may not be needed in the future.

REFERENCES

1. BRISTOW, J. A., 'Taxation and Income Stabilization', *Economic Journal* (June 1968).
2. CAVES, RICHARD and ASSOCIATES, *Britain's Economic Prospects*, Washington, Brookings; and London, George Allen and Unwin, (1968). See especially Chapter 1 on Fiscal Policy by Richard A. and Peggy B. Musgrave.
3. DOW, J. C. R., *Management of the British Economy*, NIESR, Cambridge University Press, 1964.
4. HOPKIN, W. A. B., and GODLEY, W. A. H., 'An Analysis of Tax Changes'. *National Institute Economic Review*, No. 32 (May 1965).
5. LITTLE, I. M. D., 'Fiscal Policy', in *The British Economy in the Nineteen-Fifties*, G. D. N. Worswick and P. H. Ady (eds.), London and New York, Oxford University Press, 1962.
6. ——. Review of Dow, 'Management of the British Economy', *Economic Journal* (December 1964).
7. PREST, A. R., 'Sense and Nonsense in Budgetary Policy', *Economic Journal* (March 1968).
8. SARGENT, J. R., 'Recent Growth Experience in the Economy of the United Kingdom', *Economic Journal* (March 1968).
9. SHEPHERD, J. R., 'Productive Potential and the Demand for Labour', *Economic Trends*, HMSO (August 1968).

3 Trade and Payments*

by G. D. N. Worswick

My assignment is Trade and Payments, which were covered in the original Brookings study in two chapters, on the Balance of Payments by Cooper and on British Trade Performance by Krause. Both these chapters have two features in common, a strong analytical under-pinning and a bold determination to put numbers down wherever possible. Cooper includes in his summary a table showing alternative methods for improving the United Kingdom balance of payments by £100 millions, which is reproduced here. (Table 1).

Table 1. *Alternative methods for improving the United Kingdom balance of payments by £100 million: A Summary*[1]

Course of action	Size of policy change
Rise in target unemployment rate	0·34 percentage points
Imposition of import surcharge on manufactures [b]	4 per cent
Reduction in overseas military expenditures	£143 million
Across-the-board reduction in private capital outflow [c]	£110 million
Across-the-board reduction in foreign sid [c]	£159 million
Currency devaluation [b]	1·41 per cent

[a] Per year, in terms of transactions levels of 1966. 'Medium-term' effects, after a period of adjustment.

[b] Assumes a price-elasticity of unity, allows for feedbacks, and assumes no retaliation.

[c] Each stated reduction results in a reduction in long-term balance-of-payments receipts by £4a million.

[d] Assuming other currencies devalued are limited to those devalued in November 1967.

* I am grateful for assistance in preparing this paper to a number of present and past colleagues at the National Institute – R. L. Major, Mrs A. Morgan, N. Garganas, S. Hays and R. L. Crum. I take full responsibility for all opinions and any mistakes.
[1] *Britain's Economic Prospects* p. 196.

And Krause summarizes his explanation of the decline in the British share of world trade in manufactures between 1959/60 and 1965/6 thus (Table 2):

Table 2.

Reason	Share of world trade %
Below average rate of growth	−1·5
Loss of export price-competitiveness	−2·0
Special factors relating to OSA	−0·3
R & D payoffs	+0·5
Net loss	−3·3

This approach is very much to be welcomed, though it does involve risks. Inevitably many of the calculations had to be done quickly (the whole book was produced with remarkable speed) and frequently the data are just not available for any very sophisticated calculations, so that rough-and-ready methods had to be adopted. Thus it would not be difficult to fault the authors in a number of places on points of detail. But this would be an unrewarding exercise. The figures were put forward as suggestions, as orders of magnitude which should be taken into account in considering alternative policies and alternative explanations, and they should be taken in that spirit.

Neither author offers explanations of British trade performance nor judgments about policy which are contentious. Professor Cooper does take a fairly firm position on devaluation, which occurred just as he was completing his chapter, and he believes that 'it should leave Britain's payments position – and the objectives that underly it – much firmer than during the preceding decade'. This is, of course, still an open question. But altogether the methods adopted by Cooper and Krause do not invite any kind of British 'confrontation' with an American point of view expressed in the Brookings book, nor do I feel any inclination to hunt through their texts in order to try to pick quarrels. What I shall attempt to do is to carry forward a little discussion of some of the points raised by the two authors in the original Brookings book: accordingly this paper will consist of a number of sections rather loosely connected with one another.

1. Krause confined himself largely to an analysis of the exports and imports of manufactures. This means, of course, the bulk of our exports of goods, but only the smaller part of our imports of goods. Even with this limitation there was a lot of ground to be covered, but I cannot help feeling that someone less familiar than Krause with the structure of British trade and payments might have come away with a slightly distorted impression. In my first section, therefore, I shall try to broaden the picture a little: in particular, this will give me an opportunity to say something about the income-elasticity approach which has been adopted by some writers in this field.

2. Krause goes into the interesting question of the relation between exports and growth. He adopts the position that had we grown faster we might have been able to export more, which contrasts with the alternative Lamfalussy–Beckerman approach which makes growth itself dependent upon exports. I think some additional light can be thrown on this problem by an industry analysis of which I will report some tentative findings.

3. It is still too early to judge whether Cooper will prove right in his judgment that the British balance-of-payments position will be much firmer during the coming decade than in the preceding one. However, he was bold enough to make a specific forecast as to the balance-of-payments effect of devaluation and it is interesting to examine how far he has proved right to date and to compare his forecast with one or two others which were made at the time, including that of the National Institute of Economic and Social Research.

4. Krause makes only a very brief reference to the Common Market. Since the Brookings book was published we have now had a White Paper from the British government on this question and it would seem to be useful on this occasion to summarise the conclusions of that document, although I do not propose to examine them in any detail.

I. TRADE: VOLUME AND PRICES

Krause begins his analysis with a table showing UK exports of manufactured goods and imports of manufactured goods expressed as a ratio of GDP, all in constant (1958) prices for the period 1956 to 1966. The features of this table are the virtual constancy of the export ratio at a little over 14 per cent, and the rise in the import ratio from 4·1 per cent in 1956 to nearly double, 7·9 per cent, in 1966.

Krause goes on to point out that a rise in the ratio of imported manufactured products to GDP of the kind experienced in the United Kingdom is not at all unusual among advanced European economies. On the other hand those economies also appear to have had a rising ratio of exports of manufactures to GDP while Britain has not. Consequently, on the face of it, it is the exports which are, as it were, out of line.

In so far as the trade balance has contributed to our balance-of-payments difficulties, this view that it is relatively poor export performance rather than excessive importing which has been the trouble has been held by the majority of economists and officials interested in this question, the view being held indifferently as applying to manufactured goods alone or to imports in general. This opinion has not been held unanimously. Roy Harrod has frequently argued that we should have pursued a much more vigorous policy of import restriction.[1] In summing up the experience of the 1950s I myself took the view that the root of the balance-of-payments trouble lay in the years 1953–5 'when restrictions on imports and payments were relaxed too quickly'.[2] While recognizing that I am probably out of step, I am still inclined to give the greater weight to the import side of the account, if only for the not wholly convincing reason that the National Institute invariably under-forecasts imports and, so far as I know, they are not alone in having this experience. In any case these things are matters of degree.

Krause refers to the equation $e \times r = e' \times r'$ as a useful framework for discussing the relations between the balance of payments and the growth of potential output. e = income elasticity of demand for imported goods, r = rate of growth of U.K. output, e' = income elasticity of demand of the rest of the world for British goods (exports) and r' = the rate of growth of output of the rest of the world. In the realm of economic theory, where you define your terms to fit, there can be no objection to such a formula. In the real world too, anyone who has had to produce a view about future economic prospects at rather short notice knows how indispensable a device is the ruler. But it can lead to some very strange results if used to project over long periods. We have lately had, for example, the remarkable picture painted by Houthakker and Magee of the nations in their appointed stations, growing ineluctably at rates determined by their trade elasticities, with the Japanese disappear-

---

[1] See, for example, *The British Economy*, (McGraw Hill, 1963).
[2] *The British Economy in the 1950s*, ed. by G. D. N. Worswick and P. H. Ady, p. 69.

ing in the distance, growing, to twist Ouida's expression, three times
as fast as stroke, while Britain lags ever further behind, growing only
half as fast.[1]

Krause states that in the period 1954–66 the value of *e* for Britain
was about 1·16, meaning 'that for every one per cent increase in real
GDP, imports of goods and services in real terms increased by 1·16
per cent'. I suspect that this may well be a slip. The crudest way to
estimate this elasticity is simply to take the changes from the first
year to the last year of the period. Real GDP rose by 38 per cent,
which is an annual average compound rate of 2·73; the volume of
imports of goods and services rose by 61 per cent, which is an annual
average rate of 4·05; elasticity, defined as the ratio of these two
rates, is 1·48. By simple regression we can get a figure as low as 1·38
for this period, but I cannot find any way of getting as low as 1·16.
Houthakker and Magee got an estimate of 1·66 for 1951–66, as
already mentioned, but this was from an equation in which there was
a price term with a perverse coefficient. In a simple regression they
got 1·5. Using an equation adjusted for serial correlation but re-
taining a price term they found 1·45.

If exports rise in line with production, while the import income
elasticity is greater than 1, then it might seem that two things should
be happening. Imports should bear an increasing proportion to
domestic product and the trade balance should be worsening.
Neither in fact need occur, however. The former could be avoided if

<hr>

[1] H. S. Houthakker and Stephen P. Magee, 'Income and Price Elasticities in
World Trade', *Review of Economics and Statistics*, May 1969. The income and
price elasticities are estimated, by simple or multiple regression, from time series
over past periods. The particular value of one-half for the ratio of UK growth to
the rest of the world is derived from the original import and export income
elasticities of 1·66 and 0·86. However, in these original estimations the price
coefficients, particularly in the import equations, were found to be statistically
insignificant and some of them had the wrong sign. Moreover serial correlation
was quite common. Later on the authors made revised price-elasticity estimates
and made adjustments for serial correlation. This entailed revision of the income
elasticities which were now put at 1·45 and 1·00, which in terms of the formula
would enable UK to lag rather less drastically behind. In passing it should be
noted that the German import elasticity is put down at around 1·8 to 1·9. The
original export elasticity is estimated at 2·08, but after revision it was reduced to
0·9, suggesting that Germany suffers from a serious structural imbalance in trade
of the growth-inhibiting kind!
For a fuller discussion of this question, see the article in *The Manchester School*
(Dec. 1970) by Anne Morgan, 'Income and Price Elasticities: A Comment',
from which these various figures have been taken.

E

domestic costs rise sufficiently faster than import prices, and the latter if the terms of trade change sufficiently fast.[1]

Table 3 puts down, side by side, changes in the ratios of exports and imports of goods and services to GDP, first valued at 1963 prices and then at current prices for the period 1948 to 1968. As in Krause's table, the constant price export ratio remains pretty well constant from 1956 to 1966, but of course it is at a higher figure of rather over 21½ per cent, since here we have all goods and services, while Krause had only manufactured goods. Similarly, the constant price-import ratio rises from 20·5 to 22·7, a rise, however, which is both proportionately, and also absolutely, smaller than the rise of the imports of manufactured goods alone. At the beginning of the period manufactured goods constituted one-fifth and at the end just over one-third of all imports of goods and services.

The picture looks very different when we turn to the current price ratios, for now both ratios are seen to *fall* quite considerably from around 25 per cent in 1965 to around 21½ per cent in 1966. Imports fell relatively a trifle less than exports, by about ½ per cent from the beginning to the end of the ten-year period specified, though during this period the gap between the import and the export ratio widens from time to time. It should be noted, however, that services includes here government credits on the export side and debits on the import side. Net government debits in 1956 amounted to just under 1 per cent of GDP and in 1966 to 1·4 per cent. This rise in net government expenditure is virtually sufficient to account for the relative deterioration of the export ratio to the import ratio over the ten-year period as a whole.[2]

This rather striking contrast between the volume behaviour between 1956 and 1966 and the value behaviour suggests that it might be worth looking at the trends over a longer period, and this is done from 1948 to 1969 in Charts 1 and 2. In charts 1A and 1B we have the movement of the value of exports and imports of goods and services and of the volumes as measured in 1963 prices. As regards volumes, it is a *curiosum* that the increase in the volume of exports of goods and services from 1948 to 1969 was actually greater than that of imports, but this gives far too great weight to the events in the years in the beginning and at the end. In every year from 1950 to

---

[1] Of course, it is usually stated that the elasticity formula $r/r' = e'/e$ only holds for unchanged terms of trade. What is usually lacking is any discussion of what the terms of trade have been in the past and what is expected in the future.

[2] This is, of course, a purely arithmetical statement. It does not imply that government spending ought to have been less.

Table 3. *Ratio of exports and imports of goods and services to GDP*

	Exports		Imports	
	1963 prices	Current prices	1963 prices	Current prices
1948	18·1	21·4	19·2	23·7
1949	19·8	22·9	20·1	24·7
1950	21·6	26·4	19·7	27·1
1951	20·6	28·9	20·3	34·3
1952	20·2	27·3	18·8	28·6
1953	20·1	24·8	19·4	25·8
1954	20·5	24·5	19·4	25·3
1955	21·1	24·8	20·7	26·7
1956	21·7	25·3	20·4	25·0
1957	21·8	25·1	20·5	24·8
1958	21·6	23·4	20·9	22·8
1959	21·5	22·9	21·6	23·1
1960	21·7	22·8	23·0	24·6
1961	21·5	22·2	22·1	22·8
1962	21·7	21·8	22·3	22·2
1963	21·7	21·7	22·2	22·2
1964	21·4	21·1	23·0	23·2
1965	21·8	21·1	22·6	22·1
1966	22·2	21·4	22·6	21·8
1967	21·9	20·7	23·6	22·0
1968	23·8	23·8	24·6	24·8
1969	25·4	25·3	24·8	24·9

1959 the volume of imports, as measured in 1963 prices, falls short of the volume of exports. In every year after that date it exceeds the volume of exports. There is, then, a divergent trend in export and import volumes. This divergence is less apparent when we look at the value series, although after 1960 the relative movement of the value series is similar to that of the volume series. Part of the explanation is clearly seen in Chart 2. After 1948 import prices shot ahead of export prices and both of them rose rapidly in relation to home costs (GDP deflator). These movements reflect first the 1949 devaluation and then the impact of the Korean War. We seem to be back on trend as it were, somewhere around 1954. From then until 1962 the gap between import and export prices narrows, i.e. the terms of trade improve; thereafter they show relatively little change. Meanwhile throughout the whole period, with the exception of 1949 to

67

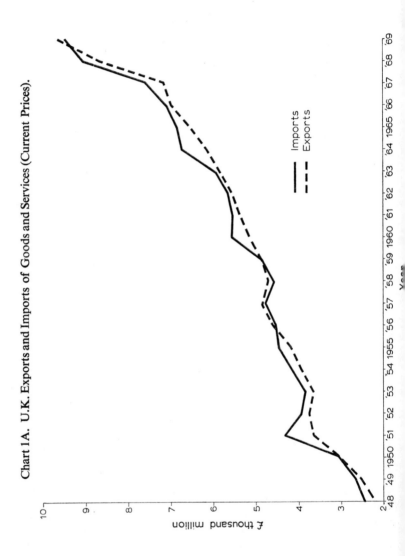

Chart 1A. U.K. Exports and Imports of Goods and Services (Current Prices).

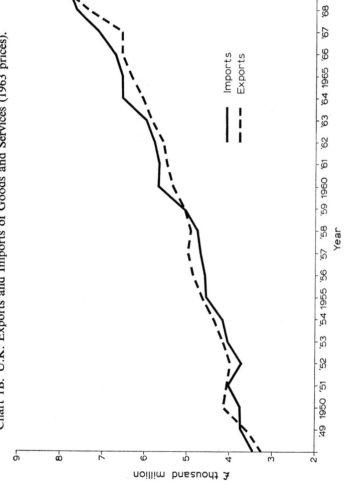

Chart 1B. U.K. Exports and Imports of Goods and Services (1963 prices).

Chart 2.

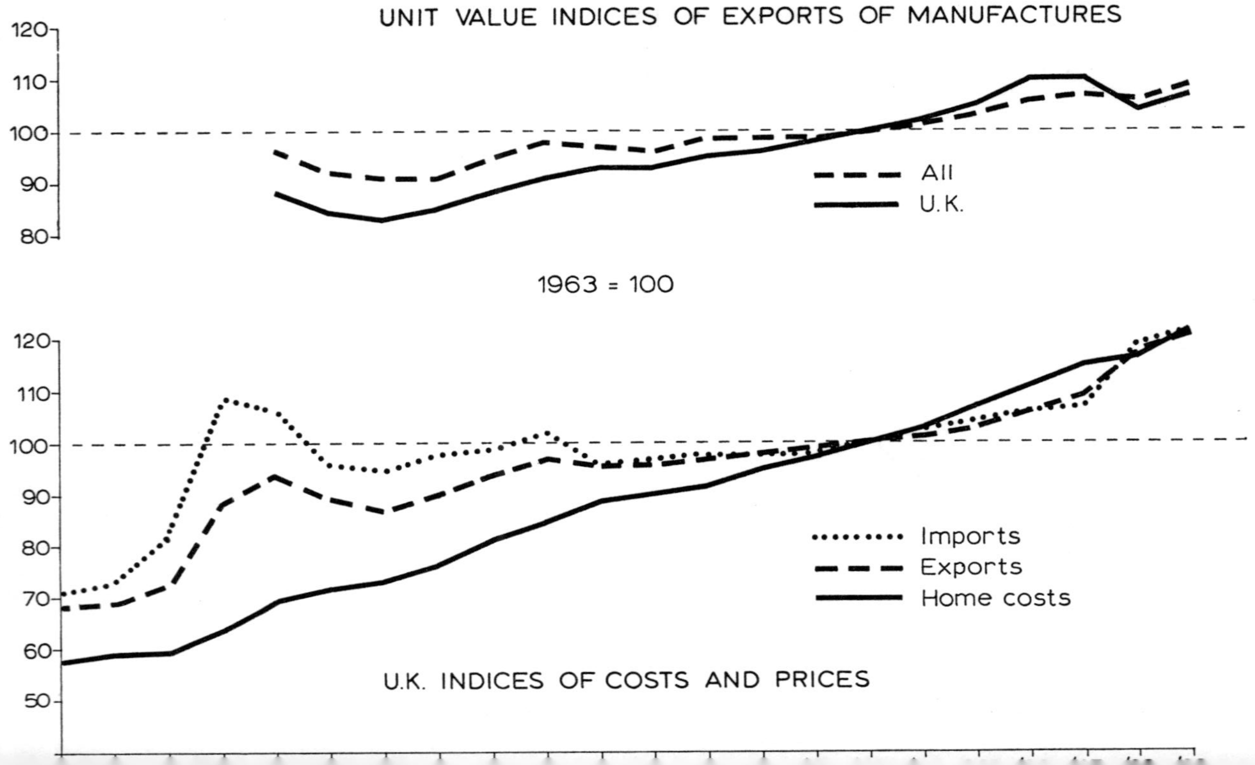

UNIT VALUE INDICES OF EXPORTS OF MANUFACTURES

1963 = 100

All
U.K.

U.K. INDICES OF COSTS AND PRICES

Imports
Exports
Home costs

1954, home unit costs have been rising faster than both export and import prices, again with the exception of the post 1967 devaluation.

Leaving aside the Korean incident, this chart suggests the following story. After the 1949 devaluation, British exports became highly competitive; British exports prices, if you wish, were too low. The limitation on expanding British exports during the earlier period was supply, and there was indeed evidence of such difficulties in the early 1950s, though they were exacerbated by the Korean rearmament. During this period a rise in British costs would do no harm because the supply of exports was below the equilibrium level, and it was positively beneficial so far as the balance of payments was concerned; that is to say, the improvement in the terms of trade improved the balance of trade at the same time. We then enter a middle period, of the later 1950s and early 1960s, in which British prices, in relation to competitors, are 'about right' and where the determination of exports is a matter both of supply and demand. Meanwhile the British cost inflation continues and in the final part of the period, the middle 1960s, British exports become over-priced relative to competitors and now export volumes become mainly demand determined. No longer can price rises of exports be taken in their stride, improving the balance of trade at the same time as the terms improve. If cost inflation goes on internally then devaluation is necessary.

An essential character in this story has not yet been mentioned, namely the movement of prices of competitors. That is shown in the upper part of the chart which shows UK export prices edging up about 1 per cent a year faster than the average for major industrial exporters.[1] The fact that all the curves cross over in 1963 is, of course, entirely fortuitous; that was chosen as the base year. It should not be judged, for instance, that because the difference between the British and competitors' prices in 1969 was 3 points, that is the size of our present margin of advantage. It we take 1959 to 1961 as the last time when British prices were 'about right', then the 1969 margin of advantage becomes zero. If the above account has any plausibility, it is a warning against looking for any single continuing factor as the sole or principal cause of British balance-of-payments problems.

I have already quoted the result of Krause's quantitative analysis of the reasons for the fall in Britain's share of world trade. He attributes a quite substantial role to export price competitiveness. I think capacity limitations indicated by his reason 'below average rate of growth' could have been operating in the early 1950s, but I

[1] (Source: Statistical Appendices of the *National Institute Economic Review*.)

really am doubtful that this was the case in the later 1950s. When we depart from the total and look at the separate trade groups, quite rapid increases in exports proved possible when markets were found. Krause attributes only 10 per cent of the loss in the share of world trade to special factors relating to the outer sterling area. In this connection it is interesting to compare the results of a study by R. L. Major published in the *National Institute Economic Review*, May 1968, on the decline in Britain's share in world trade in manufactures from 1954–66. Major analyzed trade in seven commodity groups to nine areas, and he showed that the fall in share, though widespread, was steepest in sectors of trade in which the share had initially been highest, in particular trade with the overseas sterling area and trade in textiles. These happened also to be sectors of trade which expanded relatively slowly, so that the UK's share of world trade as a whole would have fallen even if it had been maintained sector by sector. It turns out, however, that the combined effects of these factors explains only a small part, about 9 per cent, on the basis of Major's calculation, of the total loss of world share between 1954 and 1966. 'The remainder results from net losses of share in individual sectors of trade and must therefore be attributed to declining competitiveness in the broadest sense.'

This result seems to me wholly compatible with Krause's, although it leaves open the question of how much of the decline in competitivness is a matter of price and how much of some other general factor. This makes it especially important to examine, as I shall try to do later, the devaluation consequences, to see how far the price effect is working. Meanwhile I turn to a different question, namely the relation between exports and growth.

II. Exports and Growth

This section is prompted by Krause's remarks on the relations between exports and the growth of output. He mentions the two alternative hypotheses: (a) that quickly-rising exports promote growth and (b) that faster growth of output is a necessary condition for more rapidly increasing exports; and himself chooses the latter for the British case. Referring back to his table, quoted earlier in this Chapter, we see that he attributes nearly one-half of UK's loss of share in world exports from 1959/60 to 1965/6 to 'below average rate of growth'.

As Krause points out, the relation between growth and the trade balance, and especially exports, is a complicated two-way process.

Taken quite generally it is a question of great theoretical interest, but in addition it has some practical importance in the British case. For if we take the view that faster export growth is a necessary condition for faster growth of GDP, then clearly something drastic must be done to get exports moving faster: the most obvious candidate is devaluation; and if that does not do, then – presumably – more devaluation.

The theory of export-led, or export-propelled, growth has in recent years been most closely associated with the names of Lamfalussy and Beckerman, and I start with an exposition of the theory by Beckerman:[1]

'Differences in growth rates among reasonably advanced countries are largely the result of differences in the expectations that may be held concerning future long-run demand prospects. A high pressure of demand will not be enough to induce a fast increase in capacity unless it is accompanied by expectations of a fast increase in demand. Confident expectations will stimulate a greater effort to expand productive capacity, both through a higher rate of investment and through improvements in productivity per unit of total input of capital and labour. A faster rate of gross capital formation may have an automatically favourable effect on the productivity of net capital formation an account of "embodied technical progress". If the increased capacity permits the confident demand expectations to be realized, so that output is able to expand rapidly, the productivity per unit of factor is likely to rise on account of economies of scale both internal and external, as well as generally improved organization of production. In other words, the productive system, at least in most of industry, is believed to be very flexible, and the rate of growth that can be achieved is, within limits, partly a matter of the growth rate that the relevant bodies in society (particularly entrepreneurs) expect to be achieved.

'For an economy in which foreign trade is a large proportion of output the most important determinant of confident expectations about the long-run of increase in demand is the buoyancy of exports.'

One possible version of the export-led growth theory is quite simply that if domestic aggregate demand is expanded with the idea

[1] W. Beckerman and Associates, *The British Economy in 1975* (Cambridge University Press, 1965).

73

Chart 3. Changes in Gross National Product per head of employed labour force and the volume of exports–growth rates (annual averages).

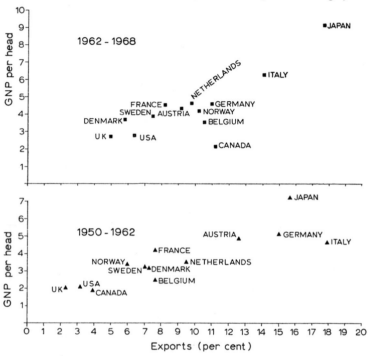

| | 1950–62 | | 1962–68 | |
	GNP per head	*Vol. of exports*	*GNP per head*	*Vol. of exports*
Austria	4·9	12·6	4·3	9·2
Belgium	2·5	7·7	3·6	10·6
Canada	1·9	3·9	2·2	11·2
Denmark	3·2	7·3	3·7	5·8
France	4·2	7·7	4·5	8·2
Germany	5·1	14·8	4·6	11·0
Italy	4·7	17·9	6·3	14·1
Japan	7·3	15·7	9·2	17·7
Netherlands	3·5	9·5	4·6	9·8
Norway	3·4	6·0	4·2	10·2
Sweden	3·2	7·0	3·9	7·5
United Kingdom	2·0	2·3	3·0	5·0
USA	2·0	3·2	2·7	6·4

of stimulating faster growth, this may lead to a surge of imports, and in the absence of a corresponding acceleration of exports the whole exercise may founder on a balance-of-payments crisis. This is the kind of story we have heard many times in the context of British stop–go. But in the passage I have just quoted there seems to be a hint of some more direct connection between exports and productivity, i.e. exports *per se* have a peculiarly favourable influence in generating confident expectations. Presumably if there is anything in this theory we ought to find an association between export growth and productivity growth in comparable countries. Chart 3 shows scatter diagrams of GNP per head and the volume of exports, both expressed in terms of annual average growth rates over two periods, 1950 to 1962 and 1962 to 1968. In the lower part of the chart, which represents the earlier period, the association seems pretty strong and positive. The upper part of the diagram is a bit trickier. On the one hand, if one blocks out Canada, it still seems that we have a good association, on the other hand if we block out Italy and Japan but retain Canada, the eye suggests that there is very little association.[1]

Another line of investigation is suggested by the last paragraph of the quotation from Beckerman. Write 'industry' instead of 'economy' and we get: 'For an industry in which foreign trade is a large proportion of output the most important determinant of confident expectations about the long-run rate of increase in demand (for the products of that industry) is the buoyancy of exports.' The Beckerman argument seems to be prima facie just as convincing when applied to 'industry' as to 'economy'. Can we find then, first of all, an association between exports and productivity by industry groups? We might ask this question in two ways. First we could look at different industries within the same country and see whether there is

[1] There are, in fact, grounds for regarding Canada as something of a special case. The growth of Canadian exports is very largely due to the exceptional growth in United States imports in general, and to the tremendous increase in imports of automotive products under the Ottawa Free Trade Agreement in particular. Between 1962 and 1968 the US dollar value of total Canadian exports increased by 111 per cent while that of total OECD exports increased by 79 per cent. But to destinations outside North America the rises were almost the same, 66 per cent for Canada and 63 per cent for the rest of OECD.

As things stand, over the period 1962–8, Canada appears as a country of fast growth of exports, but slow growth of GNP per head, and, as such, is unfavourable to the Beckerman–Lamfalussy thesis. If exports to US were excluded, Canada would still be an exception to the Beckerman–Lamfalussy thesis but less obviously so. But there seems little justification for excluding exports to US. On the contrary, they might be regarded as a conspicuous example of a good and growing market which should generate confident expectations.

Table 4. *Squared correlation coefficients*

Country	No. of industries	Productivity/Output			Output/Exports			Productivity/Exports		
		1954–9	1959–64	1954–64	1954–9	1959–64	1954–64	1954–9	1959–64	1954–64
Yugoslavia	17	0·07	0·01	0·02	0·18	0·39	0·30	0·01	0·08	0·16
Sweden[a]	11	0·14	0·31	0·13	..	..	..	..	..	..
France	15[b]	0·22	0·03	0·04	0·25	—	0·03	0·15	0·02	0·36
Greece[c]	11	0·23	0·49	—	0·35	0·03	0·01	0·14	0·02	0·15
West Germany	20	0·34	0·02	0·16	0·38	0·29	0·44	0·01	—	0·01
United Kingdom	20	0·54	0·33	0·41	0·33	0·04	0·46	0·35	0·19	0·31
Belgium	12	0·55	0·17	0·11	0·57	0·70	0·65	0·39	0·19	0·02
Norway	19	0·61	0·70	0·62	..	..	..	..	..	..
Netherlands	19	0·72	0·40	0·65	0·18	0·01	0·05	—	—	0·03
Italy[d]	15	0·74	0·31	0·50	0·13	0·26	0·12	0·08	0·01	0·01
Ireland	11	0·78	0·30	0·65	0·09	0·42	0·09	—	0·28	0·13

Source: NIESR calculations based on data supplied by European Research Institutes.

[a] Periods 1954–9, 1959–62, 1954–62.
[b] Including five sectors not normally classified as industrial.
[c] Periods 1954–8, 1958–63, 1954–63.
[d] Periods 1954–9, 1959–63, 1954–63.

Table 4a. *Squared correlation coefficients*

Country	Number of industries	Productivity/ Output		Output/ Exports		Productivity/ Exports	
		1954–69	1964–9	1954–69	1964–9	1954–69	1964–9
Italy	11	0·49	0·21	0·15	0·16	0·00	0·00
Netherlands	19	0·34	0·56	0·27	0·40	0·26	0·39
Ireland	11	0·92	0·90	0·40	0·72	0·37	0·90
Germany*	20	0·13	0·24	0·38	0·16	0·00	0·00
Belgium*	12	0·49	0·50	0·83	0·78	0·55	0·51

* 1954–68 and 1964–8.

Table 5. *Squared correlation coefficients*

Industry	No. of countries	Productivity/ Output	Output/ Exports	Productivity/ Exports
Non-ferrous metals	6	0·99	0·55	0·59
Ferrous metals	5	0·90	0·94	0·76
Drink and tobacco	6	0·90	0·84(5)	..
Chemicals	10	0·74	0·07(8)	0·03(8)
Textiles	8	0·70	0·69(7)	0·45(7)
Paper	6	0·61	0·56(5)	0·17(5)
Food	8	0·60	0·51(6)	0·20(6)
Electrical engineering	6	0·58	0·39(5)	0·32(5)
Timber and furniture	7	0·39	0·21(6)	0·02(6)
Mechanical engineering	5	0·15	..	..
Rubber	5	0·14	..	..

Note: Bracketed figures are the number of countries where less than in the main column. The period is 1954–64.

an association between export growth and productivity growth. We should not be too disheartened if we find poor results here because obviously some industries, e.g. construction, have little or no export content anyway. The alternative is to look at the same industry across countries. To make this investigation thoroughly requires the resources of an international organization, which can ensure that industry groups and product groups are really comparable one with another.

My own approach, which I made in the first instance a few years ago, was altogether sketchier. In the first instance we extracted the material for the United Kingdom and Germany ourselves at the National Institute. We then wrote to a number of colleagues in

77

research institutes in different European countries and asked them to duplicate, as best they might, the material we had got out for UK and Germany. We asked for data for output (Y), productivity (P), and exports (X), in real terms (annual average rates of growth) over the periods 1954–9, 1959–64 and 1954–64 as a whole. Tables 4 and 5 give the values of the squared correlation coefficients for the three pairs of correlations of these variables. In Table 4 we are looking at different industries within the same country and in Table 5 the same industry across countries.

I have included the productivity/output correlations to indicate that in most cases we got results similar to those which have been found by many researchers in many other instances, noting however that this correlation is not universal. The low figures for France and Germany are really quite interesting. It would, however, be too much of a digression to follow-up the output/productivity association.

Let us first look at the association between output and exports (Y, X). Except in so far as exports are themselves a part of output, it is not easy to bring *a priori* arguments for expecting to find an association between Y and X. The more direct way of looking at any possible connection would be to consider H, the rate of growth of output for the home market to be compared with X, the rate of growth of exports. Here there is the argument that if the home market is reduced (or by dynamic extension, the rate of growth is slowed down) firms will be driven to increase exports (or step up the rate of growth of exports). This argument tends to be about the pressure of demand in the short period and I think that this is the argument which Krause is using when he maintains that the fall in the British share of world exports can be partly explained by slow growth of British output. But there is an alternative argument, often adduced by British manufacturers, that a large home market is a precondition of flourishing exports, and if this argument were dynamized we would look for a positive association between H and X. Thus the *a priori* arguments go in opposite directions. Turning to the data, Table 4 provides little evidence of an association between Y and X. Five of the nine countries show none at all over the full period. Belgium shows a clear association and for the remaining three countries the connection is weak. Table 5, however, suggests a more definite connection of a positive kind, though we note that we have for many industries only five or six countries.

There is, of course, a two-way argument concerning the relation between productivity (P) and the growth of output (Y). In one direction productivity is seen as reducing costs and thus permitting an expansion of demand and hence of output. This argument may apply with even greater force where there is a large export market, simply because the elasticity of demand in such a case may be higher than it would be in the home market alone. This theoretical link between productivity growth and exports has a long history in economics. But we now also have the suggestion, adumbrated above, in the form of the export-propelled growth theory, that the growth of export demand has a peculiarly favourable quality, engendering confident expectations and the growth of productivity in particular industries. The facts, however, are not too encouraging. Table 4 shows that, over the ten-year period, nine of the eleven countries showed no correlation at all and two cases provided a rather weak one. Table 5 is a little more hopeful; there is some association at the industrial level, though rather small, except for non-ferrous and ferrous metals. Unfortunately, even in this case we have only five or six countries to provide observations.

I had hoped to get additional data for recent years to supplement the data up to 1964. I wrote again to the European Institutes and they have been very helpful. As regards the correlations between industry groups within countries, we have worked out a few of the additional ones for slightly different periods and they are shown in Table 4a. The results do not cause us to revise in any way what has been concluded from the earlier data. Unfortunately the more interesting prospect, namely, the across country correlations for particular industries, is not helped by the fact that in a number of cases the industrial classifications have been revised in recent years, so we can no longer give data comparable to that originally collected. In examining replies received from the European Institutes, it was plain that to get comparable data would now be a major undertaking. It will be seen that the results in Table 4a are broadly consonant with those of Table 4.

On the face of it, a much more detailed investigation of particular industries across countries might prove rewarding. It might also be interesting to bring into the picture the share of exports in the output of the industry, and, indeed, to go a stage further and define the industry in relations both to exports and to competing imports. Even if there is an association between exports and productivity growth which can be put on a firmer footing than it appears to be at present, we will still be left with the fact that the causal link can go either way. My own preference is for the link from productivity to exports, because I can understand the mechanism, whereas I cannot really grasp why growth in export demand can achieve something

79

which could not be achieved by a growth in home demand on the same scale, apart from special cases such as aircraft construction, where in the nature of things the home market cannot be expected to expand fast enough[1] and an international market is needed.

III. DEVALUATION

In this section an attempt is made to estimate the effect of the devaluation of November 18, 1967, when the parity of sterling was changed from $2.80 to $2.40, a fall of 14·3 per cent. Any such calculation must beg the question whether the devaluation was avoidable. The calculation presented here presupposes that the confidence crisis could have been got through in some way without devaluation, but at the same time makes no allowance for any subsequent costs to the balance of payments, e.g. interest on borrowed funds, which might have been incurred in overcoming the confidence crisis in that particular way. The calculation has to be an interim one in two distinct senses. It is made with data available up to the end of 1969 and it is quite possible that there are some further 'devaluation effects' still to come through. But it is interim also in a quite different sense. In the past few years there have been, besides devaluation, a number of events which make it difficult to pick up the underlying trends of exports and imports. There was, for example, the extended dock strike at the end of 1967 itself, and then there are the problems raised by the revision of the export statistics made during 1969, and to which reference is made later. The further away one gets from the particular event the easier it becomes to distinguish underlying trends from movements provoked by special factors. For this reason not only will an estimate be made of the most likely devaluation effects as seen at the moment of writing but it will also be indicated how sensitive such an estimate is to changes in the assumptions upon which it has been calculated.

VISIBLE TRADE

1. *Export prices*

The export unit value index, expressed in sterling, jumped at once by over 5 per cent between the third quarter of 1967 and the first quarter of 1968 and thereafter rose at a decelerating rate to the first quarter of 1969. After a brief pause it began to rise again in the third quarter. Whether we choose for comparison the third quarter, the

[1] Except in USA.

fourth quarter or the whole year of 1967 and 1969, the overall increase turns out the same at around 11¼ per cent.

Part of this rise, however, reflects the continuation of an underlying movement. In the six years prior to devaluation the export unit-value index rose on average about 2 per cent per annum. By comparing this movement with that of the indices of OECD countries and looking at how indices for those countries have moved since devaluation, it is reasonable to put down for the underlying movement of the UK export price index an increase of about 1½ per cent in 1968 and of 2 per cent in 1969. By subtracting this from the actual movement we get the 'devaluation effect' of an increase of 7·6 per cent.

2. *The volume of exports*

The method to be followed to estimate the effect of devaluation upon the volume of exports seems to be straightforward; namely to find some way of projecting what exports would have been in the absence of devaluation and then to attribute to devaluation the difference between this increase and that which actually occurred. There is, however, rather a tiresome complication which needs to be got out of the way. In a note to the Trade Returns for May 1969, the Board of Trade announced the discovery of a rather serious under-recording of exports which seemed to have been occurring on an increasing scale, both absolutely and in proportion to recorded exports since 1963. Later in the year the Board of Trade announced figures which put the records straight. This confronts us with an alternative. Either we could project the volume of exports on the basis of some past relationship and then add an extra to allow for the under-recording which would presumably have been discovered anyway. Alternatively we can reduce the actually recorded figure to take out that part of the increase which can be attributed to the discovery of under-recording. It is the second alternative which we have adopted. Specifically we have supposed that the volume of exports of manufactures in 1969 was 2·4 per cent higher than in 1967 on account of the recording correction. Put the other way round, instead of the increase of something over 28 per cent, which is what the statistics now show, we concern ourselves only with a growth of the volume of exports of manufactures of 25½ per cent which is to be accounted for by trend factors and devaluation.

It is well known that UK exports of manufactures constitute a falling proportion of the volume of world exports of manufactures. The British share of 19·3 per cent in 1956 had fallen to 11·8 per cent

F

in 1967. This is an average annual rate of fall of 0·7 percentage points in absolute terms, though the fall has tended to be greater in years when world trade was expanding abnormally fast and correspondingly less when world trade has expanded slowly. To project British exports in the absence of devaluation I have simply postulated two further falls of 0·7 in 1968 and 1969, i.e. shares of 11·1 and 10·4 per cent respectively of the volume of world exports of manufactures. Since world trade has been rising exceptionally fast, it might be argued that we should put in rather higher than average falls in the British share. But in fact constant absolute declines are, already, increasing proportionate declines; a fall of 0·7 on the British share at the beginning of the period in 1956 was 3½ per cent; a fall of 0·7 from 1967 to 1968 is nearly 6 per cent. The 1967 trade figures used as a base have been corrected for dock strikes, but might still be regarded as a little low for other special reasons.

It could also be argued that as the British share falls so the absolute amount of a further fall should be diminished on the grounds that British exports are becoming increasingly concentrated on the hard core of things like whisky, for which there is less international competition. There is plenty of room for argument here, but my own impression is that, if this projection is loaded, it is loaded slightly in the pessimistic direction, which has the consequence of leading to a slightly optimistic estimate of the devaluation effect. As we have already mentioned, the volume of world exports of manufactures grew exceptionally fast between 1967 and 1969, by a little over 30 per cent, from which we deduce that British exports of manufactures would have grown by 14 per cent in the absence of devaluation; which means in turn that exports of manufactures were about 10 per cent higher than they would have been in the absence of devaluation (not forgetting that we have made a correction for under-recording).

This is an estimate for the full year of 1969 and it can be argued that the effects of devaluation are still coming through so that the devaluation effect at the end of the year should be higher than for the average of the year. A figure of 11–12 per cent for the end of the year might seem plausible.

An alternative estimate was made by a somewhat different route which allows the use of quarterly data. This was to apply a relationship employed in the forecasting of exports at the National Institute. The equation concerned relates the value of exports to a weighted index of industrial countries, manufacturing production and a term for the ratio of this index to its own trend (to represent pressure of

82

demand). This route came up with an estimate of 11 to 12·5 per cent volume increase by the end of 1969. This was a gratifying confirmation and we choose for the purposes of calculation a figure of 11·5 per cent, but we will also indicate by how much the devaluation effect would be altered for each 1 per cent difference in the volume effect for exports.

3. *Import prices*

The total import unit-value index rose sharply by about 10 per cent between October 1967 and March 1968 and thereafter continued to rise steadily at about 1 per cent per quarter until the middle of 1969, when it appeared to accelerate again, and by the end of 1969 it was 19·5 per cent above the pre-devaluation level. As with export prices, part of this rise can reasonably be attributed to an underlying movement. Over the six years prior to devaluation, import prices rose on average by 1¼ per cent per annum. Comparing this trend with that of some other major industrial countries, and noting how the indices of those countries which did not devalue moved after November 1967, I reckon that UK import prices would have been about 6½ per cent higher by the end of 1969, leaving a 'devaluation' rise of about 12¼ per cent.

4. *Volume of imports*

In principle the procedure should be as with exports, namely to estimate what the volume of imports would have been in accordance with pre-devaluation relationships, and then to subtract to get the devaluation effect. In practice things do not turn out to be quite so easy. In the first place devaluation was reinforced in November 1968 by an import deposit scheme, applying to about one-third of imports (mostly manufactures), whereby importers of goods had to put down a cash deposit of (initially) 50 per cent of the value of the imports – a deposit which was returned only after six months. But even more troublesome is the fact that quite a wide variety of econometric relationships which have been in use for economic forecasting predict a volume of imports in 1968 and 1969 which is less, not greater, than the observed volume. This problem has been discussed at considerable length in two recent issues of the *National Institute Economic Review*,[1] and it will suffice to give here a summary of the procedures attempted and the principal conclusions.

In the aggregative approach it has been customary to forecast the

[1] Especially No. 47, February 1969, and No. 51, February 1970.

volume of imports of goods *and* services taken together. An equation of this type with the components of final expenditure as explanatory variables was fitted to the data over the period 1955 to 1967, subject to the constraint that the ratios one to another of the coefficients of the variables, consumer expenditure, public authorities' current expenditure, and gross fixed investment, should be consistent with those implied by the input/output tables for 1963. This equation predicted a volume of goods and services in 1968 of over £260 millions (in 1958 prices) less than the observed figures and that was before any account was taken of the effects of devaluation. This aggregative approach was supported by a disaggregated analysis of the various categories of import. This threw up a certain number of 'special factors' which might go towards explaining exceptionally high imports during 1968. Among them, for example, was an increase in the volume of tobacco imports by 18 per cent, which presumably reflected a massive replenishment of stocks previously run down following the Rhodesian crisis: there were also expectational imports in the semi-manufactures group of silver and diamonds. On the other hand the rise in the volume of finished manufactures of the order of 11 per cent was very puzzling, for it was in that category that one might have expected some devaluation response because of the possibility of the substitution of domestically-produced goods. The tentative conclusion of the National Institute early in 1969 was that at the end of 1968 there had been a 'devaluation' effect on the volume of imports of the order of £150 millions (at 1958 prices).

There was a very notable slackening in the rate of growth of the volume of goods and services imported in 1969. The rise of only $2\frac{1}{4}$ per cent was in sharp contrast with the experience of the previous year, when the volume of imports rose by over $6\frac{3}{4}$ per cent. If goods alone are taken, the respective figures are $1\frac{1}{2}$ per cent for 1969 against 9 per cent in 1968. This looks hopeful, but in fact much of the decline in growth could be attributed to the slackening in the rate of growth of output and the National Institute found it 'still impossible to say whether devaluation had yet begun to assert any significant effects' on imports. It is true that the import forecasting equation has begun to show signs of diminution in the amount of underestimation, but the Institute was inclined to give any credit on this account to the import deposit scheme rather than to the effects of devaluation itself, though admittedly without any decisive criterion for selecting one rather than the other.

Disaggregation of the import bill was of little help in suggesting any positive conclusion. There were falls of 4 and 3 per cent respectively in two principal categories, namely food, beverages and tobacco, and basic materials, but neither of these was covered by the import deposit scheme nor would they be thought to be particularly sensitive to devaluation. The volume of imports of manufactured goods rose by 5 per cent as compared with the increase of 14 per cent in the previous year: 5 per cent is certainly below the average of recent years (since 1966) but it is not abnormally small in relation to earlier years, such as 1958, 1962 or 1965, where growth of GDP was slow or, in the case of 1958, zero. Price elasticity of zero for food, basic materials and even for fuels can just about be swallowed, although in each case one can point to areas in which substitution of home production for imports is at least technically feasible and, one would have thought, economically feasible as well. Zero for semi-manufactures and manufactures is very difficult indeed to swallow. The amount of 'devaluation effect' is, of course, highly sensitive to the method adopted to estimate what would have been the volume of imports and goods and services in the absence of devaluation. If the method adopted is biased downwards, it will correspondingly reduce any devaluation effect: and the National Institute makes no secret of the fact that, in the past, it has systematically under-forecast imports. All things considered it seems best to record our present estimate of the import volume effect as $0+$, but also, as with exports, to note by how much a change of 1 per cent in the estimate of the volume effect of imports would alter the ultimate devaluation effect.

5. Services

Imports of services are already included in the total of imports for which a provisional elasticity of $0+$ has been put down. Something needs to be said about the exports of services. At £2,592 millions in 1969, this item was £576 million greater than in 1967. Of course, what we want is the difference between the observed value and what it would have been in the absence of devaluation. I am not aware of a good explanatory model of the determinants of the exports of services and am thus driven back to simple extrapolation from past trends. Even this is not very easy. A linear trend might be plausible between 1952 and 1963 ov even 1965, but since about that time there appears to have been a fairly smooth acceleration. The devaluation effect is thus highly sensitive to the kind of curve one fits, and precisely over what period one fits it. Purely by inspecting the graph I put down for the effect by 1969 a range of £100 millions to £400 millions, with a central guess of £250 millions.

85

6. *Property income*

Again we have no good models to turn to, but extrapolation is aided here by flukes. Property income from abroad was virtually stationary between 1965 and 1967 with an annual average of £1,551 millions, which was almost exactly the 1967 figure. The 1969 figure was £562 millions greater than this. Similarly property income paid abroad did not fluctuate much in the three years 1965 to 1967 around an average figure of £755 millions, which is also by chance virtually the 1967 figure, and by 1969 this had jumped by £259 millions. On this crude figuring, devaluation has so far been of net benefit to the balance of payments by about £300 millions. But, to set off against this, foreign taxes paid by UK residents in 1969 were £236 millions greater than the average of 1965 to 1976, while there was little change in UK taxes paid on profits due abroad. Taking property income and taxes together, there has been a gain of around £80 millions. Both current transfers to and transfers from the personal sector show increases over the years prior to devaluation, but when a rough allowance is made for recent trends, the small devaluation effects so deduced appear to cancel out. The change in parity was bound to increase the sterling equivalent of central government commitments in areas where the currency had not been devalued, but on balance it seems better to treat the central government transfers as discretionary and thus to leave them out of account.

7. *Long-term capital*

One might expect that the devaluation of a currency, which was not expected to be repeated for a long period ahead, would lead to some net inflow of funds for long-term investment. And in fact the balance of long-term capital in 1969 was positive to a small extent of £21 million and net private investment was £116 million, by contrast with the substantially negative figures of previous years. But, since 1964, a fairly stringent control has been operated over overseas investment which has been reducing the net outflow of long-term capital somewhat and it is difficult to distinguish that trend from any devaluation effects. As for the official long-term capital movement, we adopt the same attitude as that towards the government current transfers, that is to say, in estimating the devaluation effect it seems best to put aside official transfers and the long-term capital account altogether.

8. *Summary of devaluation effects*

We now pull together the results of previous sections. For exports

86

we have argued that the volume was 11·5 per cent higher, and the price 7·6 per cent higher, at the end of 1969 than would have been the case in the absence of devaluation. 'Exports' here refers to manufactures only and we now adopt the convenient device of assuming that all the trimmings (re-exports, parcel post, etc.) rose in proportion. As a base we use the seasonally-adjusted figure for exports and re-exports for the fourth quarter of 1969, expressed as an annual rate, i.e. £7,416 million. On this basis, the balance of payments gain from exports at the end of 1969 was running at an annual rate of £1,240 million.

For exports of services, we had a range of £100–400 million annual rate with a central guess of £250 million. As regards imports of goods and services, we put down the volume effect at zero and postulated a price rise of $12\frac{1}{4}$ per cent. In the fourth quarter of 1969, imports of goods and services were running at an annual rate of £9,692 millions. This yields us a devaluation cost to the balance of payments of £1,060 millions.

We found a contribution of £80 millions from net property income and tax payments.

We found no further net contribution from the remaining items in the basic balance of payments though we thought that some small positive sum might be permissible for the long-term capital account. Taking all these figures at their face value, we have Table 6.

Table 6. *Devaluation effect up to end 1969*

	£ million at current prices
Exports of goods	+1,240
Exports of services	+ 250
Property income etc.	+ 80
Imports of goods and services	−1,060
Net effect	510

These figures, however, cannot be taken at their face value. There is room for error at each separate step of the calculation. Specifically a difference of 1 percentage point in the estimate of either the price or the volume of the exports of goods is worth about £60 million on the devaluation effect. We have also already indicated a range of from £100 million to £400 million for the exports of services. An error of 1 percentage point in the volume of imports of goods and services is worth about £85 million and of 1 percentage point in the import price about £75 million. A more refined calculation could

87

yield differences in the estimates for exports of goods or services in either direction. On the other hand the present calculation implies a zero price-elasticity of demand for imports and this is barely credible. It is more likely, that is to say, that a more refined calculation might show some positive volume effect than a negative effect as the result of devaluation. We are inclined, therefore, to put the range of the devaluation effect as lying between £300 million and £800 million with our point estimate at £500 million.

According to the most recent balance-of-payments figures[1] the basic deficit of £461 millions in 1967 was transformed into a surplus of £387 millions in 1969, and if we compare the rate at which the surplus was running at the end of 1969 with the full year of 1967 the swing is of the order of £1,000 million. Of this swing we are imputing about a half to devaluation, the remainder to be accounted for by the exceptionally fast growth of world trade which would have led to a big increase in exports, even in the absence of devaluation, and to a lesser extent by the fact that the economy, after the spurt of 1968, was growing more slowly through 1969.

Two aspects of devaluation should not go without mention. Not surprisingly we have a cost inflation of exceptional severity which, among other things, is a reflection of the very success in temporarily halting the rate of increase of real disposable income in order to swing resources into the balance of payments. Secondly, even if devaluation is responsible for only a part of the swing in the balance of payments so far, that part is vital in its contribution to confidence. Without it (assuming we had somehow got through the confidence crisis of 1967) we would now have only a *small* surplus, with the prospect that a small reverse would put us back into deficit. Thus the confidence crises would still be dragging on.

9. *Comparison of estimated outcome with forecasts*

Throughout the 1960s many British economists were in favour of devaluation, or were advocating flexible exchange rates, which in the context were much more likely to lead to a falling rather than a rising exchange, and one suspects that by 1966 they constituted a large majority. Yet remarkably little work was done to estimate the orders of magnitude of the changes which might be expected to ensue. But some forecasts of the 'devaluation effect', besides that of Cooper, were published soon after devaluation occurred, and it is

[1] *Preliminary Estimates of National Income and Balance of Payments 1964 to 1969*, Cmnd. 4328.

of some interest to look at one or two because at least they manifested what some economists did know, or thought they knew, at that time. Besides Cooper's own forecast, therefore, I will look at the first forecast made by the National Institute published in the *Economic Review* within a fortnight of devaluation, and that of the London Business School, published at the end of 1967 in *The Sunday Times*.

Let us begin with the exports of goods. All three forecasts adopt the same line of attack, namely to put down a figure for price elasticity and then try to get the effective degree of 'price reduction' to the foreign buyer. Both Cooper and NIESR put down a figure of 2 for an overall elasticity;[1] LBS 'varied our estimates between 1·5 (the base assumption) and 2·0'. This looks like near unanimity, but in fact it seems that the London Business School applied their price elasticity to only about half of exports; working backwards from their forecast increase in volume of from 7–10 per cent and their estimate of price advantage of 8 per cent, the range of elasticities, if applied to all exports, is between 0·9 and 1·25 per cent, which is, of course, very much lower. The National Institute did not expect that the whole of the devaluation effect would have come through on exports by the end of 1969. They thought the price effect would have been fully through at 9 per cent, but for the volume effect they reckoned that 10 per cent of the ultimate 16·6 (the 14·0 to be found in the November 1967 *Economic Review* was a mistake subsequently corrected) would have come through. The NIESR forecast for the volume effect was a little low for the end of 1969, and sterling export prices rose a little less than was forecast. But the implication of that forecast – that there is still two-fifths of the volume effect to come through – now looks unlikely. LBS and Cooper gave no time profile, but it looks as though the former's elasticity estimate will prove to be nearer the mark.

The situation with regard to imports is summarized in Table 7. There was close agreement between all three forecasters with respect to the probable increase in sterling import prices and this was a very good forecast. The forecast price elasticities varied from the 0·5 of the London Business School to nearly 1 by Cooper. As regards what many people hoped would be the most sensitive items, Cooper gave an elasticity of 2·68 for finished manufactures and 1·06 for semi-finished. The National Institute gave figures of the order of 2·0 for the more competitive components of both manufactures and semi-manufactures and 0·3 or so for the less competitive components.

[1] The NIESR was a 'performance elasticity' – which comes to estimating price competitiveness on the basis of costs alone.

As we have seen, the best estimate to date of the overall elasticity is zero, and this is undoubtedly the most disconcerting difference between the forecasts and the outcome so far. NIESR forecast an increase in net invisibles by £125 million in 1968 and rather more in 1969. Earlier we showed a zero volume effect for goods and services together and imputed a common price rise of 12¼ per cent. Assuming the volume effect and the price rise to operate for goods and services separately, this means that the increased cost of services might offset the central estimate of £250 million on the export side, leaving the net increase in property income of £80 million. Cooper also forecast some increase in the invisible balance but he gave no separate figure.

Table 7. *Comparison between outcome and forecasts of the effect of devaluation on the volume of UK imports*

	Outcome	Forecasts		
	NIESR estimate	NIESR Nov. 1967	LBS Dec. 1967	Cooper Early 1968
Increase in import prices: per cent	12¼	13·5	12–14	13[a]
Price elasticity of demand (−)	0+	0·70	0·50	0·99
Decrease on import volume: per cent	0+	9·5	6–7	−12·9

[a] Deduced from the estimated impact of devaluation after allowing for the fact that some supplying countries also devalued.

Those who mentioned it said that they expected some improvement on the long-term capital account, and that is in accordance with the developments, though quantitative comparison is not possible.

The acid test is not how many marks were scored for the individual components, but whether the overall estimate of the swing in the balance of payments to be attributed to devaluation was right. The National Insititute had a swing amounting to an annual rate of about £1,000 million by the end of 1969, but that was before allowing for 'second round' effects which would have taken quite a lot off. On the other hand there was still, on their then assumption, quite a lot to come. The implication of the assumptions made in November 1967 in that forecast certainly was for an ultimate swing of over £1,000 million. Cooper gave a figure of £800 million for the full effect on the balance of trade to which an unspecified amount should be added for the balance of invisibles. Moreover he was working in 1966 prices so that his 'devaluation effect' also amounts to something over £1,000 million in the terms being used here. The London Business School made no overall forecast of this kind.

Thus, the National Institute and Cooper were both forecasting swings in the balance which are very much the order of the swing which actually occurred between 1967 and the end of 1969 but which on my earlier calculation (of a point estimate of £500 million) is about twice as much as can be attributed to devaluation, the rest having to be attributed to the remarkable increase in world trade in the past two years and slow British growth during 1969. The figuring on the export side was not far out in its estimates of the effects up to the end of 1969, but may turn out to have been optimistic as regards the full effect. It is on the import side where everyone seems to have been wrong. It is barely credible that there has been zero devaluation effect on this side, but that is what is shown by the orthodox type of calculation which is in current use. Most disconcerting is what appears to be zero response to the price advantage on the part of imports of semi-manufactures and manufactures.[1] If this is correct then it would seem that we should revise our views that it is our exports which are abnormal in their behaviour and our imports are similar to those of other countries, and turn back once more to worrying about imports, especially of manufactures.

In the discussion at Ditchley Park, Professor Harry Johnson pointed out that there were objections to the traditional 'elasticity' approach to the analysis of the effects of devaluation. It tended, for example, to treat imports as simple substitutes for home production in the home market with the implication that they ought to fall after devaluation, whereas in reality a variety of possible outcomes of devaluation was possible. The case of higher exports and lower imports was one of them, but another possible case was very much higher exports accompanied by somewhat higher imports leaving still a net favourable balance. The point is well taken and suggests further empirical investigation.

[1] Besides apparently having a low price-elasticity, UK imports of manufactures have a high income elasticity – by international standards. ECE Geneva have estimated a hybrid elasticity of change in *value* of imports to change in volume of GDP over the period 1953 to 1967 (Economic Bulletin for Europe, Vol. 21, No. 1, 1970, p. A 54). Comparative figures are:

France	3·4
Germany	4·3
Italy	2·8
Sweden	2·6
UK	5·7

On the other hand, the elasticity concept was not essential to the three forecasts to which we have referred. They could have been formulated entirely in terms of what was expected as regards the movement of export and import prices and volumes. It is therefore quite proper to test them in their own right against the actual out-turn.

Professor Cooper raised a different point, namely that the calculation ought to be conducted in terms of foreign exchange rather than in terms of sterling. But it is important to be clear what the case for doing this is. If a calculation in terms of sterling shows an improvement in the balance, so also it should show an improvement if done in dollars. Of course the proportion of the improvement in the balance expressed in sterling will be greater than the improvement expressed in dollars. Indeed, if the improvement in sterling is less than the proportion of devaluation then there will be a worsening expressed in dollars. That is, of course, when there was a positive balance in the first instance. If there were a deficit expressed in sterling before devaluation and a surplus expressed in sterling after, so there would be a change from deficit to a surplus if expressed in dollars. We have here an example of the index-number problem, ubiquitous in economics, and there is no presumption that one method is more correct than the other in any absolute sense. If foreign exchange were regarded as persistently scarce by comparison with home resources there would then appear to be a case for working in foreign exchange terms for the devaluation exercise. But inasmuch as devaluation itself is designed to eliminate this scarcity, even this argument needs to be treated with care.

IV. THE COMMON MARKET

At the end of his chapter Krause makes a brief reference to the Common Market but he makes no policy judgment. Denison, in his chapter on economic growth, however, takes the view that a mistake was made by the British in not joining the Common Market at its inception. Denison, it will be remembered, enumerates some twenty-two sources of growth of real national income and estimates the contribution of each of these sources to the growth in nine countries, USA, UK and seven other European countries. Among these twenty-two is a factor entitled 'Reduction of International Trade Barriers'. This source contributed fractionally less to growth in the USA than in the UK. On the other hand it contributed more to growth in all the other European countries. Denison's method of attribution to the sources of growth is not without its critics, but even if his figures were accepted his conclusion does not necessarily follow. Five of the European countries which he considers belong, it is true, to the Common Market, but two of them, Denmark and Norway, do not, but are members of EFTA. Yet the reduction of international trade barriers apparently contributed as much to their growth as to countries within the Common Market. Why then is the Common Market singled out as a reason why Britain gained less from reductions of trade barriers than other countries? Denison's comment is misleading in quite a different way in implying that 'joining the Common Market' and 'reduction in international trade barriers' are one and the same thing.

I have not any new thoughts or insights of my own to add to the Common Market debate and more especially the question whether Britain should join, if the other members will have it, but since this was one of the topics dealt with rather sketchily in the original Brookings Report it may be useful to summarize here the contents of a White Paper issued in February 1970 entitled *Britain and the European Communities: An economic assessment.*[1]

The White Paper attempts to make quantitative estimates of the consequences to Britain of joining the Common Market in three important areas:

1. agriculture and food,
2. trade and industry,
3. capital markets and invisible trade.

It takes for given the rules of the Community as they exist or can be foreseen at present and the estimates are of the full impact of joining, but the White Paper stresses on more than one occasion that it is very likely that the effects of joining will be spread over a period of years.

1. *Agriculture and food*

It is assumed as a basis of these calculations that the Irish Republic, Denmark and Norway will join the Common Market at the same time as the United Kingdom.

The broad distinction between the methods of protection of agriculture in the United Kingdom on the one hand and the Common Market on the other is that in the former the price paid by the consumer is based upon the world price. British farmers would suffer

[1] Cmnd. 4289.

heavy losses if they attempted to sell their product at these prices but they receive considerable subsidies, mainly in the form of deficiency payments which bring the ex-farm prices of the principal products up to a level which is considered in the Annual Price Review to be sufficient to give adequate return to the farmers and to inject sufficient capital into the industry (there is, of course, an annual dispute between the farmers and the government as to whether the actual guaranteed prices fixed are sufficiently high). In the Common Market the consumer pays a price much higher than the world price, not so high as to cover the costs of the marginal farmer but sufficient to cover a great many of them. This entails two things. First, there has to be an import duty or levy on agricultural products coming in from outside the Community at otherwise lower prices. Secondly, several members of the Community have substantial exports of various foodstuffs but in order to compete in world markets it is necessary that they should be subsidized.

So far as the consumer is concerned the outcome is shown in Table 7 on page 16 of the White Paper which lists the relative prices at current exchange rates of certain main foodstuffs in the EEC and the UK in October 1969 in terms of shillings and pence per pound. In virtually every case except milk, the British price is lower than in all other countries and in no case is the British price the highest. The most famous case is butter, which was in October last year 3s 4d per pound in Britain and more than twice this in every Community country except Italy, where it was nearly three times as much.

If Britain joins the Common Market a number of consequences follow. The price to consumers of most products would rise steeply. The White Paper estimates that the rise in the retail index of food prices would be between 18 and 26 per cent with a corresponding rise in the cost-of-living index of 4–5 per cent. This is, I think, a first-round calculation and takes no allowance of any wage increases which might be induced by the rise in the cost of living. In general, British guaranteed prices are not as high as the Common Market support prices, so that British farmers will probably get in some cases, though not all, a higher price than at present. This has a number of consequences. It may stimulate British production, thus reducing somewhat the British import bill. It will largely abolish the need for the present agricultural subsidies. On the other hand, import duties will have to be imposed, otherwise the British market would be swamped by food imports coming in at world prices. The proceeds, however, of these duties would not be at the disposal of the British government but paid over to the Agricultural Fund of the Community.

It will be seen that an attempt to estimate the cost to the balance of payments is difficult on two counts. First, it requires some estimate of the effects of the price changes on food production in this country and indeed on food consumption. Secondly, it needs a guess about how the Agricultural Fund of the Common Market will be financed in the future and particularly what the British contribution will be. The White Paper gives estimates of the change in UK food imports and the estimated levy receipts, on different assumptions concerning prices and the production response which would occur. As regards food imports, these calculations range from a saving of £85 millions to an increase in imports of £255 millions. The contribution to the Agricultural Fund is reckoned to be at least £150 million and it could conceivably be, according to the interpretation of various rules, as much as £670 million. On the other hand, it is reckoned that perhaps between £50 and £100 million might come back to the UK from the Agricultural Fund.

2. *Trade and industry*

The Treaty of Rome provides for the ultimate establishment of a Common Market with free movement of goods, persons, services and capital. Since its inception there has been a steady reduction of tariffs and quota restrictions among the members, and a Customs Union was completed on July 1, 1968, which has involved the complete abolition (other than in exceptional circumstances) of tariff and quota restrictions and the replacement of national external tariffs of the member states by a Common External Tariff (CET) which is applied against imports from non-member countries except those with preferential arrangements with the Community.

The duties on most raw materials are zero in the CET as in the UK tariff, with certain notable exceptions, such as aluminium, lead, zinc and newsprint which are dutiable under the CET. In the agricultural and food sectors, duty-free imports from the Commonwealth preference area represent a considerable part of UK imports and in certain cases Commonwealth supplies at present coming in to the UK duty free would become subject to quite a high rate of duty under CET – for example, mutton, lamb and bananas. Duties on machinery and chemicals, clocks and watches, optical and photographic equipment, musical instruments and many kinds of precision instruments are higher in UK. On the other hand the present plastics tariff is lower. For the rest, the two tariffs are at present

95

broadly similar and both are due to be further reduced in 1972 in the final stage of the Kennedy Round.

If Britain joins the Common Market the White Paper distinguishes two kinds of effect. There are 'dynamic' effects which would follow from becoming a member of a much larger and faster growing 'home market' for British industry, which would provide the stimuli of much greater opportunities and competition than exist at present and would otherwise exist in the future. There would be further advantages from membership stemming primarily from the opportunities of greater economies of scale and increased specialization. Besides these long-run dynamic effects there are 'impact' effects resulting from changes in tariffs and food prices which would come about if Britain joined the Common Market, and it is possible to make rough estimates of the possible cost to the balance of payments of these impact effects.

At present Britain enjoys preferential trading relationships with the Commonwealth preference area, EFTA and the Irish Republic. If we join an enlarged Common Market, these relationships would be adversely affected. If we start applying the CET against imports from the Commonwealth, for example, we can hardly expect to continue to enjoy preference in Commonwealth markets. For two reasons no quantitative exercise on this kind of problem can be precise. First, if Britain joins, other EFTA countries may join the Common Market at the same time, but it is not known exactly which. Secondly, the present structure of tariffs and preference arrangements is not necessarily permanent; the White Paper suggests that there is already some tendency for Commonwealth countries to wish to make new preferential trading arrangements with the Community. The method of calculation adopted is to postulate elasticities for exports and imports, both of demand and supply, which are taken to apply when there is a change either way in tariffs or costs. For imports, it is assumed that, given a change of 1 per cent in prices, the response in the quantity imported would lie between $\frac{1}{3}$ per cent and $1\frac{1}{2}$ per cent and for exports the corresponding volumes are between $1\frac{1}{2}$ and $2\frac{1}{2}$ per cent for a 1 per cent changes in prices. Suppliers faced with a tariff change to their advantage are assumed to absorb a quarter of the change. This increases their unit profits and it is assumed that a 1 per cent increase in unit profits leads to a $\frac{1}{2}$ per cent increase in the volume exported, on the lower assumption for elasticities, and to 1 per cent on the higher assumption. If on the other hand suppliers are faced with a tariff change to their disadvantage, they are assumed to absorb a quarter of this by cutting prices.

With these assumptions it is found that the balance of trade worsens, with the lower elasticities, by £125 million at 1968 prices, and with the higher elasticities by £275 million.

When it turns to the benefits, the White Paper does not provide any estimate of the static gains from trade. A number of such estimates have been made in the past by Scitovsky, Johnson and others, and their common feature is that they come up with a very small amount, less than 1 per cent of GNP. The White Paper draws attention to the rapid growth of intra-trade among community members and the faster rate of growth of GNP per head in community countries than in EFTA countries, and particularly than in the UK, and it believes that Britain will react favourably to the opportunities created. It points to the possibility of an increased inward inflow of investment into UK from America, and mentions certain special advantages in the case of high-technology industries where the minimal optimal scale of R & D is very high, and where in general Western European suffers from lack of companies of a sufficient size to command R & D on the necessary scale. The White Paper acknowledges that various forms of technological co-operation are possible without the Common Market, but thinks that such co-operation can only be fully productive within an enlarged economic union. It points out also that what is a monopoly situation within the UK under present arrangements would not necessarily remain one if UK formed part of a larger market to which French and German companies have duty-free access.

To sum up, the White Paper treats the impact effects essentially in terms of the cost to the balance of payments and makes an estimate of between £125 and £275 million on this count, and it says nothing about the gains from trade association with the changes. It enumerates the dynamic factors of larger markets and accelerated growth. The dynamic factors are not quantified but the impression is left that they are nearly all favourable. The possibility that Britain or parts of it might actually be retarded by joining the Common Market and become peripheral in the way that, for example, Scotland or Southern Italy and parts of France may be regarded as peripheral to their national economies, is not mentioned.

3. *Capital movements and invisible trade*

Under the Treaty of Rome it is intended that ultimately capital movements, whether for direct investment, quoted portfolio investment, real estate or other personal transactions should all become completely free at the official rate of exchange. At present, restrictions on capital movements are operated through exchange control by UK. Thus the normal method of financing direct investment in EEC is the ploughing-back of the earnings of subsidiaries and the use of foreign currency borrowing. The financing of direct investment by a transfer from UK at the official rate is permitted only for oil investment and certain other cases under strict conditions. The use of the official exchange for the acquisition of private houses in the EEC is not allowed.

The White Paper takes the view that normally the net flow of capital would be from UK to EEC, possibly on a considerable scale. It is probable too, that there would be a net outflow on personal account for the purchase of houses. It is pointed out, of course, that where the outflow entails the acquisition of an earning asset, that in the longer run will benefit the balance of payments on current account. As regards current invisibles, it is thought that the City of London might well increase its earnings if Britain joined the Common Market, being able to offer a very wide range of financial and commercial services. While diagnosing the direction of change in these items, the White Paper makes no quantitative estimate.

4. Summary

The results of the examination can be summarized in a table in which a minus sign denotes a gain to the balance of payments and a plus sign a loss. The balance-of-payments effect is estimated to lie somewhere between £100 and £1,100 million, with perhaps a point estimate of £500 million.[1] The size of the entry fee is, of course, negotiable, and set against it are the many unquantifiable net gains from the so-called dynamic effects. It is obvious that the White Paper has been written by many hands, some of them belonging to enthusiasts for joining and others to pretty thorough sceptics. The White Paper sums up by saying that 'the estimates set out earlier in this White Paper of the balance of payments cost of membership would involve, at most, an additional claim on the annual rate of growth over a period of a few years of considerably less than 1 per cent of our GDP'. Another way of putting the comparison would be to say that the range of costs to the balance of payments overlaps our earlier estimate of the range of the benefit to the balance of payments of devaluation and the point estimates seem to be about the same.

[1] The White Paper gives no point estimate. The 'central' figure is of course £600 million, but my reading of the balance of arguments suggests that the authors of the White Paper would put a point estimate lower. Nevertheless the figure of £500 million is my responsibility, and not theirs.

98

Thus the effort, the amount of 'hard slog', entailed in joining the Common Market on the terms as they are known at present, seems to be of the same order as that which has been involved in the devaluation effort. Whether this is large or small and whether the effort is worth it are matters of opinion.

Table 8. *Impact effect on balance of payments* (*1969 White Paper*)

	£ million	
	Lower	Upper
Food imports	−85	+255
Agricultural Fund:		
Contributions	+150	+670
Benefits	−100	−50
Impact effect on trade	+125	+275
Total	+100	+1,100

V. CONCLUSION

I conclude briefly with two reflections.

Earlier on I showed how differently things look according as we work in volume or value terms. Our perennial problem, in an increasingly complex world, is to be sure that we have the facts marshalled in the right way to fit the right conceptual framework. Economic theory is apt to treat exports and imports, for example, as independent and distinct, given in exchange for one another, but anyone adopting this conceptual framework in using British trade returns must have been puzzled by the substantial import into the United Kingdom from developing continues of aero-engines and scientific instruments. When this sort of thing happens one wonders if we have the right facts.[1] Nevertheless I think that imports of manufactures into UK are, in some sense, a problem. Doubtless the persistent tendency to under-forecast imports is because we have the wrong model, but when the price elasticity goes bad on us as well, then the least one can say is that the sooner we get a full understanding of the determinants of British imports, the better.

How far British balance-of-payments problems are questions of structure, of the characteristics of the economy, and how far questions of policy, is a matter of judgment. To some extent it reduces to what one believes to be politically practicable. In so far as policy is invol-

[1] The explanation is that until lately British import statistics have not distinguished between goods genuinely imported from abroad and goods in British ownership re-imported after a period of use abroad. This omission has now been partially repaired. Cf. Anne Morgan, 'Re-imports and Imports for Process and Repair', *National Institute Economic Review*, November 1969.

99

ved, I think there may be something in Cooper's charge of vacillation, that the authorities have shifted from one measure to another, though even the best policy would be apt to appear in this light simply because there is a multiplicity of objectives. Besides being concerned for the national economy, British governments have continued to believe that they have some sort of role in the world, of a military and political kind, which has on occasion entailed embracing economic policies that on narrower economic grounds might have been rejected. Perhaps, however, I may add my own contribution to this criticism, which is to say that I believe that throughout the post-war period the British authorities have usually been too optimistic with respect to the balance of payments. Crises have occurred, dams have been erected to hold back the flood, order has been restored, whereupon promptly the dams have been dismantled. Surprise has often been expressed that sometimes the floods have engulfed us again. One suspects that it will be as hard to sit on the surplus as it was to dispose of the deficit.

4. Labour Policies: Productivity, Industrial Relations, Cost Inflation

*by E. H. Phelps Brown**

I. PRODUCTIVITY

Lloyd Ulman's study of Collective Bargaining and Industrial Efficiency was focused upon productivity. The level and the rate of rise of British productivity are central to much else in the Brookings team's enquiry. At the outset, therefore, it is useful to place them in an historical and international setting. In more than one way our diagnosis of what is unsatisfactory in recent British performance will be guided by what we find here. Comparisons of different periods and economies enable us to discard some possible diagnoses, and attach higher probability to others. If the relatively low rate of rise of British productivity proves to be something new in recent years, we shall look for factors that themselves are new, at least in magnitude; if it is of long standing, we shall look for factors that themselves are persistent. A factor that attracts contemporary attention will seem less likely to be important if the effect ascribed to it appears no less at times when it has not been present. The probability that a factor has been active will be raised if differences in its activity in a number of times and places are found to be associated with differences in performance.

How, then, does the British performance of recent years appear in a wider setting? Some impression is offered by Figure 1.

Here we have productivity not in the whole economy but in industry – that is, generally, in mining, manufacture, construction, transport and the public utilities of gas, electricity and water. (There are minor differences of coverage, and for the UK in the inter-war years and the USA before 1945 the coverage is only of manufacture.) This limitation of coverage has the advantage for our present purpose of excluding the greater advances in productivity in the whole economy that have been made where people have moved in large numbers out of

* I am greatly indebted to those many British participants in the Conference who gave much time to reading this paper in draft – and in one notable case carrying out computations – that enabled me to improve it at many points.

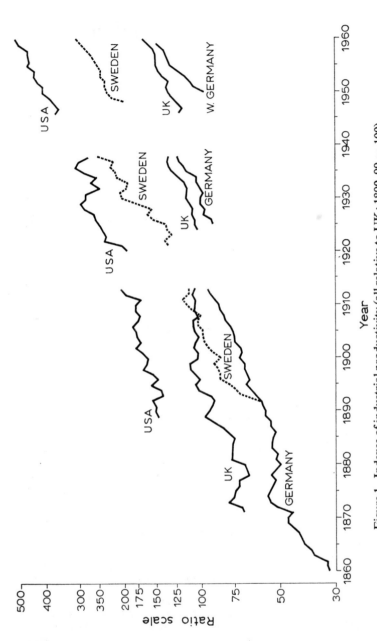

Figure 1. Indexes of industrial productivity (all relative to UK: 1890–99 = 100).

Source: Phelps Brown & Browne, *A Century of Pay* (1968), Adjusted as described in Addendum to present Chapter.

agriculture and self-employment into industry. A movement of this kind has been going on in the UK, but in comparison with most other industrialized economies in the last hundred years it has been restricted narrowly – already in 1871 nearly 53 per cent of the whole occupied population of Great Britain was in industry, and by 1951 the percentage had become only 55. In considering the comparative British ability to improve given processes over time, it is therefore helpful to abstract from the shift of workers from processes where value added per worker is lower to those where it is higher. The possibility remains that a shift of this kind has been going on within industry itself, but the effect of this on the movement of productivity as between one country and another is likely to have been smaller.

Within the bounds of industry, the course of change in productivity has generally been estimated by dividing the aggregate value added at constant prices by the total number of persons occupied, in whatever capacity. Productivity is thus measured in output per man-year, and a country that reduces its annual hours will tend (save so far as hourly effort rises as a consequence of shorter total hours) to impair its performance as that is reckoned here. The consideration is important if the calculation is right that 'down to the Second World War the wage-earner' in Germany, Sweden and the UK 'had taken out his gains about equally in the forms of purchasable goods and leisure'.[1] This consideration apart, there remain the familiar uncertainties in any estimate of real output. Probably the greatest arise from the inherent difficulty of forming an index of the prices of highly fabricated products. The measure of the change in each country that Figure 1 presents must therefore be received with caution, not least in respect of the extent of displacement through the upheavals of the two world wars.

Nonetheless, Figure 1 makes bold to offer estimates not only of the course of change of industrial productivity in each of the four countries, but also of the level attained by each relatively to the UK. One way of comparing levels is to convert the value added per worker in terms of domestic currency into common terms by applying a rate of exchange between currencies. This rate ought to be based on the comparative prices of industrial products. When such a rate has been calculated,[2] it has proved to differ substantially from the current par

[1] E. H. Phelps Brown and M. H. Browne, *A Century of Pay* (1968), p. 345, and pp. 206–12.
[2] D. Paige and G. Bombach, *A Comparison of National Output and Productivity of the United Kingdom and the United States* (OEEC, Paris, 1959), at Table 5, give the net cost ratio in manufacturing in 1950, in $ per £, as 4·1 weighted by UK

103

of exchange: in recent years, notably, applying the par of exchange seems to have exaggerated the superiority of American productivity. Unfortunately no other means of conversion is available over most of the range of Figure 1. We can apply some check, however, to the results of using it. The relative levels of British and American productivity that it yields for 1913, for instance, imply certain relative levels in the inter-war years when each country's level of 1913 is carried forward to those years by its own index of productivity; and the relative levels so obtained can be compared with those obtained directly when we take the values added per worker in the inter-war years and convert then at the current par of exchange. We can do the same as between the inter-war years and the 1950s. This, it is true, is only to check one hazard by another, for the price index that must be used in each country to bridge the years of either war is itself hazardous. The check does in fact throw up some wide disparities. It has been assumed that the estimates of relative levels were most likely to be improved if the disparities were removed by the adjustments that fell equally on the rates of exchange and the domestic price indexes. The method, together with the sources, is described in the Appendix.

Some further check is provided by Table 1, in which the relative levels of productivity shown in Figure 1 for the USA and the UK may be compared with those found by the investigators who have worked in detail on the censuses of manufacture or production in the two countries. There is fair agreement between the two sorts of estimate in the three comparisons since 1930, but in the three earlier ones the census estimates are higher – in 1907–9 very much higher – than those of Figure 1. It seems unlikely that much of the disparity in 1907–9 arises from the estimates of Figure 1 covering all industry in the UK but only manufacturing in the USA, for at least in later years in the UK productivity seems to have been rather lower in manufacturing

---

prices, and 3·6 weighted by USA prices; the par of exchange then was $2.80 per £. Milton Gilbert and Associates, *Comparative National Products and Price Levels* (OEEC, Paris, 1958), Table 5, give the following equivalents, in units of domestic currency per USA $, over the whole range of GNP, in 1955:

	France	Germany	UK
Official exchange rates	350	4·21	0·358
Purchasing power parity,			
USA quantity weights	394	3·51	0·319
European quantity weights	287	2·54	0·272

Table 1. *Real net output per operative or per employee in USA manufacturing industries as a multiple of that in UK manufacturing industries, as reported in the Censuses of Manufacture or of Production, compared with the corresponding multiple of real net output per occupied person derived from the series of Figure 1.*

					From Censuses	From Figure 1		
		Dates			Multi-	Multi-	Coverage	
Source	USA	UK	Units of output		ple	ple	USA	UK
1. Flux	1909	1907	Net value output converted at par of exchange		2·26	1·66	Mfrg.	Indy.
2. Flux	1925	1924	As for (1), but par 10 per cent below that set for the £ in 1925		2·82	2·48	Mfrg.	Mfrg.
3. Flux	1929	1930	As for (1)		2·93	2·56	Mfrg.	Mfrg.
4. Rostas	Comparable years in 1935–9		Physical units as reported		2·15–2·18			
	Av. 1935–8					2·18	Mfrg.	Mfrg.
5. Frankel	1947	1948	Physical units as reported		2·69–2·74	2·86	Indy.	Indy.
6. Paige and Bombach	1950	1950	Net value output converted using product prices		2·56–2·92	3·06	Indy.	Indy.

Sources:

1. A. W. Flux, 'The Census of Production', *Journal of the Royal Statistical Society*, 87, 3, May 1924; the overall multiple of 2.26 is taken from sources 2 and 3 below.

2 and 3. A. W. Flux, 'Industrial Production in Great Britain and the United States', *Quarterly Journal of Economics*, 48, 1 Nov., 1933.

4. L. Rostas, *Comparative Productivity in British and American Industry* (1948).

5. Marvin Frankel, *British and American Manufacturing Production*, (Univ. of Illinois, Bulletin Series No. 81, 1957).

6. Deborah Paige and Gottfried Bombach, *A Comparison of National Output and Productivity of the United Kingdom and the United States* (OEEC Paris, 1959).

than in industry as a whole.[1] Both sorts of estimate in 1907–9, moreover, rely on the par of exchange. The disparity remains unexplained, and disturbing.

[1] Col. 1 below gives the relative contribution to GDP per employee (before providing for depreciation and stock appreciation) in the UK in 1965. The estimates are made by dividing the number of employees in GB alone into the product in the whole UK, and the absolute product per head will therefore have

Yet this and the other disparities of Table 1 are a small matter in comparison with the excess of American over British productivity that remains even if we take the lower of each pair of estimates. By the census estimates this excess does not appear to have grown since the 1920s, but by the estimates of Figure 1 it does appear to have grown progressively except in the inter-war years, and Figure 1 also indicates that the level of industrial productivity in Germany and Sweden rose faster than the British throughout most of the hundred years. This predominantly slower rate of rise of British productivity is summarized in Table 2. This Table also draws on the data of Figure 2, which carries the story on into the 1960s, and shows that throughout the post-war years industrial productivity was rising faster in France too.

Table 2. *Five countries, periods between 1871 and 1968: rates of growth, annually compounded, of industrial productivity (net annual real product per operative, employee or occupied person, in manufacturing and industry).*

	France %	Germany %	Sweden %	UK %	USA %
1871–1913		1·81		1·03	
1892–1913		2·27	2·95	0·84	1·40
1920–1938			5·80		
1924–1937				2·05	
1925–1938		0·26	4·80	1·77	0·40
1948–1967	5·35		4·06		
1948–1968				2·84	3·39
1950–1968		4·89			

Sources: As for Figures 1 and 2.

been overstated by 1 or 2 per cent, but the effect on the relatives of col. 1 will be negligible. Col. 2 provides for comparison the relative net outputs per employee recorded for the same sectors of industry except transport and communications in the UK Census of Production of 1924.

	Relative productivity	
	1965	1924
Manufacturing	100	100
Mining and quarrying	93	90
Construction	107	98
Gas, electricity, water	206	191
Transport and communication	133	
All industry	108	

Sources: 1924, A. L. Bowley, *Studies in the National Income 1924–1938*, Table A, pp. 124–5. 1965, *National Income and Expenditure 1969*, Table 17; *Statistics on Incomes, Prices, Employment and Production*, June 1969, Table E.1.

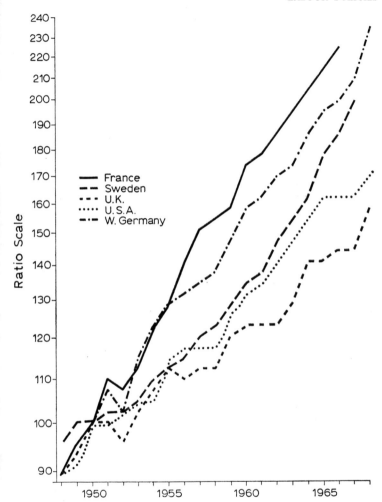

Figure 2. *Indexes of industrial productivity* (base for each country: 1950 = 100).

Sources: UN, *The Growth of World Industry* (1963, 1967, 1969); ILO *Yearbook of Labour Statistics* (1965, 1969).

This is not a story that does British industry credit. Its relatively slow advance goes back at least a hundred years. It comes out in comparison not only with the richly-endowed American economy, but

107

also, and even more markedly, with the more comparable economies of Germany and Sweden and, since the Second World War at least, of France. In these last years, it is true, productivity has been rising much faster than before in British industry; but so it has in Germany and American industry too.

What are the differences between industry in the UK and the other economies that will account for the inferior British performance? To find an answer, let us first note what the factors are that the comparative study of the industrialized economies has found to be generally associated with differences between their growth rates; and then bring these findings to bear on the differences in Figure 1.

There are three factors that comparative studies have found to be positively associated with high or rapidly rising productivity – the amount of capital per worker, the relative size of a given industry as a part of the whole economy, and the rate of expansion of the total product of industry.

Within any one economy the amount of capital per worker in different industries is not very systematically associated with value added per worker, so that the capital/output ratio varies from industry to industry. But between one country and another the capital/output ratio in a given branch of industry generally varies less than the output per worker – in the countries where output per worker is high, capital per worker is generally high too. Paige and Bombach have applied this relation to the difference in productivity between British and American manufacturing industries as a whole. 'It would seem', they say,[1] 'that, although output per worker in the United States is rather more than two and a half times that of the United Kingdom, output per unit of capital employed may be about the same in the two countries. Thus it follows that capital available per worker in the United States may also be about two and a half times that in the United Kingdom. . . .' But this does not mean, they warn us, that the higher output per worker in the United States is due predominantly to the greater capital per worker there. We might express the warning by saying that it is the higher rate of return to resources generally that warrants the higher investment, as much as it is the higher investment that raises the output per worker. This generally higher rate of return is due to such factors as the skill of management, the training and energy of the worker, the natural environment, and the scale of operations. Sad experience with ICOR has reminded us that product-

[1] D. Paige and G. Bombach, *A Comparison of National Output and Productivity of the United Kingdom and the United States* (OEEC Paris, 1959), p. 69.

ivity cannot be raised far by raising capital intensity alone while these other factors remain unchanged.

There is another way in which capital intensity appears as the consequence no less than the cause of the achieved level of development. How far it pays to carry investment in a given process depends on the relative cost of the equipment to be installed and the labour it will displace, and it has been noted that British managers are justified in not installing equipment that is used by their opposite numbers in the United States, because the relative cost of the displaceable labour is much lower in the United Kingdom. But this does not mean that British investment will be stimulated by raising the cost of labour, as for example by a payroll tax, for (unless engineering were exempt) this tax would raise the cost of the equipment too, and would not raise the cost of the labour relatively. The relative cost of labour is higher in the United States because output per worker in the making of equipment is higher there. To him that hath shall be given: it is the achievement of higher productivity that makes it feasible to raise productivity.

Another way of making the same point is to note that though capital per worker may be two and a half times as great in America industry as in British when we measure capital at market value, when we measure it by labour content the amount per worker in the two countries comes out much the same: $2\frac{1}{2}$ units of equipment, where the unit is of market value, are the product in America of no more man-years than 1 unit is in the United Kingdom.

Capital intensity is therefore as much a consequence as a cause of the achieved level of productivity. In so far as it is a consequence, moreover, the determining factor seems to be largely the human factor. Natural advantages apart, it is the skill and dynamism of management, and the training and adaptability of labour, that determine what output will be achieved from existing equipment, and hence what inducement there is to install more.

The second association that has been established is that between relative productivity and proportionate size. Formally, an industry whose proportionate share in the total output of industry is greater in country A than in country B generally shows a productivity that stands higher relatively to the national average in A than in B. Absolute size is not at issue here – the industry in A may be small, that in B big. There is therefore no easy explanation by way of the economies of scale. Why should it be the size of an industry relatively to other industries in the same country that matters? One evident answer is that here again we are dealing with an effect of productivity

109

no less than a cause: it is the industries which achieve the higher productivity that we should expect to have grown relatively to the others. The initial achievement they may owe to natural endowment. They may owe it also, as the early history of particular industries and their localization suggests, to a nucleus of able and enterprising men attracting others of like kidney to set up alongside them. It is a basic principle of economic growth that birds of a feather flock together.

The third association, that between the level of productivity attained and the rate of expansion of output as a whole, is readily intelligible for a number of reasons. In part it is a case of positive feedback: in more rapid expansion a higher proportion of current equipment will be of recent installation and design, and since annual recruitment bears a high ratio to the labour force that force will be flexible. But in great part also it must be through the human factor that expansion takes its effect on productivity. The experience of expansion, and the expectation of its continuance, reduce the attraction of defensive and restrictive practices for both management and labour. The expectations fostered by expansion warrant investment and innovation that carry the expansion on. For a particular industry the growth of exports generally provides a more sustained expansion than the home market alone can sustain, and the effect of such expansion on expectations will make rising exports a cause of rising productivity as well as an effect. Where output has been rising faster than labour input, the prevailing expectations will call for investment in forms that will raise not only total output but also output per worker.

The three established associations have thus brought us back to the human factor. Higher capital intensity goes with higher productivity because (natural advantages apart) it is only where men have the ability to use resources efficiently that high capital intensity is warranted. Industries of greater relative size achieve a higher relative productivity because (natural advantages again apart) it is the industries that attain an initial magnetism for enterprising men that are most likely to grow relatively to others. A high rate of expansion of total output fosters expectations that warrant productivity-raising decisions, and lowers resistance to them.

This line of diagnosis converges with the conclusions of some particular studies of comparative growth. Rostas,[1] in his comparison of British and American manufacturing industry by industry, noted that 'in a number of industries (or firms) where the equipment is very largely identical in the US and UK, e.g. boots and shoes, tobacco,

[1] L. Rostas, *Comparative Productivity in British and American Industry* (1948). p. 64.

strip steel (or in firms producing both in the UK and US in such fields as electrical appliances, soap, margarine, etc.), there are still substantial differences in output per worker in the UK and US'. On a wider front, Denison[1] has found the importance of 'residual efficiency' – of the sources of growth that cannot be quantified as inputs, and include the rate of application of advances in knowledge. Aukrust's[2] review of research into the differences of growth rates between the Western economies led him to the conclusion that 'it is the ability of man to devise new technological possibilities . . . [and] increasing insight and cleverness alone which determine the speed of technical progress', whether 'the rate of capital accumulation is being kept permanently high or permanently low'.

If such are the findings of the comparative study of growth, what light do they throw on the difference between the performances of industry in the United Kingdom and in the other countries of Figure 1? Three features of that difference attract attention and challenge explanation. First, of the four countries, it is in Sweden that the rise of industrial productivity has been the most rapid. Second, the relatively poor performance of British industry goes back at least to the 1870s. Third, it is in the years since the Second World War that British industrial productivity has risen faster. Let us consider these in turn.

The comparison with Sweden should be specially instructive for the British. In some ways it is unfortunate that British endeavours to improve the performance of industry have relied so much on learning from the United States – that it was there that Alfred Mosely took his team of trade unionists in 1902, and that the Anglo–American Council on Productivity sent its sixty-six teams in the years after the Second World War. For much that underlies American productivity is peculiar to the American heritage. The abundance of natural resources; the conquest of a continent by a vigorous, adventurous people, self-selected for enterprise and freed from the constraints of traditional societies; the rich rewards of the frontier for bold endeavour; the sheer size the domestic market has attained – all these assets a European economy can envy but not reproduce. Small wonder if some of the visiting students could only feel on coming home the discouragement that the countryman conveyed when he

[1] E. F. Denison, *Why Growth Rates Differ: Post-war Experience in Nine Western Countries*, (Brookings Institution, 1967); Chapter VI of R. E. Caves and Associates, *Britain's Economic Prospects* (Brookings Institution, 1968).
[2] Odd Aukrust, 'Factors in Economic Development: A Review of Recent Research', *Weltwirtschaftliches Archiv*, 93, 1, 1964.

111

was asked the way to Barnstaple – 'if I wanted to go there I wouldn't start from here'. For the British there may be more to learn from the facts that Germany, save for the inter-war years, and Sweden throughout, have been raising their industrial productivity faster than the UK – faster even than the USA.

The example of Sweden is specially instructive. Here is a country of limited natural resources; a country that at one time was drained by emigration instead of gaining by it; and a country that still remains small, with a labour force of less than 4 millions: yet one that has raised its material standard of living above all others in Europe, has developed the manufacture of cars and aircraft as might be thought beyond the reach of so small an economy, and maintains the exports by which it earns a quarter of its national income despite a level of hourly wage cost which in manufacturing was more than 50 per cent above the British even before the devaluation of sterling in 1967. The factors to which observers ascribe this achievement are human factors. The exceptional progress of the Swedish economy in the 1930s marked an ability rare at the time to apply economic analysis to public policy. The level of education in Sweden is high, and the Swede attaches great importance to the qualifications to be attained through it. By the same token, he brings to the tasks of administration and design a thoroughness of reasoning and vigour of imagination that he combines with readiness to follow in practice the course they mark out. In the same way he combines a disciplined acceptance of decisions reached collectively with a strong sense of individual responsibility: the cohesion of the employers' association in collective bargaining does not sap the competitive drive of management. It was to similar factors that the German industrial achievement was attributed by British observers, when that made so sharp an impact on British economic prospects in the twenty years before the First World War: particular stress was laid on the thoroughness of management, the ability to co-ordinate action without slackening individual effort, and the patient and far-sighted application of science to industry. There is an obvious risk in explaining the performance of an economy by national characteristics, when the chief evidence for these lies in the performance; but our inability to quantify them, or otherwise establish them objectively, does not warrant our passing them over. For it is to them that the process of eliminating possible causes leads when we compare the performance of British industry with that of the Swedish and German.

The second outstanding feature of Figure 1 is that the British retardation which in recent years the Brookings team was concerned

112

to account for is in fact nothing new, but goes back for most of a century. It is always possible that the same effect was produced by different causes at different times, and we have reason to think that this was so here, at least in part. Germany and Sweden, having come later than the UK to industrialization, were both compressing into the fifty years down to the First World War advances in technique and changes in structure that in the UK were realized over a longer period, and so took less effect year by year. The United States had the advantage in earlier years of developing vast natural resources, and of the stimulus to enterprise that is imparted when those resources are exploited by a rapidly-growing population. In later years it has had the advantages of having already attained a size that affords great economies of scale, and of continuing to possess the natural resources that are called for by current developments of technique. But it is hard to find special advantages that have been enjoyed by the German and Swedish economies since 1914, unless it be the Swedish neutrality in the two world wars. Nor can we readily point to special disadvantages that have operated at different times to retard British development. We must therefore turn to the possibility that some part at least of the retardation of the British economy has been due to factors that have differentiated it from the others persistently.

That there have been such factors is indicated when we look to the diagnosis of the lag in British development in the years before the First World War: for this leads to some of the same factors as the Brookings team has put its finger on in recent years. Figure 1 shows British industrial productivity as no higher in the cyclically rising phase of 1910–13 than in that of 1896–9. The discussion of the apparent 'climacteric of the 1890s' has represented the stasis of the ensuing years as the deepening of a deceleration that had set in from the 1870s.[1] It has brought out, it is true, some factors peculiar to the times – the exhaustion of the best coal measures, the wasteful extension of railway mileage, the completion of the phase of the rapid exploitation of the economies of steam and steel. But this inevitable check to the rise of productivity in the older industries would not have taken so much effect on the performance of industry as a whole if the UK had kept pace with other economies in the innovations of the time – in electricity, the internal combustion engine, chemicals and man-made fibres. There was no overt bar to its

---

[1] The literature is surveyed and the discussion summarized in A. L. Levine, *Industrial Retardation in Britain, 1880–1914* (1967), and S. B. Saul, *The Myth of the Great Depression 1873–96* (1969).

H

doing so: on the contrary, one would have said that no country was better placed to take the lead, by reason of its resources of industrial manpower, capital and know how. But it seems that it was the existing attainments themselves that inhibited innovation. The effective check has been found in the conditioning of men's minds by the traditions of existing industries, engrained by long usage and enforced by great achievements. The time had been when the men of enterprise, keen to seize any new opening for making money, saw the scientists of their day as a main source of openings, and worked with them closely;[1] but as industry grew it developed its processes from within, by trial and error, and the link with the laboratory was broken. The British manager became above all a practical man, and prided himself on it. Typically, he had served an apprenticeship to his trade, and his identification with it was inflexible. His education had not encouraged his mind to range widely: scientists he regarded as cranky and impractical. As the age of empiricism gave way to the age of technology, he remained staunchly empirical.

At the same time labour resisted the introduction of new methods in the workshops of established industries. Here the traditional craftsman had enjoyed substantial autonomy, because the operations could be performed only by the skill of his hands, and he was left to use them in his own way. This autonomy was now threatened by new methods that gave managers more control over the way and speed of working, and by new machines that enabled semi-skilled men to do craftsman's work. The resistance of craftsmen to both tendencies raised the issues of the prerogatives of management and workers' control. We have no measure of its effect, but in the judgment of contemporaries there was no question but that the British workers were less willing and adaptable than the American or the German. Many of the latter, it is true, were more adaptable simply because they were new to industry, and had had no time yet to become set in their ways, or to organize in defence of them. But it appeared in addition that the American worker was keener and more vigorous, the German more industrious and better disciplined.

These characteristics cannot simply be regarded as innate, for it was remarked that British emigrants to the United States soon picked up the pace of the native Americans around them.[2] A differ-

[1] R. E. Schofield, *The Lunar Society of Birmingham* (1963).

[2] Arthur Shadwell, *Industrial Efficiency* (1906), Vol. II, pp. 110–11: 'The prevailing, though not universal, spirit at home' (in the UK) 'is that of getting as much and doing as little as possible. . . . In this frame of mind they go to America

ent working environment induced a different attitude towards work. What was it, then, in the working environment of the UK that induced a less willing attitude there? There are three linked factors to which the effect seems attributable. First, there was the force of example by which management exert leadership, positively or negatively: the British employers of the later nineteenth century were taking life more easily than their predecessors, they had more interests outside the business and worked shorter hours there.[1] This was linked with a second factor, the worker's sense of the basic unfairness of his position over against the owner, his resentment at toiling to make profits for one whose birth spared him the need to toil. This in turn was linked, thirdly, with the values, perceptions and expectations of the working class, formed under the impact of past experience and so liable to change as experience changed, yet showing a persistence, as father handed them down to son, that made them at any one time an independent factor in current behaviour. To work harder, it seemed to the wage-earner, meant not getting on in the world but working yourself or your mate out of a job. In any case it would be more likely to put more money into the boss's pocket than your own. He is out to get more out of you, and you must resist that; by strong trade unionism you may even get a bit more out of him. You are not living in a world where there are great rewards in prospect for energy and enterprise: you cannot expect to rise

and start working; but after a few months they fall under the spell of the prevailing spirit, and lay themselves out to earn all the money they can; they extend themselves and put their backs into it . . . as they never did before.' See also Vol. II, pp. 130–1.

[1] Alfred Marshall observed in 1903 that the advantages British manufacturers had enjoyed in the 19th century, and the distraction of their rising competitors in the United States and Germany by wars in the 1860s and 1870s, had encouraged 'the belief that an Englishman could expect to obtain a much larger real income and to live much more luxuriously than anyone else, at all events in an old country; and that if he chose to shorten his hours of work and take things easily, he could afford to do it. . . . This combination of causes made many of the sons of manufacturers content to follow mechanically the lead given by their fathers. They worked shorter hours, and they exerted themselves less to obtain new practical ideas than their fathers had done . . .' (Sec. L of *Memorandum on Fiscal Policy of International Trade*, completed August 1903, published as H. of C. No. 321, November 1908). Arthur Shadwell observed in 1906 that 'the once enterprising manufacturer has grown slack, he has let the business take care of itself, while he is shooting grouse or yachting in the Mediterranean' (*Industrial Efficiency*, Vol. II, p. 453). Shadwell was a careful observer of industrial and social conditions in Great Britain, Germany and the United States, but it is only fair to state that the present quotation comes from a declamatory final chapter which finds the great cause of demoralization in the diffusion of wealth.

out of your class. You can expect only to earn less as your working life goes on. The best you can do for yourself is to stand shoulder to shoulder with your mates to resist those who are more powerful than you and will exploit you if they can.[1]

We come here on the characterization of British labour that Lloyd Ulman has noted as one theory to account for uneconomic practices in British industry in recent years – a theory he evidently allows to have something in it. 'A combination of alleged laziness, suspiciousness of class and of progress, and an atavistic opposition to redundancy is what appears to constitute the syndrome known as bloody-mindedness.'[2] But is there any reason to believe that there has been and is more of this among British workers than among those of other industrialized countries? We might well turn the argument round, and say that the syndrome being a natural response to the position of the worker in industry is likely to appear wherever industry is developed, and it is only where it does not appear that we must look for something differential in the man or his environment. For to the extent that the relations of employer and employed reduce to those of a labour market, in which work is bought and sold at so much per hour, and an excess of supply threatens the worker with partial or total loss of income, he will surely react as the farmer has always done in like case: he will seek income security by combining to restrict output. It is where he does not do this that we must look for countervailing forces that may well be specific to the country concerned.

We can find them readily in the United States, where – as we have remarked – so much of the labour force or its forbears has been self-selected for enterprise through migration, has broken out of the stratification of traditional societies, and has found itself in a Continent where land was to be had for the asking and fortunes were made by the bold. But these are not forces we can find in Germany or Sweden. The world in which the industrial worker finds himself there is much more like the British. The industrial counterpart of the British worker's outlook is trade unionism, and German and Swedish labour have been and are highly unionized. The political counterpart is socialism, and there have been and are strong socialist movements in Germany and Sweden. Yet there is a general

---

[1] See the 'ideal-typical' specification of the 'working class perspective' at p. 147 of John H. Goldthorpe and David Lockwood, 'Affluence and the British Class Structure', *The Sociological Review*, 11, 2, July 1963.

[2] Richard E. Caves and Associates, *Britain's Economic Prospects* (1968), p. 332.

belief among those who have practical knowledge of industry in the three countries that the attitudes of the workers in Germany and Sweden make a distinct contribution to raising productivity there relatively to that of British industry. That different attitudes should have been formed in settings so much alike may be explained by either or both of two possibilities. One is that the attitudes which the position of the wage-earner would of itself engender are modified in all countries by national characteristics of wider coverage and of historic, perhaps in part even of genetic, origin. The other possibility is that wage-earners' attitudes are much affected by the quality and style of management: in particular, that in Germany and Sweden a more professional and harder-working management has reduced the wage-earners' rankling sense of the disproportion of reward to effort, and been able to exert more authority because it commanded more respect.

So far our quest for factors operating persistently over most of the last hundred years to keep the rise of industrial productivity in the UK lower than in some other countries has led us mainly to the culture of managers and workers – their culture in the sense of the habits of mind, the values and expectations, and the ways of perceiving the working life, in which they were reared, and which were linked with socially sanctioned norms of behaviour. In no society are these things subject to sudden or spontaneous change. It is therefore possible to link them – if that seems warranted on other grounds – with a characteristic of the economy that has continued to be manifest while much else in it has changed greatly.

But that characteristic has been less manifest of late: though its relative showing has continued to disappoint, British industry has at least improved greatly on its own past performance. This was the third feature we noted for discussion in Figure 1.

One explanation to offer itself immediately is that industrial investment has been running at a much higher level – as a proportion of income generated, twice and more than twice as high as in the inter-war years. Certainly this has been a necessary condition of the recent advance, but we have already argued that though investment will generally be raised if other factors are making for growth, little can be done to promote growth by raising investment above what those factors call for.

It is therefore to those other factors that we must attend. In particular, if it was the distinctively British culture that largely accounts for the poorer performance of the earlier years, is it a change in culture that accounts for the better performance of the later? Let

117

us consider what changes there have been in the setting of industry, and their probable effects, whether by way of culture or directly, on productivity. These changes fall under three heads: full employment with cost inflation; government intervention; and management development.

The experience of full employment sustained for twenty-five years might be expected to have reduced the wage earners' sense of the need to uphold those restrictive practices that are designed to safeguard jobs; but though it has made workers more ready to leave their jobs voluntarily, it does not seem to have reduced their sensitivity to any threat of imposed redundancy, and it has increased their ability to resist any reduction in manning quotas or any squeezing out of the under-employed. In general, the new indispensability of the individual worker, and his awareness of it, are alleged to have loosened discipline and slackened effort. Speaking, it must be supposed, from his experience in the chemical industry and on the railways, Lord Beeching has said that '. . . accelerated wage inflation is not the only effect of over-employment, nor even the worst one. Many other things happen. Union leaders lose control over their members; managements lose control over employees to the point of having to condone rank indiscipline; and improvements in working methods are most unreasonably opposed.'[1]

'Productivity bargaining' has worked to the opposite effect, but only in the last three or four years on any scale. But whatever the attitude of labour, the 'cost plus economy' that is created when full employment is maintained despite rising labour costs has reduced the pressure on management to keep costs down: the cost of a stoppage cannot be covered by raising prices, but experience has shown that the cost of the wage rise that will avoid it can be. Lloyd Ulman has called our attention to the conclusion reached by a group of directors and senior managers of firms in the Midlands, that 'over-manning in much of British industry stems more from management weaknesses than from trade union restrictive practices'.[2] In sum, it is hard to find in the effects of full employment upon labour any clear balance towards raising productivity.

With the effects upon management, however, it must have been far otherwise. Though the progressive expansion of monetary demand by which full employment has been maintained has relieved management of much of the pressure to keep labour costs down, it has

---

[1] House of Lords, 276, 46, August 1, 1966, 1102.
[2] Ministry of Labour, *Efficient Use of Manpower* (1967), p. 5 cited at p. 335 of R. E. Caves and Associates, *Britain's Economic Prospects* (1968).

118

encouraged it to plan for growth. Though there has been much complaint of the disappointment of expectations and the upsetting of plans by 'stop' and 'go', the setbacks this has brought have been slight and transient by comparison with those that the eight year cycle used to impose. The expansion of monetary demand has at the same time increased the internal flow of funds to finance investment: Richard and Peggy Musgrave have reminded us that 'companies in the United Kingdom have operated at a substantially higher internal funds-to-investment ratio than have corporations in the United States', and that 'by 1964 the United Kingdom ranked among the lowest of the high income countries with respect to the effective tax rate on corporate profits'.[1] A higher rate of investment means a wider and prompter application of technological advances. In sum, it seems clear that the expansion of demand to maintain full employment has exerted a positive influence on the rate of rise of productivity through its effects on the expectations of managers and their ability to act on them.

The second feature noted as distinctive of the years since the Second World War was increased government intervention. The intervention intended to raise productivity has taken many forms, some of which will have been dealt with elsewhere in this symposium – those notably that concern investment, price competition, and the formation or maintenance of efficient units of management. There remain the measures designed to promote the mobility of labour and to improve the personal quality of workers and managers. Grants and retraining to help workers move to new jobs, though of importance in particular cases, can have taken no more than marginal effect on the large movements that have been taking place in the deployment of labour, both industrially and regionally. The Redundancy Payments Act of 1965 is bound to have reduced what might otherwise have been an obdurate collective resistance to the closing down of uneconomic units. But meanwhile, on a wider front, the proficiency of workers has been raised by increased education and training. The number of years of schooling of the average entrant into industry has been rising. Technical education has been greatly expanded. Since 1964 the entrant into industry – and sometimes the worker of standing – has had the benefit of the Industrial Training Act, a radical departure in that for the first time it makes the provision of training in an industry a charge upon all firms in it.

Government has also intervened to raise the proficiency of

[1] Richard E. Caves and Associates, *Britain's Economic Prospects* (1968), p. 59 and p. 51.

119

management. Three public agencies have diagnosed weaknesses and spread information about better practices – the Anglo–American Council for Productivity in the days of the first Labour Government; the National Economic Development Council and its sub-councils – the 'little Neddies' – industry by industry, since 1962; and since 1965 the National Board for Prices and Incomes, providing what is in effect a free consultancy service on means of raising productivity. In all these last measures, what has probably taken most effect is not so much the particular prescriptions made for improving the performance of management as the diffusion of a heightened awareness that improvement is possible and that managers will be judged by their ability to achieve it.

But the changes that have been coming about in management go much beyond what can be ascribed to these stimuli. They form the third of the ways in which the last twenty-five years are marked off from the years before. They can be seen as part of a movement common to many countries that have learned, largely from the USA, that management is a profession with its own body of principles capable of application to concerns of many different kinds, and its corresponding requirement of formal training as well as practical experience. So widely is this accepted and acted upon today that we may forget how different it is from the view that prevailed in the United Kingdom at least as late as the 1930s – the view that management in each industry is bound up with that industry's technical processes and can be performed adequately only by those who have come up through them; that the really good manager is born and not made; and that 'an ounce of practice is worth a ton of theory' – indeed that academic qualifications are a handicap that entrants have to overcome. At least in the more prestigious universities, this view was cordially endorsed by the graduates themselves, extraordinarily few of whom (save for the technicians) went into industry.

The change that has come about since then is manifest in several ways. Business Schools have been set up, largely on the motion of management itself, while the universities have developed business studies. The larger firms pay great attention to the recruitment of graduates, and many able graduates (though not all) regard management as a challenging and socially beneficial career, no longer of lower intellectual and moral status than the learned professions or the public service. Firms have development policies for their own junior management, plan their experience, and provide spells of formal training in their own schools or in college courses. There is generally believed to be more movement of young executives from

120

firm to firm than used to be thought permissible; something like a market in managerial abilities has grown up, and salaries are competitive. No doubt all this has done little to make the best management of today better than that of former years, and no doubt it has left some tracts untouched; but it must have done a great deal to raise the level of the average.

The answer we have found here to the question why British industry has been raising its productivity faster in the last twenty-five years than before cannot be established by quantitative analysis or even by rigorous reasoning from the qualitative evidence. What factors have been significant, and what relative weights should be assigned to them, must remain a matter of personal judgment. But the question is still inescapable, and discussion by observers who bring different experience to it should serve at least to show what answer is most probable. The answer now submitted is that two features of recent years stand out as most likely to have raised productivity: the maintenance of full employment, through its effects on the expectations of management; and the raising of the professional status of management, as that is viewed by the community and governs the performance of managers themselves.

It is thus contended here, as we review the preceding discussion as a whole, that the comparative course of British productivity over past years, distant and recent alike, is to be accounted for largely by two types of consideration. One is that the level of productivity attained by any economy at a given time depends upon its antecedent course of growth, and cannot be sharply raised by the importation of features of other economies whose course of growth has already carried them further up. This explains why British productivity has been lower at any given time than the American, and why much study of American practice by the British has not enabled them to close the gap. But it does so simply by assuming that the British were behind the Americans on a path along which both were climbing: what it does not account for is that the British path also rose less steeply as a rule than the American, and not the American only, but, even more, the German and the Swedish. This the second types of consideration does account for: namely, that the culture of British managers and workers was generally less propitious to change and development than, in their different ways, the cultures of those other countries.

In some respects it has not been the worse for that. A society that puts humanity before productivity, and weighs satisfaction in the

121

working life against satisfaction by consumption, may go further in 'the pursuit of happiness' than one that drives itself hard in the pursuit of growth. At various points the intervention of British governments in industry has been deliberately counter-productive by the usual criterion for the allocation of resources – in keeping high-cost pits open, for example; in rural electrification; and in much regional development policy. The justification lies in human values that GNP fails to take into account. But when the material standard of living is held back in order to uphold a chosen way of life the price should be paid deliberately. Where it is not, the constraints of a customary culture may be merely wasteful. We cannot, moreover, hope to have it both ways – both keep to the wellworn paths, and achieve a high and ever higher material standard of living. But that such a standard shall be achieved has now become a settled expectation of the British people.

The diagnosis offered here indicates that the principal means of achieving it lies now in the training and development of management – directly, through its effect on the performance of managers themselves, but also not less indirectly, through its effect on the performance and attitudes of labour.

II. INDUSTRIAL RELATIONS

Lloyd Ulman noted some adverse effects of two distinctive features of British industrial relations: the 'occupational striation' of the trade unions, and the concentration of formal collective bargaining on industry-wide negotiations.

He saw British trade unionism as striated because, in the patchwork of its structure, so many of the boundaries between unions coincide with those between occupations; and he pointed out a number of drawbacks that this entails, in contrast with the industrial unionism that organizes in a single union all the manual workers in common employment. When the skilled men are in separate unions, and are able to enforce the closed shop and admit to membership only by apprenticeship, they can cause a shortage of skilled labour. Since the semi-skilled and unskilled are denied the prospect of advancement to skilled status, they try to raise the rates for their jobs relatively to the skilled rate, and the differential for skill becomes too small. At the same time, when a number of unions take part in the same negotiation, and have to agree among themselves on a common form of claim and settlement, the easiest course is to conserve existing differentials. The reservation of particular operations to the members

122

of a certain union reduces the adaptability of the labour force and makes for the under-utilization of labour. The differentiation of the craftsman by union membership enhances his attachment to his mate as a status symbol. A technical change affecting the work of the members of an occupational union disturbs a higher proportion of union membership, and is alleviated by a poorer prospect of redeployment, than if the affected workers belonged to an industrial union: they will therefore be more resistant to change.

Two qualifications of this analysis suggest themselves. One is that restriction of membership of craft unions to the apprenticed, and restriction of skilled jobs to members of craft unions, are much less complete in practice than in principle. Practice varies from one locality or even one workshop to another. In engineering, the unapprenticed man has more access to skilled work in London and the south-east than in the north-west. Even in printing there remain some houses in which men can acquire skill without apprenticeship; in building the opportunities are widespread. Where not a few men acquire skill in this way, even a union that can exclude them from its strongholds has to reckon with their competition as they work elsewhere, and the safer course is to admit them to at least some grade of membership. Union policies concerning the proportion of apprentices to journeymen, moreover, are not necessarily calculated to impose scarcity, for union members have sons they want to see follow them in the craft. The other qualification is of the argument that occupational unionism makes for too small a differential for skill – too small, that must mean, to induce enough men to go through the needed training. This implies that the presently effective limitation of numbers in the skilled occupations is through lack of volunteers. One cannot then at the same time ascribe it to the restriction of entry.

But these qualifications do not affect the main consideration, that occupational unionism is bound to have an interest in restricting movements across occupational boundaries. Members of the British productivity teams visiting the United States noticed by contrast the flexibility in the deployment of the labour force from day to day, and the incentive of the prospect of advancement to higher-paid jobs, under industrial unionism. A lurid light has been thrown on the British demarcation lines when they have been in dispute, and an implacable struggle has been waged between unions about 'who does what'; but the cost of these stoppages, though conspicuous, is probably much less than that of the many peaceable and unreported understandings that are wasteful of man-hours.

123

British observers are therefore bound to look wistfully at the industrial unions that took shape in the United States under New Deal legislation, and in Germany under the reconstruction of unionism after the Second World War. Even more wistfully must they look at the achievement of the Swedish unions in advancing from a patchwork unionism very like the British to an almost complete grouping by industry, even though this took them most of the thirty years after 1909. The governmental guidance that is effective when workers are being unionized for the first time, or after old institutions have been razed to the ground, can do far less to refashion unions whose roots are sunk deep in tradition, and whose executives have an identity to maintain. That the Swedes were able to transfer members and draw new boundaries between unions may be attributed to several factors – besides the Swedish capacity for not only reaching thoughtful decisions but acting upon them – that are not present in the United Kingdom: the biggest of their unions were still small in comparison with the British; all were of comparatively recent origin; and the need for unity by industry was enforced by employers' associations acting with a cohesion made possible by national character and – again – smallness of scale.

But is there then nothing that can be done to improve British trade-union structure? Motions favouring greater unity have met with little opposition in principle within the Trades Union Congress, but enquiries into how to attain it have found the obstacles easier to list than the means of overcoming them. It seems that governments could help restructure unionism only if they could offer some powerful inducement – if, for example, the legal protection of combination ceased to cover all unions as such, and could be enjoyed only, in each defined bargaining area, by the union or association of unions that was certified as the sole bargaining agent within that area. This is to depart much further from tradition than would be considered remotely practicable, short of the social or economic earthquake that shatters existing structures of thought as well as institutions; but today there are at least tremors, and lines of reconstruction demand consideration.

There is also much change in union structure in fact proceeding. The total number of unions has been halved since the Second World War. A number of important amalgamations have taken place – though by no means always on the lines of industrial unionism – and more are pending. The unions that have been growing fastest are those that are open without bar of occupation or industry: these extend across many industries, but can and do act for a number of different occupations within any one of them.

Public policy, moreover, is now to be exerted, 'to encourage reforms in trade union structure and services' through the good offices of the Commission for Industrial Relations, and the financial assistance it is to be enabled to provide for trade-union mergers.[1]

But the developments that seem likely to do most to change the effective structure of British trade unionism are those now taking place not at the national level but at the place of work, and not through the allotment of membership but through spontaneous regrouping. The ability of workers under full employment to defend and assert their interests by direct action has endowed their shop stewards with powers not derived from their particular unions, and thereby has brought shop stewards from different unions together in common counsel and joint initiative. In twenty years' time it may appear that what has set up the new problem of workshop bargaining has gone some way to solve the old one of trade-union structure: the development of recent years may be seen as a turning point in the notion of union membership, away from sole and exclusive membership of a national union, and towards joint membership of the national union and what we may call the works association. This is a form of dual unionism, in which the duality corresponds with the two tiers of bargaining. The works association performs the functions of an industrial union for the purpose of works agreements. For that purpose, what trade union a man belongs to becomes distinct from how he associates with his fellow workers. Membership of the works association can be changed readily on a change of workplace. But membership of a national union will continue to confer its own form of citizenship in the polity of labour, and it is on the national union that the many workers outside the scope of works agreements must continue to rely.

These developments mark the impact of full employment on the structure of British collective bargaining, but in that structure it is still industry-wide bargaining that predominates, and this is the second distinctive feature of British industrial relations whose adverse effects were noted by Lloyd Ulman. These effects all stem from the industry-wide negotiations being necessarily conducted at a remove from the place of work, where alone so much that affects the relations of managers and workers can be regulated. The national officers of employers' associations and trade unions lack the opportunity for involvement in local issues. Managers may neglect industrial relations because they see them as being regulated outside their own

[1] *In Place of Strife* (Cmnd. 3888, Jan. 1969), para. 36; and paras. 71-5, 'A Trade Union Development Scheme'.

125

sphere of responsibility, and disputes that crop up within it as being properly referred away. In the gap left at the firm by the absence of the charter that is provided by the plant contract in the USA, issues arising in the shops can only be handled informally. There can be no distinction between issues of rights under the agreement, that must go to arbitration, and issues of interests, that must be deferred until the fixed date of renegotiation: so there cannot be a 'no strike clause', nor is management secured executive freedom in matters not regulated by the agreement, subject only to the right of the union to bring any such matter into negotiation on its expiry. So long, moreover, as working practices are left to custom and to pressures exerted at particular points on the shop floor, management cannot negotiate changes in them as part of a pay settlement.

We may ask why the gap thus manifest in the firm did not give trouble before. It used to be filled by an interplay between the prerogatives of management, as they were called, and the adherence of unions to policies and procedures endorsed by their unions and administered by its district officers. In days of endemic unemployment there had always been the threat to any group of workers who struck that the firm could replace them permanently. Even where in fact it could not, the worker's sense of his individual dispensability was apt to restrain him from striking even in concert with others, unless he was assured of the support of his trade union for his reinstatement. But full employment has substituted a sense of indispensability, and this in turn has endowed the shop steward with bargaining power. This power emerged under the full employment of the First World War; in that of the last thirty years the shop steward has grown in numbers and gained an authority commensurate with the ability of the small group to strike. At the same time the growth of industries whose products are assembled from many components has increased the number of small groups that can at will stop a whole firm or even most of a whole industry. The worker's new power is used not only to vary terms and conditions of employment such as have long been subject to negotiation, but to reduce the discretion of management in other matters. These are mostly such as bear directly on the worker's own job, but there are signs of his increasing concern with wider issues of managerial policy.

The exercise of a still novel power is at present largely unregulated. The major task of British industrial relations in the 1970s is to develop rules, procedures and institutions for its regulation. This development must serve two purpose: it must provide for local bargaining on the terms and conditions of employment, but also for

126

the association of the worker with management in the reaching of decisions on other matters of concern to him.

The development of procedures for local bargaining leading to factory agreements became the prime concern and recommendation of the Donovan Commission. It found in the growth of two-tier bargaining, and particularly the use of the strike in the lower tier, the major problem of British industrial relations in our day. 'Its central defect', the Commission found, 'is the disorder in factory and workshop relations and pay structures promoted by the conflict between the formal and informal systems'.[1] Again, 'We have no hesitation . . . in saying that the prevalence of unofficial strikes, and their tendency (outside coalmining) to increase, have such serious economic implications that measures to deal with them are urgently necessary.'[2]

The aim of the Commission accordingly was the development of orderly procedures for bargaining and dispute settlement at the place of work. It made several positive recommendations, and arrived at one major negative conclusion. These, and the debate about them, constitute the main development in British industrial relations since the Brookings team reported.

The positive recommendations are designed to promote the growth of 'the factory agreement', which in all save its legal aspects is a close counterpart to the American plant contract: 'effective and orderly collective bargaining is required over such issues as the control of incentive schemes, the regulation of hours actually worked, the use of job evaluation, work practices and the linking of changes in pay to changes in performance, facilities for shop stewards and disciplinary rules and appeals'.[3] To bring this about, the Commission looked first and foremost to voluntary action. Employers' associations and trade unions meeting at the national level should agree guidelines for factory agreements, and should advise their own members on the negotiation of those agreements. Henceforward it should be the main purpose of employers' associations to help their members 'develop orderly and efficient systems of industrial relations within their undertakings'.[4] On the union side, 'the processes of union government should be altered to accommodate shop stewards and work groups more adequately'.[5] The union branch should be based on the place of work, and its meetings should be held

---

[1] Royal Commission on Trade Unions and Employers' Associations 1965-8: Report (Cmnd. 3623, June 1968), para. 162.
[2] *Ibid.*, para. 415.   [3] *Ibid.*, paras. 162, 1019.
[4] *Ibid.*, paras, 735, 1084.   [5] *Ibid.*, 696-8, 1079.

127

there. Trade-union rules should provide more fully for the election and the functions of the shop steward, and unions should do more to train him, especially in day-release courses. The TUC should give a lead to its affiliates in these things: in particular, it should encourage them to reduce the present competition between them for members by endorsing the principle of 'one union for one grade of work within one factory'. But to push this voluntary action forward the Commission also recommended that all firms with 5,000 or more employees, together with the public sector, should be required to register with the Department of Employment and Productivity the agreements they have made at company or factory level – or account for their absence. The Commission for Industrial Relations should investigate such issues thereby raised as the Department referred to it. The Government has put first among the concerns of the Commission 'how to promote suitable company-wide procedures'.[1]

In all this the Commission abided by the British tradition of voluntarism in industrial relations. But it had been bound to ask itself whether it was right to rely on that tradition, in the face of so much that was new and disturbing in industrial relations. In particular, it had to consider whether the disorder that it diagnosed as arising out of the loss of control by industry-wide negotiations and the lack of procedures for negotiation locally, did not call for the provision of legal sanctions against the breach of agreements and departure from procedures. Its consideration of this question led it to its major negative conclusion.

The legal provisions it examined were the extension of arbitration to unofficial strikes; the imposition of a compulsory pause for fact-finding and conciliation, on the lines of the provision for national emergency disputes in the Taft–Hartley Act; and making collective agreements into contracts enforceable at law. It also examined the proposal that, within at least certain categories, strikes to be lawful must first have been endorsed by secret ballot. All these proposals it dismissed with substantial unanimity.

Its reasons for so doing – if we pass over difficulties raised only by particular proposals – were mainly three. First, the introduction of legal attitudes, procedures and penalties was alien to the British tradition of unhampered negotiations leading to agreements based on and reinforcing mutual respect and understanding. Second, legal pains and penalties are hard to apply to workers acting in combination: to penalize a union for the action of some of its members is likely only to disrupt the union; to try to enforce penalties

[1] *In Place of Strife* (Cmnd. 3888, Jan. 1969,) para. 35.

against the workers individually is likely only to bring the law into contempt. Third, the law cannot in any case give the force of contract to an agreement that would be void for uncertainty, nor penalize departures from procedure when there is no defined procedure to depart from. It followed that the first step would have to be the formulation of clear and comprehensive agreements, and the definition of procedures. Only after this had been done would it be possible, and only if disorder should persist would it be necessary, to consider bringing in the law.

The Commission, in its Report, did not examine the possibility of overcoming the present lack of defined procedures by instituting one that would be generally applicable, save that it did consider – only to reject – a statutory 'conciliation pause' on the lines of Taft–Hartley. But when the government set out its proposals for action on the Report, it went beyond the Commission in taking this possibility up. It proposed,[1] namely, that the Minister should be given 'a discretionary reserve power to secure a "conciliation pause" in unconstitutional strikes and in strikes where, because there is no agreed procedure or for other reasons, adequate joint discussions have not taken place'. If voluntary agreement was not reached by the end of a pause of twenty-eight days, the parties would be free to strike or lock out. If any party – employer, trade union or individual worker – failed to comply with an order to continue working during a pause, it could be fined after a hearing by an industial Board. The difficulty in any proposal of this kind is that the order is bound to prescribe the terms on which work shall be carried on during the pause, and when workers are objecting to a change brought in by management this can hardly be done without anticipating the final decision. The attraction of the proposal is that without withdrawing the right to strike, or substituting an award by a third party for a negotiated settlement, it offers a means of checking the wildcat strike. But it came up against not only the resistance of trade-union leaders to any constraint on the freedom of action of their members, but the traditional sense of the Labour movement as a whole, powerful in the Parliamentary Party, that the scales of justice are inherently weighted against the workers, and that after their long struggle to free themselves from the shackles that the law lords with persistent cunning had devised for them, any suggestion that they be fined for striking was abhorrent on its face. On June 18, 1969, the government ceded the field.

The date may well figure in history as that of the first major

[1] *In Place of Strife* (Cmnd. 3888, Jan. 1969), paras. 93–6.

collision between traditional attitudes towards industrial relations, and the changed locus of the forces which those relations must accommodate. A survey of industrial societies indicates that attitudes towards industrial relations differ more widely than differences between the present circumstances of those societies can account for. This suggests that those attitudes are a legacy of history, it may be even of an accident of history. Australian trade unions, for instance, derive from the same origins as the British, and operate in a society conservative of British traditions, yet they generally accept and work with a system of compulsory arbitration that most British unions would reject as repugnant to the institutions of a free country, save in direst emergency. The Australian unions accept it because it was brought in nearly seventy years ago at a time of their great weakness, when it offered them vital protection and support; and because, now that it has worked so long, they see no readily available alternative. At the time of its introduction in Australia, the weaker unions were appealing for it in the United Kingdom. Had they prevailed then, the British attitude to the role of law in industrial relations must have been very different today.

When, therefore, we consider the benefits that other countries derive from their legal framework of industrial relations – the working of the labour courts in Sweden, for example, or of the Taft–Hartley Act in the United States – we cannot dismiss them as irrelevant to us on the ground simply, in the words of the Donovan Commission, that 'to transplant from one country to another legal institutions or principles which have stood the test of time . . . may be useless or even harmful if the social conditions of the country which seeks to adopt them differ from those which have given rise to their growth in their country of origin'.[1] What is thought and found practicable in these matters depends greatly on attitudes that are received by tradition, not imposed by the present circumstances of the particular society. But when traditional attitudes manifestly fail to meet the need of the hour, they are thrown into relief and subject to question,

It is therefore significant that the Conservative Party, formulating its approach to industrial relations before the Donovan Commission reported, was concerned to survey the role of law in the industrial relations of some other countries, and to propose changes in the law as the chief means of improving industrial relations in the United Kingdom.[2] The proposals owe much to Taft–Hartley. The

[1] Royal Commission, *op. cit.*, para. 461.
[2] *Fair Deal at Work* (Conservative Political Centre, April 1968).

130

most far-reaching were, that collective agreements should become legally binding as contracts between employers and trade unions, save for such provisions as the parties agreed to exclude; that 'strikes to enforce a closed shop, inter-union disputes, "sympathetic" strikes or lock-outs, and strikes called for the predominant purpose of preventing management from engaging certain types of labour would no longer be protected "trade disputes" ';[1] and that in disputes threatening the national interest the Minister would be empowered to refer the case to the Industrial Court for arbitration, to apply to the Court for an injunction against strike or lock-out for a limited period, and within this period to hold a secret ballot among the employees. The Industrial Court, which would sit by divisions in the principal industrial centres, would deal with cases arising under the above proposals, and with those brought by individuals, trade unions or employers' associations in pursuance of rights conferred on them elsewhere in the proposed code of law.

It is by the first of these proposals that the problem of the unofficial strike would be tackled. There would first have to be a procedure agreed between trade unions and the firm or employers' association. If members of a trade union struck in breach of this procedure, the union itself would become liable to civil action for damages, unless it had used its best endeavours to get its members back to work. Where the union did this the employers, in Mr Heath's words, would 'be able to take disciplinary action without the union being able to complain, against those who break agreements and flagrantly encourage others to do so'.[2] There may be some response here to the view urged by some employers that the crux is getting rid of a small number of agitators without a general stoppage being called on a cry of victimization. But the Donovan Commission no less held that if a procedure has been established, and

'the majority of the workers in a factory accept the procedure and have confidence in its effectiveness, those who defy the procedure may be isolated from that majority. It may then be possible for the employer to do what at the moment he cannot do: to take such action as the law allows him to take against this minority. That action may in the first place consist in the use of the most obvious remedy which the law puts at his disposal, that is to dismiss those who foment strike or similar action in defiance of the procedure agreement.'[3]

[1] *Op. cit.*, p. 64.   [2] *The Times*, 6 April, 1970.
[3] Royal Commission, *op. cit.*, para. 508.

The difference between the two proposals is that the Donovan Commission relies wholly on the acceptance of the procedure by the majority, making them unwilling to strike in defence of those who breach it, and provides no sanction against them if they do strike or against their union if it supports them in so doing; whereas under the Conservative proposal a union that did not use its best endeavours to get the majority back to work would make itself liable to action for damages. Another Conservative proposal provides some sanction against the majority themselves, in that participation in an unofficial strike would terminate the individual contract of employment, as participation in an official strike does not.

So far we have been discussing the need created by full employment to develop procedures at the place of work. But the changed balance of power there has reinforced another need, one recognized long since but becoming more insistent now, the need to bring the worker into the managerial process of problem-solving and decision-taking in matters that concern him. The ground here is littered with the banners, dropped from disappointed hands, of workers' control, syndicalism, industrial democracy, co-determination, joint consultation, co-partnership, profit-sharing and participation. It would be well to leave idealism aside and start afresh from realism. Where a decision can be implemented effectively only with the concurrence of the worker, and that concurrence cannot be enforced by the threat of the sack, the decision is not within the discretion of management. 'If you can't beat 'em, join 'em'; if a man has a veto on my actions I had better clear them with him before I try to take them. But once managers accept that the veto is there, they do not find that it is wielded by an invariable adversary, for though some ways of achieving management's aim of keeping costs down and output up do involve a direct clash of interests with the worker, there are others that advance his interests in high earnings, security of employment, and greater satisfaction in the job. The best way forward, therefore, seems to be to eschew comprehensive and formal schemes based on political analogy, and to begin with the jobs of the individual worker and the working group, with the aim of providing the workers with as much autonomy as possible in the arrangement of their own work, and, where management wants to make a change, engaging them in a joint attack on the problem of how to make it best. In this way a variety of practices may grow up, and some of them may prove capable of extension to the reaching of decisions affecting larger numbers.

Here is a problem that is likely to assert itself increasingly, but

132

on which as yet we are ill-informed: at least we know much more about the attempted solutions that have failed than those that have succeeded. The reason may well be that the failures have depended on provisions that can be reduced to writing and reported, whereas the successes have been achieved simply by the style of management and the way in which managers have been given to understand that their own job should be done. In view of one experienced observer and practitioner of industrial relations, there is room here for a great development in British management. Mr L. F. Neal recently asked,[1]

'Is industry really satisfied that the training it still gives to plant managers and first-line supervisors is adequate to these new tasks? . . . Is there still too great a tendency to think of Management as the management of things rather than of people? What we need is an acceptance by top management that the management of human resources is an extremely important part of every Line Manager's job and that he must allocate time to it, be trained to do it, and find that he must have skill at it to get promoted.'

The changes in the balance of power we have been discussing here do not exhaust those that full employment has brought: there are also those that bear on collective bargaining as a means of regulating the structure and the general level of pay, and have resulted in cost inflation. Full employment has thus imposed on British industrial relations the need to develop three kinds of procedure – for local negotiation; for joint problem-solving and decision-taking; and for regulating changes in pay. Let us now in conclusion consider the case for the third of these.

III. COST INFLATION

Lloyd Ulman has remarked how 'during World War II and thereafter, the prevalence of full employment, coupled with the legal potential for the extension of the terms of collective agreements . . . ensured that British employers would emphasize the tranquillizing effect of federation bargaining on costs and correspondingly minimize its potential for united resistance'.[2] Since those words were written, industry-wide bargaining under full employment has shown that it can bring about not only a progressive rise in costs at a moder-

---

[1] In his paper 'Industrial Relations in the 1970s', read to the Manchester Statistical Society, 20 January, 1970.

[2] R. E. Caves and Associates, *Britain's Economic Prospects* (1968), pp. 351–2.

ate rate but an outright wage explosion. It should prove instructive to enquire why the workings of the system in recent years have been so different from what they used to be.

The system served certain purposes of wage regulation well under the inflationary pressures of two great wars and the deflationary pressures of the years between. It was, indeed, to serve the purposes of wage control during the First World War that it was first extended widely and largely generalized: in part this was a response to a doubling of union membership, but it was also promoted by government, which found that to bring all firms and workers in an industry under a common code was essential to uniformity in wage adjustments. No such control was attempted during the Second World War. On the contrary, it was the faith of the Minister of Labour, Ernest Bevin, that provided the government kept down the rise in the cost of living, the parties to collective bargaining would do more to check cost inflation if that were left to their own public spirit in voluntary negotiations than if the government relieved them of responsibility and harassed them with regulations; and his faith was justified in the event. Between the wars, the British system has shown its ability to limit cuts in wages during long years of unemployment and downward pressure on prices and costs, that included a world depression of exceptional severity. At the time there was concern at the inability of industry to get its labour costs down more; but looking back now we must reckon it to have been an advantage to the British economy that from 1929 to the trough of 1933 the average annual money earnings of an employed worker fell by only 5 per cent, against more than 30 per cent in the USA.

With these achievements behind it whatever quarter the gale blew from, the British system came out of the Second World War with great prestige, and the TUC for its own part saw no reason to admit more interference with it in time of peace than had proved necessary in time of war. Yet the way it now began to work made the Labour government change its own mind: in its White Paper of 1948[1] it revealed its reluctant conclusion that unless the parties to collective bargaining could check its present tendencies, interference would be unavoidable. The tendencies that disturbed the government were the 'annual round', in which a general increase arose through the gains made initially by certain groups being extended over the rest; and 'wage drift', through the competition of employers for workers. Times in fact had changed. Full employment had already begun to make the system function very differently.

[1] *Statement on Personal Incomes, Costs and Prices* (Cmd. 7321, Feb. 1948).

134

The twenty and more years that have elapsed since then have made the differences even greater.

They centre upon the expectations in the light of which firms consider a wage claim. Under the old order money wages had risen in the more active years of each eight-year cycle, but the rises obtained at any one time were limited by the employers' willingness to take a strike rather than go beyond a certain sticking point. For some industries with a standardized product sold under international competition – notably certain sectors of the coal and iron industries – sales proceeds were set by the impersonal working of markets from day to day, and the wage above which it would not pay to hire the man was set at the same time – so clearly so that in both those sectors the workers accepted for a good many years a sliding scale that raised and lowered their wage-rates automatically from quarter to quarter according to ascertained sales proceeds. The absence of such arrangements elsewhere suggests that other producers were not simply price-takers, but evidently they were chary of wage settlements that would require them to raise their prices to maintain their profit margins. Foreign competition in a free-trade market may have counted for much here again, even though its impact was less certain and immediate. It is probable also that though each employer, if a wage rise were negotiated that made him want to raise his own prices, could count on most of his competitors at home having to pay no less, he did not feel he could count on them to raise their prices too. Resistance to a wage rise was in any case more likely when most employers were proprietors who would see it prima facie as reducing their own incomes.

These constraints had their counterpart in the expectations of trade unionists. They would hold out doggedly for the ruling 'rate for the job', but generally accepted it as a fact of life that this rate could be raised only when their industry was prosperous, and might have to come down when it was depressed. This meant that wages in different industries, even in the same locality, varied relatively to one another from time to time: the force of custom and sense of equity probably stabilized differentials between grades within one industry, but did not bear on those between industries, which varied with capacity to pay. In taking the opportunity of a rise in the activity of his own industry to make good a wage claim, the trade unionist had it in mind that the improvement might be temporary: there was little appreciation in any quarter of the potentiality of economic growth with its 'annual improvement factor'. The main purposes of the union were seen as the defence of the individual

135

member against unfair action by his employer, and of 'the union rate' against undercutting when there were two men after one job. But the union could not push that rate up above a point set from time to time by the capacity of industry to pay, which was beyond the power of the employers no less than of the workers to vary at will.

If this account is right, the non-inflationary operation of multi-firm collective bargaining depended essentially on the expectations of the parties to it, on both sides of the table. The way it worked depended on how it was expected to work. The essential change of the last twenty-five years then appears to be that old expectations have been dissolved, and new ones have been fostered.

The threat of foreign competition has been reduced, partly perhaps because the increased diversification of products has reduced price competition, certainly also because the sectors of industry that can sell only in so far as they can quote an internationally competitive price are less concentrated and conspicuous than they were. It has been the experience of recent years also that if we have had to raise our prices, most of our competitors abroad have been raising theirs. In any case, even if our wage and price rises have checked our exports and raised our imports, home demand has been so sustained that it has been the balance of payments and not the level of employment that has suffered. Employees who understood and accepted the connection between the rise of pay and the troubles of the balance of payments in the past have still felt and contended strongly that their own present claim had its particular justification that was not to be dismissed on the ground merely that if everyone got as much those troubles might recur. Employers seeking to justify a settlement took the same line.

The fear that other firms in the industry will not raise their prices as one will need to raise one's own has been reduced if not dispelled by the continued experience of price rises. It is still far from the case that firms needing to raise their prices to maintain their profit margins can count on doing it at will without harm to their businesses: each annual rise in labour costs has put firms under a pressure that has been unwelcome to all and to some has been acutely embarrassing. Yet the record shows that an escape route is there. Prices have doubled in twenty years while the volume of sales has expanded progressively.[1] For most of the time, profit margins in money have risen very nearly as fast as unit labour costs – between

---

[1] *National Income and Expenditure 1969*, Table 16: Price index (1963 = 100), all final goods and services sold on the home market: 1948, 58·9; 1968, 120·9.

1950 and 1964 these costs rose by 74 per cent, but over the same span gross profits (and other trading income) per unit of output rose by 69 per cent[1]. Latterly there have been signs of a profit squeeze. But the market environment has remained one in which managers generally have not had reason to believe that a strike would hurt their businesses less than the wage rise for which they could settle.

Managers have also been largely relieved of the fear that whatever their present ability to pay, a present wage rise would prove damaging when the tide of business turned. The lesson of the last twenty-five years is that though governments are concerned to reduce the rate of rise of aggregate monetary demand, they are even more committed to prevent that demand from falling. It is true that governments cannot do much to maintain demand from abroad, short of devaluing, but they have devalued. Because other countries, moreover, have been inflating too, the rise of domestic costs has operated to slow down the expansion of British exports and not to stop it. Where, as in shipbuilding, it has gone further than that at times, the government's intervention has called much about the industry in question, but not its wage level.

Any one industry, indeed, now finds it virtually impossible to stand apart from the general movement of wages, whatever the state of its own market. The principle has been too firmly established that the unprofitability of an industry is no reason for its paying its workers less than is being paid in comparable jobs elsewhere. Charging the same price for a given factor of production in all its uses promotes the efficient allocation of resources in a non-inflationary economy, but when factor prices are rising in a cost inflation it accelerates the rise. The generalization of rises has been enhanced by a much more complete and rapid transmission of information about particular rises that makes those who lag behind aware of their position quickly. Collective bargaining has come to be seen as a procedure through which at least once a year claims are presented, and ought to be made good, to advance most wages and salaries in much the same proportion. Any who for some reason get left behind have an undoubted right to restore their relativity. Their catching up brings the announcement of a big rise that others then aspire to match.

Collective bargaining has thus come to work very differently

[1] *Ibid.:* Home cost per unit of output (index, 1963 = 100)

	1948	1950	1964	1968
Income from employment	56·0	58·9	102·5	120·3
Gross profits and other trading income	60·1	61·0	102·8	111·8

137

because it is carried on with very different expectations. The former expectations that kept settlements on a non-inflationary course have given way to new ones that permit and foster rises in pay that raise costs progressively. The actual rate of rise has varied somewhat from year to year under the influence of three factors: whether unemployment was rising or falling – not its current level; the size of some prominent settlement that could be taken as striking a keynote; and the degree of restraint exerted by government.

In the winter of 1969–70 the first of these factors was neutral, the other two operated powerfully to raise expectations and the size of the advance needed to satisfy them. The amount of one settlement, the dustmen's 17 per cent, was seen more vividly than the extent to which it made up for less than average rises in previous years or for the absence of wage drift. It also had a symbolic and emotional impact. With the wider choice of jobs that full employment has been affording, and the extension of opportunities for schooling and training, the supply of labour to the less pleasant and less skilled occupations has contracted, that to the more pleasant and more skilled expanded. As the economist sees it, the natural and beneficial consequence is a narrowing of traditional differentials. But that is not how the schoolteacher sees it: to him that narrowing is a derogation of his status and a blow to his self-respect. Evidently the interplay between the market forces narrowing a differential and the conventional restoring it sets up perpetual motion. Some recent rises have also had a special impact on expectations because they were won by strikes. The government's abandonment in June 1969 of its proposed legislation to check the unofficial strike, and the approach of a General Election, were seen as disabling it from maintaining even such moderating influence as had held the rise in wages rates of the two past years to an average 7 per cent; while a dramatic improvement in the balance of payments had released it from the compulsion to try to do so. At least it came about that after the government's White Paper on *Productivity, Prices and Incomes Policy after 1969* had laid it down in December 1969 that 'most wage and salary settlements need to fall in the range of $2\frac{1}{2}$–$4\frac{1}{2}$ per cent increase in a year',[1] the government was allowing settlements to pass big enough to raise the *average* of hourly wage rates between January and March 1970 at an annual rate of over 12 per cent. This explosion marked the extent to which the working of British collective bargaining had changed. Evidently the old constraints were no more. The new system of forces allowed of, even fostered, cost

[1] Cmnd. 4237, para. 36.

inflation. There seemed to be nothing now in the system to stop that inflation accelerating; it might even run away.

If the view advanced here is right, and the basic difficulty is that the old constraints have gone, what new ones can be devised? One suggestion has been that we might restore the expectation that cost-raising settlements will harm those who make them, by announcing and enforcing a limitation of the rise of aggregate demand. Notice, for instance, might be served on all concerned that the stock of money was going to be increased by an amount sufficient, but no more than sufficient, to mediate a growing real turnover at constant prices, so that if settlements of pay were such as to raise costs and prices, they would bring a credit squeeze down on the heads of those who made them. Proposals of this kind are attractive because they avoid interventions and administrative controls, let accustomed procedures alone, and leave market forces at least as free a field as they ever had before. But there are great obstacles in the way. Unless the effect of the proposed sanction is to impose a general standstill, we cannot be sure that individual infringements will be deterred by it when it will be activated only if infringements are general. Unless there is a compensating effect on efficiency, to leave resources idle, even marginally, is wasteful; and to concentrate the loss of pay on those men and their families who are unemployed is invidious. But the greatest obstacle in practice is that no democratic government can deliberately keep the economy throttled back for long, and allow unemployment to rule far above the level to which governments are now known to be able to reduce it if they choose. Limitation of monetary demand remains indispensable as a weapon of the last resort against external imbalance or a threatened runaway at home, but it can hardly be built in as an automatic regulator in permanence.

An alternative proposal would rely basically upon administrative control: in whatever way the permissible rise in any rate of pay was arrived at, statutory penalties would fall upon those who exceeded it. The principle was applied, albeit within limits, by the Prices and Incomes Acts of 1966–9, which empowered the government to delay the implementation of a pay rise for a period of some months, and provided for the fining of any employer who did implement it, or of any trade union or other person who tried to make an employer implement it. Experience has shown the acute difficulty of trying to enforce such controls when not the workers only but the employers too want to get round them. Paradoxically but intelligibly, it is when pay is rising fastest that employers are most anxious to do this, for it is then that the embarrassments of postponing the settlement loom

139

largest. In other circumstances, such that the employers support the control, the problem of enforcement shifts from the detection of evasion to the repression of strikes. At all times there is this basic difficulty about enforcing an externally prescribed term of employment on workers to whom it is unacceptable, that forbidding them to strike against it implies requiring them to go to work and do a normal day's work under it, and this is not a requirement that legal sanctions can enforce.

But this is not to dispose of the possible usefulness of a legal framework for the avoidance of inflation through collective bargaining. Legal sanctions against a refusal to work that constitutes a breach of procedure are to be distinguished sharply from those against a refusal to work under the terms and conditions at which the procedure arrives: they are more acceptable in principle and more applicable in practice. Legal sanctions of all kinds, moreover, are impracticable if they meet with a general resistance, but they do not do this when they are seen as the necessary adjunct to a system that is accepted voluntarily by the great majority of those concerned, so that they serve to keep in line the minority who are recalcitrant in principle or would like to steal a march on the others.

Voluntary acceptance is in any case so much the most effective way of regulating innumerable dealings, if only it can be attained, that the natural course is to consider first whether it is indeed attainable, and only then to ask what part controls should play, whether as adjunct or alternative. In Sweden, and at times in the Netherlands, the employers and unions at the national level have taken comprehensive control of the movements of pay themselves, if only to keep the government out. It has been much in the mind of the General Council of the Trades Union Congress that it should do the same, and at one time it raised the possibility of at least some discussion of the prospective scope for pay rises with the Confederation of British Industry. But despite the Joint Declaration of Intent of December 1964 there has been no attempt at joint administration. The CBI may well be inhibited by its own nature, as a voluntary association of employers' associations, without authority over its members, who in their turn have seldom much if any power in practice to regulate the wages paid by the firms who belong to them. On the side of the TUC, however, one development deserves more attention than it has received. The Congress of September 1965 agreed to set up a committee of the General Council to 'vet' – that is, to scrutinize and advise upon – the claims being entered by affiliated unions, which were laid under an obligation to notify the Council of them. Of some 460 claims vetted between May 1967 and March 1968, nearly 200 were found to be incompatible, in whole or in part, with the incomes policy accepted by the Council.[1] This policy has not necessarily been that of the government. At a time when the government's criteria were accepted, they were applied with more regard to the difficulty of changing expectations abruptly; and in 1968 the TUC produced its own *Economic Review*, with its own assessment – more hopeful than the government's – of the prospective scope for non-inflationary rises in pay. But the *Review* also raised the possibility of the principal claims coming forward in 1969 being considered together in the autumn and – presumably after adjustments had been negotiated internally – being submitted simultaneously in the following spring. In the event, the *Review* was approved by a Conference of Executives by so small a margin that no more could come of this suggestion. But here, as in the vetting system, what is remarkable about a new idea is not what has come of it but the mere fact of its ever having been entertained. That would have been quite unthinkable only ten years ago. It is in the logic of the situation, however, that the authority of the TUC over its members should be strengthened. As Mr Frank Cousins, at that time General Secretary of the Transport and General Workers Union, said in the Congress of 1966, 'If the trade unions themselves are going to surrender their authority, I suggest they will want to surrender it to this body here and not to a government'.[2]

If collective control is not undertaken by the trade unions and employers' associations, then it must continue to be attempted by government. Past governments have laid down guidelines in the hope that they would be observed voluntarily. The hope was disappointed, through the lack of any procedure for bringing guidelines down to particular applications so as to meet the need of the worker for assurance, on the one hand that some externally prescribed norm will not be imposed on him mechanically without regard to the merits of his own case, and on the other hand that if he does himself toe the line he will not simply find himself left behind the others who do not. But in 1966 the government was constrained to develop a procedure: it took statutory powers to refer particular claims or settlements for investigation by the National Board for Prices and Incomes, and to hold up implementation for a period, but at the end of this the parties were at legal liberty to do what they would. Two principles are im-

[1] Derek Robinson, 'Implementing an Incomes Policy', *Industrial Relations*, 8, 1, October 1968.
[2] *TUC Annual Report, 1966*, p. 464.

plicit here: that there may be a statutory requirement to follow a certain procedure without any obligation to accept the terms at which it arrives; and that detailed enquiry is necessary to find the best way of applying guidelines to the circumstances of a particular case. But hitherto this investigation has taken place only after the event. The need now is to inject the public interest at the point where decisions are taken. This might be effected if the members of a national service – an expanded National Board for Prices and Incomes – took part in the negotiations leading to the principal pay settlements. They might do so as members of formally constituted tripartite councils, or of boards, national or local, to which either party to a negotiation might take the other. But they would have no casting vote or veto in the councils, or arbitral authority in the boards; their role would be rather to obtain such information from the parties, and make such representations to them, as the National Board has been doing. Their participation would therefore be effective only to the extent that there was acceptance of the need to take the public interest into account, but we have seen reason to believe that comprehensive provision for their participation would make that acceptance easier.

At least the line of development is clear. Because there is a common interest in the rate of rise of pay as a whole, the common interest enters into the decision of each individual rate. If cost inflation is to be avoided under full employment, that decision cannot be left to the bargaining power or mutual understanding of the parties to it alone. There are now three parties concerned in it. The problem for the United Kingdom is to devise a three-point suspension for it.

ADDENDUM

E. H. Phelps Brown and M. H. Browne, in *A Century of Pay* (1968), provide an index of productivity in industry (or manufacturing) for each of Germany, Sweden, UK and USA in each of three periods: I, 1860–1913; II, the inter-war years; III, 1946–60. To set these out as in Figure 1: (a) the three indexes for each country must be linked from period to period so as to provide a continuous index; and (b) the indexes for the different countries must be set in an appropriate relationship to one another, according to the level of productivity attained by each at a given time. The links required under (a) are provided in *A Century of Pay* between periods I and II, but not between II and III. To obtain these last, we can take the series of annual income generated per occupied person in industry (or manufacturing), in current money, also provided in *A Century of Pay*, and apply a price index to express this series in real terms common to both periods. But indexes of the prices of industrial products are hard to find or form: what has been done here is to combine money-earnings per worker and wholesale prices with weights 2, 1. The links required under (b) equally require price indexes, but indexes that run through space, not time, and enable us to express the money incomes generated in different countries in common real terms. For lack of measures of purchasing power parity over industrial products, the pars of exchange have been taken here.

With these links, we can arrive at the appropriate level of productivity in one country in say period II relatively to that of the UK in period I along two paths, as illustrated in Figure 3.

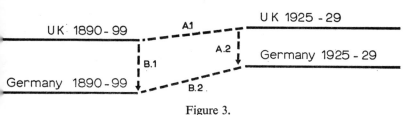

Figure 3.

Expressing the links as ratios, we have

A.1, UK 1925–9 relative to UK 1890–9	1·050
A.2, Germany 1925–9 relative to UK 1925–9	0·807
Path A, Germany 1925–9 relative to UK 1890–9,	
$1.050 \times 0.807 = 0.847$	
B.1, Germany 1890–9 relative to UK 1890–9	0·657
B.2, Germany 1925–9 relative to Germany 1890–9	1·536
Path B, Germany 1925–9 relative to UK 1890–9,	
$0.657 \times 1.536 = 1.009$	

Thus the terminal of path B proves to be as much as 19 per cent above that of path A. Divergences are found likewise for the other two countries and for the transition between periods II and III. We might assume that the four links in any one case such as that set out above are equally unreliable, and bring the terminals together by equal proportionate adjustment of all four. But the link A.1 is common to the calculations for all three of the other countries, and after adjustment should be the same in each case. We therefore begin by taking all three terminal gaps as they appear initially (path

143

B, which we have seen ends above path A by 19 per cent for Germany, ends above it by 21 per cent for Sweden and 23 per cent for the USA), and applying a quarter of their average as the adjustment to be made in A.1 throughout – it proves to be of the same effect as lowering the UK price index for 1890–9, with 1925–9 as base, by about 5 per cent. The gap that remains after this adjustment is then removed in each of the three cases by equal proportionate adjustments of A.2 (to expand it) and B.1, B.2 (to contract them).

The paths from period II to period III can now be traced, using for the B.1. the A.2 of 1925–9 as adjusted above. The terminal of path B now proves to lie *below* that of path A by 21 per cent for Germany, 28 per cent for Sweden, and 25 per cent for the USA. The same procedure as before is followed to bring the terminals together.

The inter-country relatives of 1925–9 given by the B.1 as now adjusted differ from those given by the A.2 in the adjusted transition from period I to period II. The same procedure as before is now worked through for both transitions, with the adjusted B.1 obtained from the first working of the II–III transition inserted as the A.2 of this second working of the I–II transition. The disparities that remain in the inter-country relatives for 1925–9 after the second working of both transitions prove not to exceed 0·6 of 1 per cent.

5 Industrial Policies and Growth

by M. V. Posner

I. INTRODUCTION

When the Brookings study first appeared, I did not read it with as much attention as has now been necessary; hence my first comment is one of admiration. In particular, to read Professor Caves' own chapter is to receive a complete education from the footnotes alone, and, since my own preoccupations in the last few years have been fiscal and monetary policies (a point which has the advantage that I can claim with honesty that none of the views I express in this paper reflect the opinion of government departments for whom I have worked) I was much in need of this refresher course. I have taken as my fair field for comment the whole of Part III of the Brookings study, with the exception of Professor Ulman's chapter on collective bargaining: within this field I have concentrated most on the essays by Professors Caves and Shepherd. Having had the pleasure of reading an early draft of Professor Phelps Brown's paper for this conference, I have steered clear of some of the issues he analyses so magisterially.

May I start by putting 'industrial policies' (and industrial change) in the context of general economic policy? It is common ground, surely, that most of the changes that take place in individual factories are independent of government policies, certainly in the short run and to a large extent in the long run. The constant minor improvements of product design, or factory lay-out, or progress chasing, that account for so much of the 'trend in productivity', are grassroots activities: in any system, with even the minimum degree of devolution of control, these are shop-floor responsibilities. (In the British system, one result of the weakness of higher management techniques is the very considerable degree of independence exercised by lower management.) Of course, these changes take place in the context of conjunctural policy, and there are some grounds for believing that changes in the conjunctural environment would set free, to a significant extent, the energies of those responsible for improvements at plant level. Moreover, although the absolute success of each industry might be largely independent of policy, the weights given to different industrial sectors by government policies might change, and so improve the weighted average result. Again, the structure of ownership and control, and the market environment in which firms operate, can be changed substantially in short time, and this may lead to a speeding-up of a sort of 'transfer mechanism' by which the best practice is generalized throughout an industry. Finally, long-term changes in the quality and training of various categories of the labour force may have an effect on the capacity of firms to improve themselves. These four possibilities are examined below.

There is, however, an initial question which must be confronted. The fruits of industrial policy, the general consequences of diffused industrial change, emerge in the recorded figures of output and employment; but the growth of output is much influenced by the growth of demand. In asking, therefore, whether the trend of productive potential has accelerated in recent years it is not sufficient to rely on the observed growth of GDP. (In any case, divergence among the several estimates of GDP in the last few years makes it extremely difficult to detect small changes in growth rates.) At the very least we have to examine productivity per man employed (and, at higher levels of sophistication, the effects of, and future expectations of, changes in annual hours worked). It is generally held that employment in mid-1970 was well below the level that would have been predicted on the basis of regressions of employment on output over the previous decade, and this 'negative residual' in the employment equation emerged particularly strongly in the last two or three years (in particular, after the period to which the Brookings study statistics referred). If it could plausibly be argued that the size of the residual would go on increasing a turning-point in the trend of productive potential could be identified – perhaps as much as $\frac{1}{2}$ per cent per year.

Dispute on this question rages, and will not be resolved here. Perhaps the major question is the degree to which the impact of SET has released labour from the distributive trades, and the extent to which we can expect repeated bonuses from this tax in the future. (An optimistic conclusion could come *either* by assuming a strong once-for-all SET effect and predicting further dollops of the tax in future; *or* by assuming a generally more rapid trend of productivity in the SET trades which happened by chance to coincide with the introduction of SET. There are several possible pessimistic assumptions as well.) If we assume that the effect of SET was once-for-all, and decline to regard the recent increase in average hours worked in manufacturing as an increase in underlying productivity, only a little evidence is available from orthodox methods of any accelera-

146

tion in productivity trends. Indeed, because the future demographic change in the labour force will probably be quite small, the trend of productive potential (i.e. the maximum growth rate consistent with a constant number of unemployed) could be lower in the future than in the previous decade.

But we have no proof positive that this is so. Just as Professor Phelps Brown suggests that the Phillips curve relationship is best construed as one between changes in unemployment and changes in wages, our past evidence on productive potential is a record of changes in unemployment in response to changes in the growth rate: from this sort of cyclical evidence no firm predictions can be made about what could be achieved under steadier demand conditions.

However, while the growth of productive potential must be the main interest of conjunctural policy makers, it is perhaps possible (using a microscope of exceptional resolution) to detect some small acceleration in what might be called 'underlying output per hour' – productive potential before taking account of demographic factors or increasing leisure. This evidence is too slight to prove that the changes in the last decade have had any effect: but it is at least not inconsistent with such a hope. Since recent estimates suggest that perhaps $\frac{1}{2}$ per cent of the $3\frac{1}{4}$ per cent per year growth in productive capacity over the last decade have been due to favourable demographic factors which will not persist, and most of us can list inflexible demands on available resources which would be hard to constrain below a growth rate of at least 3 or 4 per cent over the next decade, the 'hope' of an acceleration in underlying productivity must be fervently cherished. This paper attempts to assemble some of the (necessarily inconclusive) reasons for nurturing such a hope.

II. The International Productivity Gap

As I understand Professor Denison's main result,[1] much of Britain's 'failure to grow' can plausibly be explained away: it is the *level* of our residual efficiency which is particularly low. Professor Matthews comments that 'if it is a matter of trying to improve general efficiency and attitudes, it may not make much difference to policy whether it is our growth or our level that is at fault'. I certainly agree, though I must confess that I find it hard to see this result as a new idea: I was

[1] Brookings Report, p. 274. This result is stressed by Professor Phelps Brown, and Professor Matthews makes much of it in 'Why Growth Rates Differ', *Economic Journal*, June 1969, p. 268.

brought up on the Rostas productivity study[1] which emphasized differences in the organization of the work force and the market, as well as differences in 'capital per head.'[2] as causes of our poor performance. But this view, if correct, provides the strongest grounds for optimism about the growth of productivity in the UK: it is far easier to expand towards an existing production frontier than to fight the frontier outwards.

This is really the basic reason for believing that an increase in the rate of investment should yield large returns to the UK: provided the investment is well directed, the outcome should be the transformation of more British firms into replicas of their American equivalents. Investment, in the British economy, is to be seen not as a mode of increasing capital intensity, or even as a necessity for the embodiment of the latest blueprints into physical plant, but rather as a necessary counterpart of any act of reorganization, small or large.[3] It is for this reason that I doubt the relevance of Professor J. R. Sargent's results,[4] when he suggests that an increase in the investment /GDP ratio may have no permanent effect on the growth rate: my case would be rather that the increase in investment (or, admittedly, its redirection) would be an inevitable concomitant of most improvements in our residual efficiency.

I am not sure how to select and identify a specific example of 'residual inefficiency', but consider two examples that might serve. It has frequently been suggested that excessive product differentiation, perhaps associated with our stratified social system, is a cause of inefficiency, probably quite separate from any failure to take account of economies of scale.[5] Now, in his study of firms making small electric motors, Cole found an extraordinary heterogeneity of output (associated more with a failure of price competition to force

[1] L. Rostas, *Comparative Productivity in British and American Industry* (1948). Professor Caves uses M. Frankel, *British and American Productivity: A Comparison and Appraisal* (1957), to illustrate similar themes with more up-to-date information.

[2] See Professor Phelps Brown, p. 110 above.

[3] I draw on the experience reported in the series of articles by H. J. D. Cole and associates entitled *Factory Productivity and Efficiency* (Bulletin of the Oxford Institute of Statistics, 1960-1). This extremely detailed comparative study of three plants in the light electrical engineering sector supports few generalizations but does exhaustively illustrate the complexity and catholicity of industrial progress.

[4] J. R. Sargent, 'Recent Growth Experience in the Economy of the United Kingdom', *Economic Journal*, March 1968.

[5] See Caves, *Brookings Report*, p. 285, and particularly note 27 on page 290. See also Matthews, *op. cit.*, p. 263.

the benefits of standardization on industrial customers than with any peculiar sociological qualities of the British consumer). At least one plant eventually took the obvious plunge of segregating the standard product on to a series production line, taking the opportunity to introduce various other improved practices at the same time. This involved fairly substantial investment in new machinery, and also an increase in the scale of operation (note that this need not appear in the *Census* as an increase in size of plant, since the production of other ancillary output could be readily reduced or transferred elsewhere to make room for greater output of motors). Doubtless many factors are involved in this little story – changing market structure, changing factory organization, changing size of market – but I would emphasize:

(i) The resulting increase in productivity may be analytically a reduction in residual inefficiency, but statistically it will appear as an increase in productive potential.

(ii) Investment was necessary to bring about the change.

A second example may be provided by the gas and electricity industries. As is well known, there are several alternative ways of meeting expected final demand 'at peak' in the fuel industries: discouraging peak demand by appropriate pricing policies; installing various alternative peak-lopping plant (of low capital cost and high running cost); disconnecting specific customers (and suffering a penalty in consequence); expanding the base-load capacity of the industry. The choice amongst these several possibilities is a highly technical matter, involving the calculation of shadow prices by the solution of a programming model, and finding some (politically acceptable) method of signalling these prices to different sections of the fuel industry and to the final customer. The more rapidly and smoothly these calculations are made, the appropriate signals transmitted, and rational responses calculated by the final customers, the less will be the absorption of resources into the fuel sector for a given basket of final satisfactions. For this sort of 'improvement', what is required is a skilled and efficient managerial class, receptive of new ideas and able to convince a large number of decisionmakers elsewhere in the economy that the sums are worth doing. This case shares property (i) with the example in the last paragraph, but not property (ii).

It is impossible to give other than casually empirical responses to the question – which of these examples is more typical? But it seems evident to me that acceleration of growth in productive potential

149

will require ample doses of both types of change, and that we cannot ignore the importance of maintaining and increasing the investment ratio so as to get as much of the first sort as we can without inhibiting the second. Unfortunately the reasoning of an earlier paragraph above suggests that coaxing resources from consumption or public expenditure into investment is not costless, and is certainly not easy. Indeed, simple ICOR calculations suggest that the investment necessary for an extra $\frac{1}{2}$ per cent growth of GDP per year could be obtained only by abandoning most of the normal year-to-year growth in consumption.

III. Technical Change: Innovation and Imitation

There is one other element which we must dispose of before we approach 'policy' in the strict sense. Professor Peck's Chapter 10 in the Brookings study gives (Table 10.8) an illuminating comparison of the distribution of research and development expenditure between industries in the US and the UK. R & D expenditure, of course, requires skilled manpower, and Britain's shortfall in this factor input is a typical example of the chicken-and-egg controversy in economic development: have we insufficient development engineers because we are poor, or are we poor because of a deficiency of development engineers? It has been plausibly suggested that, in many industries, market advantage whether in the home or foreign markets) is a function of the rate of change in technology rather than the level of technology at a point of time.[1] But innovation is an activity that costs resources – new knowledge does not fall like manna from heaven – and poorer countries can benefit by imitating the progress of others. There is some evidence for the proposition that the UK has been slow to imitate as well as slow to innovate.[2]

Although this is not the place for an exhaustive treatment of the problem, it has been vigorously argued[3] that the substantial UK investment in nuclear R & D was a mistake, and the licensing of the American boiling-water reactor would have been a better bet. The computer story (where great efforts have been made to sustain a

[1] See, e.g., R. Vernon, 'International Trade and International Investment in the Product Cycle', *Quarterly Journal of Economics*, 1966; and C. Freeman and associates, 'Chemical Process Plant: Innovation and the World Market', *National Institute Economic Review*, August 1968.

[2] See G. Hufbauer, *Synthetic Materials and the Theory of International Trade* and M. V. Posner 'Technical Change and Economic Growth', *Oxford Economic Papers*, 1961

[3] Duncan Burn, *Political Economy of Nuclear Energy*.

viable UK producer) raises similar questions. But, apart from these rather grand decisions of national strategy, product development in the mass of British industry has tended to be an isolated, esoteric activity, in which engineers pursued the internal logic of the technical processes without due regard to commercial pay-off.

An economist is bound to approach this sort of problem by asking whether the institutional arrangements and market forces are operating in a way which would encourage appropriate management behaviour. As regards institutional matters, the broad lines of the former government's Green Paper, recommending that government research establishments in 'applied science' should be organized on a more frankly commercial basis, are appealing and (given that government has a weight of at least 30 per cent in R & D) of great importance. Market forces, particularly those that depend on a market in knowledge, do not seem strong, and it may be that international mergers or takeovers are the speediest route by which new methods and products can be spread.[1] The only danger to which I would draw attention[2] is illustrated by Sir Dennis Robertson's well-known parable about the rich, constantly innovating business man and his sluggish, imitative servant:

> 'The simple fellow who, to the advantage of both, has been earning a living by cooking the dinner for a busy and prosperous scientist, wakes up one day to find that his master has invented a completely automatic cooker, and that if he wants to remain a member of the household he must turn shoeblack. He acquires a kit and learns the technique, only to find that his master has invented a dust-repelling shoe, but would nevertheless be graciously willing for him to remain on and empty the trash-bins. Would he not do better to remove himself from the orbit of the great man, and cultivate his own back garden?'

The hope must be that the innovatory habit, once implanted, will grow in its environment, and the autarchic conclusion of this parable prove false. But it seems to me inevitable and right that the process of international investment and takeovers should be, in Whitehall language, 'closely watched'.

IV. LONG-TERM GROWTH AND SHORT-TERM POLICY

We now come to the first of the four conditioning factors which

[1] See H. G. Johnson's *Wicksell Lectures* for 1968.
[2] See my article in P. Streeten (ed.) *Unfashionable Economics* (1970).

determine the environment within which micro improvements happen. The side heading deliberately evokes the title of the basic Godley–Shepherd article,[1] enshrining (as far as UK economists are concerned) the maximum-growth-rate hypothesis: that growth rates above an (identifiable) natural rate cannot be achieved without encountering ever-increasing pressure of demand. Nothing in that article (nor, as I understand them, in the views of its authors) denies the possibilities that:

(a) the underlying growth rate *may* be functionally related to the time-path of effective demand (e.g. a cyclical or 'stop–go, path of demand may induce a lower growth rate of productive capacity);
(b) a fairly lengthy period during which demand increases (and is confidently expected to increase further) at a rate faster than productive capacity has grown in the past *might* induce a faster rate of improvement at the micro level and hence accelerate the growth of productive capacity.

Perhaps it is not otiose to produce simple examples of these effects.[2] The segregation of output into 'standard' and 'special' lines requires a reasonable stability in the output of the standard product. Resources (labour and machinery) are made, by reorganization, specific to particular productive processes, and fluctuations in final demand for the standard product (due, in the case cited, to hire-purchase controls) leave resources idle. The mere expectation of such uncertainties, when the (e.g. industrial relations) costs of change are substantial, will rationally inhibit the speed of change. Competitive pressures from other UK suppliers are limited by the tendency of (industrial) customers to spread their purchases among many suppliers on 'eggs and baskets' grounds; and in this field of consumer durables competitive pressure from abroad has had at least as much effect on the 'propensity to import' as on the efficiency of UK production.

As regards the relationship between alternative steady-state growths of demand and the rate of growth of efficiency, it is far harder to find, and claim some general significance for, convincing examples. The innumerable small improvements (together aggregating to a growth of overall efficiency of between 3 and 6 per cent a year in the Cole study) are a function of the strength of managerial and design-staff initiative and, for any given size of the design team,

[1] W. A. H. Godley and J. R. Shepherd, 'Long-term Growth and Short-term Policy', *National Institute Economic Review*, 1964.
[2] See Cole and associates, *op. cit.*

of time. An increase in the growth of the market might induce the employment of a larger team and hence a more rapid rate of improvement; or alternatively, cost reduction might loom less important when selling prices are less constrained than are delivery dates. In so far as the effect we are seeking is to be found at all, it will probably consist in a speeding up of the rate of introduction of the large changes (e.g. the new production line for standard products) which we have already examined. Certainly tooling-up for faster growth involves substantial costs (to the firm[1] and the economy) if the growth is held back, but equally cost advantages should be obtained if demand follows its expected path. This will be particularly true of firms which seek to rationalize and improve their mix of final products but fear competitive constraints on any attempt to increase market shares.[2]

These arguments are not now as fashionable as they were in the early 1960s, and even at that time their chief exponents were careful not to make excessive claims.[3] But, of course, nothing that has happened in the UK in the last decade has remotely resembled a proper test of optimistic hypotheses. The period 1963–6 was admittedly one of high and increasing pressure of demand, but from so short an experiment (against a background of justified fears of nemesis to come) little can be deduced.

Probably most observers, whatever their theoretical presuppositions, would agree with the following prescription. Starting from a position where sterling is somewhat undervalued, and the pressure of demand historically low, an attempt could be made over a four- or five-year period to allow the growth of demand to accelerate slowly (from perhaps $2\frac{1}{2}$ per cent p.a to 4 per cent p.a.). Early symptoms of increasing demand pressures would generally be expected, but if there were sufficient initial slack, and if the exchange rate were such as to ensure that growing exports were a chief source of growing demand, these symptoms could be noted philosophically. Optimists

[1] See G. B. Richardson, *The Heavy Electrical Plant Industry* (1969).

[2] This argument is distinct from the straightforward static scale-economies discussion, since it seeks to relate the growth of the final market to the number of new (or standardized old) products which can be introduced in a given period. This notion has a respectable antiquity. See S. Kuznets, *Economic Change* (1953).

[3] See W. Beckerman, *The British Economy in 1975*, p. 46. 'In other words the productive system, at least in most of industry, is believed to be very flexible, and the rate of growth that can be achieved is, *within limits*, partly a matter of the growth rate expected.' (My italics.) Beckerman adds elsewhere that high expectations do not guarantee high growth, but low expectations do bring about slow growth.

would expect that towards the end of the experimental period the increase in demand pressures would begin to tail off, as we approached a new equilibrium growth path; pessimists would predict the need for eventual new restrictions. Whether the present position of the UK economy perfectly exemplifies the optimum conditions for such as experiment may be disputed, but it is difficult to see any positive effect of conjunctural policy in industrial growth unless such conditions can be created and taken advantage of.[1]

V. THE APPARATUS OF PLANNING

The National Plan of 1965, like its informal predecessors,[2] placed great emphasis on the relationship between growth performance, on the supply side, and the growth of demand: hence the position of this section in the structure of the present paper. It is, I think, correct to say that the inspiration of this particular round in the fashion of planning was the idea, supposed to characterize French[3] planning, that expectations, consistently held by most decision-makers, of an overall growth rate of X per cent might tend to be self-fulfilling, at least for values of X in the range 2–4. Hence the increasingly vigorous attempts to fit the growth projections together through the use of input–output analysis, drawing in particular on Stone's Cambridge work,[4] and requiring initial forecasts of the structure of final demand. Over-simplifying, the slogan of '*l'economie concertée*' applied the expectations analysis (of crucial importance in most theories of cyclical fluctuations) to the analysis of trends; it was an attempt to raise the Harrodian warranted growth rate towards the natural growth rate.

From this point of view, planning is the natural complement of any attempt to allow the growth of output to be coaxed upwards by a controlled 'taking in of slack' in conjunctural policy. The trouble is that the 'Plan' reached its peak of vogue in 1963–6, and now is widely regarded as a failure; while the conjunctural conditions for its opera-

[1] Most of the participants at the Ditchley conference would place less weight on demand management as an aid to faster growth than is implicit in the last few paragraphs. My own view remains that it would be a mistake to adhere too rigidly to a mechanistic model which treats the maximum output of an economy as if it were akin to the rated output of a motor.

[2] The NEDC publications of 1963 and 1964.

[3] In turn the French claim to have derived some notions from post-1945 British 'planning'. See V. A. Lutz, *Central Planning for the Market Economy* (1969).

[4] See, for instance, *Exploring 1970*, No. 6 in the series 'A Programme for Growth' (1965).

tion lie, hopefully, in the future (at any rate not in 1963–6). Echoing Beckerman,[1] I would venture the unfashionable remark that planning, in the sense of making rational expectations mutually consistent for a chosen growth rate, will have to be resuscitated one day soon.

But the difficulty with this proposal is not just its unpopularity but its dubious analytical standing. Mrs Lutz[2] has presented a coherent and impressive statement of one set of reasons for doubting the logical compatibility of national plans and managerial initiative, and Professor Perroux[3] long ago drew attention to the necessity to complement a 'physical' plan with a consistent set of projected financial flows. The Lutz argument is that if we have roughly forty industry groups for which output is forecast (as in the 1965 National Plan) and at least 400 important decision-making units, there is every reason to suppose that the result of individual decisions will not be merely the allocation *within* industries of the 'planned' output for each industry, but effectively also a reallocation *between* industries in a necessarily 'un-planned' way. She uses the French record, with notorious deviations between plans and outcomes, to illustrate this case, and there is no doubt similar fun to be had with the UK projections. Perroux would, as I understand him, explain some of these deviations. by the failure of the planners correctly to understand the formation of prices, profit distributions, savings ratios and indeed wages: all these financial decisions have feedback on investment decisions and on the distribution of final demand (to say nothing of their effects on the government accounts).

For these reasons the best-laid plans will be likely to go astray. Nor is it possible to retort that the errors should 'cancel out', since each enterprise is concerned with predicting the ease of selling in a number of separate (though interconnected) markets in which it might plan to intrude its technology in the future. Vague statements that the 'growth rate' may rise from $2\frac{1}{2}$ to 4 per cent over a run of years are meaningless unless translated in detail by each firm's own market researchers, aware of the special characteristics of that firm's products. The central planners have neither the information nor the willingness to do this job.

Nevertheless, I remain of the view that a general notion of the way in which the authorities envisage the course of aggregate demand developing over the coming five years (on a 'rolling forward' basis) can serve a useful purpose in providing a common 'key' into

[1] See above, p. 153, n.3.
[2] V. A. Lutz, *op. cit.*
[3] See his *The Fourth French Plan*, in English translation (1964, NIESR).

which the projections of corporate planners can be fitted.[1] But I would agree that the *Tableau Economique* of the Stone model should not be seen as throwing up output 'targets' for arbitrarily chosen (and heavily aggregated) industry groups;[2] instead these exercises should be used in an attempt to identify the types of problems that might generate bottlenecks to (partial constraints on) growth. This last thought represents a familiar strand in British thinking in the period 1963–5 and is worthy of a little elaboration.

Both the NEDC publication *Conditions Favourable to Faster Growth* (1963) and the 1965 National Plan recognized the need for action to improve efficiency, in the broad sense. The National Plan incorporated a 'Check List of Action Required' – mostly of the form 'Government will promote management education . . . Economic Development Committees will be set up . . . studies will be made, industry by industry (of methods of achieving standardization and longer runs)'; there was also promise of specific action on individual items – 'Government Training Centres will be expanded'. The main emphasis was put on the work of the Economic Development Committees (EDCs), and the notion was that these bodies would identify specific problems arising in their own industries and try to solve them. The EDCs were duly set up, and a large volume of glossy literature in due course began to find its way through academic letter boxes. It is difficult for the outsider to assess the worth of these studies, many of which were doubtless no more than pious hot air. But two examples that I do know of are possibly good specimens of the modest nuggets of good sense that arguably justify the whole exercise.

Civil engineering contracts have traditionally been let, for the most part to public local authorities, on a 'one-off' competitive tender basis. The traditional division of function between architects, consultant engineers and contractors has great merits for honesty

---

[1] For this reason I am frankly astounded at the views reported in Lutz, *op. cit.*, and more extensively in Chapter 2 of the useful PEP volume *Economic Planning and Policies in Britain, France and Germany* (1968), which claim that there is some argument of principle against allowing government authorities to make or elaborate such forecasts at all. These ideas, particularly strong in post-war Germany (where they apparently derive from the work of Walter Eucken), seem to represent a classic case of following a principle *ad absurdum*. On the other hand, the notion of 'removing specific obstacles to faster growth' (Anglo-Saxon) is readily translatable into the notion of 'permissible interventions by the State' or 'Marktkonformität' (Teutonic). (See PEP, *op. cit.*, p. 43.)

[2] But see below (page 159) for a more *dirigiste* approach to output targets for nationalized industries.

and sound design, but great difficulties for the efficient conduct of contractors' business: if specialized machinery is to be kept fully employed, and contractors encouraged to equip themselves on a long-term basis with both machinery and skilled manpower, there are great attractions in a system of so-called 'serial tendering'. In such a system, both contractor and customer (or groups of customers – hence one reason to welcome the larger local-government units now proposed) would have a partial obligation, subject no doubt to variation clauses, to repeat existing contract terms in successive jobs. The EDC for the industry has organized much discussion and revision of practice with this idea in mind (building, incidentally, on the work of committees set up on government initiative several years earlier).

Secondly, the Machine Tools EDC has struggled to seek some reorganization of the industry's practice, both to change the habits of their customers and to reduce the traditionally high marginal propensity to import at the time of investment booms. This has involved government development contracts, management education, some consequential mergers, and so on. In this case it is perhaps fair to say that the degree of energy and activity has been greater that the degree of success.

These examples illustrate conditions which I think are fairly general:

(a) There is some connection between the Plan projections (of construction activity or machine-tool imports) and the problems studied by the EDCs, but no close numerical connections.
(b) The EDC discussions take place in a context of previous and subsequent independent committee reports.
(c) Often EDC discussions are overtaken by specific commercial initiatives (e.g. merger actions).
(d) The government is often involved as customer, or provider of research contracts, or influencer of the market (demand management or fiscal policies), or setter of a legal framework (for competitive tendering).

Naturally, since 1964 the government has presented much of its own role in these discussions as 'active intervention', or 'deliberate action to encourage growth points', but it would be easy to justify much the same actions according to a more market-orientated philosophy.[1] I myself would conclude that this sort of 'planning'

[1] See p. 156, n.1.

157

activity needs to be done somehow, and the apparatus of EDCs and consultation with industry is as good a method as any. Its quantitative contribution to the growth of productive potential will be for ever unknown.

But, to most people, planning means more than this: the projected outputs for individual industry groups are to be treated as control data,[1] and divergence between plan and outcome creates a presumption that the projection of aggregate GDP is at risk. We have already noted the analytical difficulty with this approach, but nevertheless any bureaucrat charged with responsibility for 'watching closely the prospects for growth' will want to know how far the micro-data flowing across his desk are consistent with his macro-projections (upon which, *inter alia*, government action on public expenditure or taxes are posited); and, under some regimes, will wish to tell Ministers what action might be taken to correct the divergence. The only serious attempt to lay down suitable decision algorithms that I know of has been suggested by Bray[2] in a way that most economists will find unsatisfactory but is certainly worthy of discussion. He postulates a series of 'bargains' (which perhaps need not be formal) between industries and government; e.g. 'growth industries' (with high income-elasticities or time-trends in their demand functions) may be offered assurances about demand-management policies in return for offers to stabilize their capital expenditure trends or to reach export targets.

Such 'bargains' have in fact been openly discussed only in the case of the motor-car trade, and the government has been understandably reluctant to make even half-promises which experience in the last decade has shown to be hard to keep. Nevertheless, the notion is not without merit, and will doubtless develop in an informal way, not necessarily through the EDCs, but through informal contacts between the Ministry of Technology and individual firms: certainly the recent increases in concentration at the large end of industry has made it possible for senior officials and even Ministers to be on first-name basis with most of the 50 or 100 key managing directors.

But how far all this will contribute substantially to growth will depend on how far the obstacles to faster growth are internal to the firm, and on how far the external conditions are manipulable through conscious action rather than by market forces (acting through motivations ostensibly very different from policy desiderata). It seems to me that there must be some role for conscious 'planning' in the sense

---

[1] In the same sense as the French '*contrôle des billets*'.
[2] J. W. Bray, *Decision in Government*, 1970.

in which I have developed the notion in the last few paragraphs, but it would be unwise to bet too heavily on it in advance.

VI. The Choices for Public Expenditure

I propose to hang a critique of Professor Shepherd's chapter in the Brookings volume on the peg of my second question – how far can government influence the weighted growth rate by redistributing through its own actions the weight given to different industrial sectors? I come to the conclusion that nothing can or should be done to this end. The preceding discussion of planning serves to remind us that, with public sector expenditure on 'resources' alone of £13 billion,[1] the influence of government on the rate of growth of demand must be substantial, and so must be also the reciprocal interest of the rest of the economy in projected government expenditure and its ramifications. But the amount of feedback is small, save in so far as the government is moved to constrain the growth of expenditure overall to avoid the necessity for taking an increased proportion of the GDP in taxation.

It may be useful to distinguish between three types of public expenditure. In the first, there is a straightforward resource allocation problem; take 'fuel policy' as an example.[2] Investment in the nationalized fuel industries is heavily dependent upon the choice of technique between nuclear and conventional power generation, and on the speed of conversion of the existing gas industry to the use of natural gas. Given the calculations of the resource cost of oil products and natural gas at beachhead, and the computation of an appropriate shadow price of coal-mining labour which takes account of the potential unemployment of redundant miners, the pattern of investment is entirely determined by the interest rate ('test discount rate') imposed by the central authorities. To suggest that investment could be reduced (with the result that resources could be released for more productive investment in manufacturing industry) is to suggest either:

1 *that the government has done its sums wrong.* This is certainly a strong possibility in any complex calculation, and there is little doubt that excessive investment in nuclear energy was made in 1956–62. Any decision on choice of technique involves the complex balancing of technological risks, and, although this is not the

---

[1] See the projections in Cmnd. 4234, Table 17.
[2] See Cmnd. 3438 of 1967.

place for the necessarily lengthy discussion required, my own conclusion is that the nuclear or conventional-power choice is very nicely balanced.[1] The recent decisions on power-station choice,[2] although excessively kind to coal, seem to reflect that balance. I am quite certain that within a very few years the balance will swing decisively to nuclear energy, but I would admit that past experience does suggest an excessive British tendency to back technological horses before they are really fit to run (the Comet, the Concorde, nuclear energy) which is part of that misallocation of research and development expenditure to which Professor Peck draws attention. However, this does not mean, *pace* Professor Shepherd, that investment resources can usefully be saved in the future by materially altering the present pattern of choice; or

2 *that the level of nationalized industries' prices is too low, thus both aggravating the government's fiscal problem and allowing demand to attract excessive resources into the nationalized sector.* As far as the fuel industries are concerned, there is no reason to suppose that price levels are lower than long-run marginal resource costs, or that the ratio price/marginal cost is lower in the public sector than in the competing oil industry. However, I would admit that this is true in 1970 only after a significant rise in public sector 'mark-ups' in recent years; in particular the recent rise in telecommunications charges, whose aim was no doubt in part to postpone, instead of immediately satisfying, that increase in demand which Professor Shepherd foresaw; or

3 *that the Test Discount Rate (TDR) is too low* – capital resources are more scarce than official calculations assume. I revert to this possibility below.

In a second type of expenditure decision – on transport – the problem is a mixture of a cost-minimization exercise (with externalities playing a major role) between road, rail, and underground expenditure;[3] a basic choice on the total of 'non-competitive' road expen-

---

[1] Comparing oil-fired stations with nuclear stations, a rise in the discount rate to 12 per cent would in my view push nuclear energy out of court; but comparing nuclear energy with coal, the nuclear victory is far more robust in regard to discount-rate variations.

[2] Four new power stations recently authorized comprised two oil-fired, one coal-fired, and one nuclear station.

[3] To make this sort of decision properly, flexible pricing by the railways and the relation of railway investment to road utilization have to be carefully combined, as Shepherd points out. For guidelines, the NBPI Report on Commuter Fares (Cmnd. 4250 of 1969) is an excellent starting-point.

diture; and a distribution of that total amongst projects on some quasi-economic criterion. The real issue is of how the 'basic choice' should be made. This can be related only to the mass of non-market public expenditure, since although it might in principle be possible to establish a 'return' on road expenditure (in terms of man-hours of travel saved, etc.), economic science provides no conclusive method of weighing this sort of return against the benefits from other forms of expenditure.

The distribution of public expenditure amongst a third main category of non-economic services, like health or education, is essentially a matter of political choice, which can indeed be enlightened by statistical information and knowledge of individual choices, but cannot and should not be determined by them.[1] The difficulty is that some bits of the expenditure total (roads, telecommunications, narrow parts of technical education) do have measurable returns, and that, if the total of public expenditure is constrained in any short sequence of years, successful bids from these programmes limit expenditure elsewhere. Moreover, the TDR can be used to choose optimal distribution between capital and current expenditures within any given programme (even within non-economic programmes), and hence can cut slices from the public-expenditure cake in early years that would otherwise be devoted to 'non-economic' expenditures.

The practical handling of these allocation problems involves much complexity. An outsider who has not been concerned with recent decisions might, drastically simplifying, describe the decision-making process as follows. Assume that a constrained path of total government claims on current resources[2] has been established, either by a consideration of the minimum requirements for other types of expenditure (private consumption, investment, exports) or by a choice between various possible paths for the tolerable increase in tax revenue. Then choose totals for the non-economic programmes, distributing programme expenditures through time (or between capital and current items) using some initial assumed TDR (say, 10 per cent). Work out the level of the TDR that would be required to fit the economic expenditures (chiefly nationalized industry invest-

[1] Despite a formidable literature on public goods (e.g. *Public Economics*, ed. by Margolis and Guitton, 1969), I think this conclusion holds. If not, rapid steps should be taken by the economic profession to reveal the philosopher's stone to governments.

[2] The translation of expenditures into resource claims has taken a formidable step forward since the Brookings study by the publication of the 1969 Green Paper *Public Expenditure: A New Presentation*, Cmnd. 4017.

L

ment) within the constrained total; then iterate back to the level of the TDR initially assumed.

The difficulties with this method, in ascending order of importance, are that:

1 in practice, because of the devolution of investment decisions, the TDR tends to be set in advance for several years. Hence the iteration process, and the consequent adjustment of programmes, takes time and equilibrium need never, in general, be reached.
2 The elasticity of investment to changes in the TDR may be small, and large changes may be ruled out for reasons of continuity and long-run considerations.
3 The TDR has to serve the purpose of allocating investment between the public and the private sectors, as well as simply *within* the public sector, and private sector discount rates cannot be readily influenced through acts of policy.

For all these reasons, the government will from time to time find it necessary to reallocate expenditure *ad hoc* (quite apart from particular conjunctural emergencies). The constraints on total expenditure may be broken; or the desired path of non-economic expenditures may be modified; or capital rationing for economic expenditures may be practised; or (as in the recent rise in the financial targets for, and hence the price-level of, the telephone and postal services) steps may be taken both to reduce the growth rate of particular elements in the demand for nationalized industry output and at the same time, effectively, to 'tax' the consumers of this output by raising prices. Fiscal policy, the distribution of public expenditure between programmes, and the allocation of industrial resources, may all thus be manipulated at the margin in a way which may be formally non-optimal but seems unavoidable save in a golden age.[1] Only if there are grounds for believing that, over a run of years, misallocations are large, and repeated marginal adjustments inconsistent with the main approach, can we seriously question the pattern of decisions on economic grounds.

Professor Shepherd does suggest that there have been serious misallocations, first because of the lack of consistency in decisions within the 'economic' category , and secondly because of a bias against those items of social expenditure with high (external) bene-

---

[1] This description of planning expenditure was written before the 1970 election. To judge from press comments during the first months of the new government's life, the basic framework of decision-making has not dramatically changed.

fits. But if the broad criteria which I have described are used, I cannot see grounds for worrying unduly about the first head: as regards the second, I would readily agree that decision-making in this area is primitive, and could be much improved by the application of skilled manpower and open discussion.[1]

Our economic interests in UK growth, however, are not closely involved in this question. Marginal reallocations of resources between coal and other sources of fuel will, in the 1970s, make a significant contribution to the growth of productive capacity, provided the major proportion of 'released miners' – or rejected entrants to the industry – are employed elsewhere. The growth of the electronics industry, and conceivably also the rate of improvement in its efficiency depend on the growth of telephone investment. The efficiency of road transport can make a significant contribution to a smooth regional redistribution of industrial investment. At the risk of charges of complacency, I believe we have these decisions broadly 'right'.

There are two particular issues of public expenditure that merit comment. Practice in recent years has led to a number of relatively small *special expenditures* designed explicitly to prop-up firms – in the shipbuilding and aircraft industries for the most part – that would otherwise have risked failure. In some cases the justification has been regional policy, in others a sort of 'contribution to overheads' in lieu of research and development contracts. The process of technical change is never smooth, and there may be in particular cases strong welfare-economic reasons for postponing or preventing change: in general, however, the notion that change should be braked is not conducive to growth, nor to the rational distribution of public expenditure. These expenditures are more important as symbols than quantitatively, and are certainly small compared with general R & D expenditure and investment grants,[2] which raise the second particular problem.

Investment grants are estimated at around £530 million per year in 1969–72, and can be compared with expected corporation tax receipts in 1970–1 of £1,900 million. Whatever the 'resource cost' of investment grants (in the Green Paper sense), a reduction in investment grant expenditure, if it were to be accompanied by no change

[1] The work of the Roskill Commission on the third London Airport will be a monumental contribution to cost-benefit analysis in this field, but I hope its authors will bear in mind Professor Shepherd's warning that cost-benefit studies 'are not a magic wand'.

[2] See Cmnd. 4234 of 1969, pages 33 and 35.

163

in real capital formation or dividend distribution in the private sector, would increase the financial deficit of companies accordingly: whether or not this is desirable is more a matter for monetary policy than for industrial policy as such. The new government is expected to do away with investment grants, but no doubt most of the funds saved will be channelled back in the form of tax concessions to the company sector. But a reduction in investment grants might also have some effect on the calculated *ex ante* profitability of certain investment projects and (although the analysis is complex) hence reduce real investment. It is beyond the scope of this paper to explore the industrial consequences of the present mix of tax sticks and carrots in manufacturing and service trades: I would make the point only that a reduction in grants would, *ceteris paribus*, either have merely 'monetary' consequences or would reduce the sum of real capital formation plus profits distributions. We cannot expect much direct help to 'growth' from such a move.

VII. COMPETITION AND AMALGAMATIONS

The third policy impact on productive potential is the attitude to competition and size. As a result of successive Restrictive Practices Acts, formal price agreements and associated restrictions, and resale price maintenance, have virtually disappeared from the British economy. Although informal agreements linger in many trades, they last only until abrupt changes in technology or the structure of ownership change accustomed ways and demand the acquisition of new habits. Indeed, there is reason to believe that the end of price agreements, and the abandonment of 'Buggins turn' in much public sector purchasing,[1] have provided the initiative for many mergers.

Mergers and takeovers have accelerated very substantially in the last two or three years (no doubt since the Brookings study was prepared). Sutherland[2] suggests that, after a gentle acceleration in the early 1960s, both the number of acquisitions and even more their size increased radically in 1967 and 1968. Moreover, 'the 28 biggest companies in 1961 owned 30 per cent of the total net assets of large UK manufacturing companies. By end of 1968, the

[1] See G. B. Richardson, *op. cit.* Purchases by the CEGB and the Post Office were dominant elements in the demand for heavy electrical equipment and electronics.
[2] See a clear and vigorous statement of the position, and attack on official policies by A. Sutherland in A. Cairncross (ed.) *The Managed Economy*, (1970), and the official Green Paper *Mergers* (HMSO, 1969).

(new) 28 biggest owned 50 per cent of the total assets owned by the survivors of these large companies'. Indeed, the industrial economist returning to his muttons after three years on other work finds it difficult to recognize the names of many companies, so sweeping have been the changes.

Finally, the National Board for Prices and Incomes has now completed four years of life and something like 150 reports. No firm or union that has been investigated by the NBPI has a good word to say for the Board's reports – from the clearing banks to the Gas Council, from university teachers to the brewers, they unite in opposition; but there is no doubt that the questions asked and the hares started by these investigations have been a major source of change and adaptation in British society (the effect on the movement of incomes and prices is, alas, more questionable).

The impact of these related changes on the organization of production must be substantial. The opportunities for the achievement of longer runs, for economy in development overheads, for expressing cost differences adequately in price differentials, have all materially increased. Moreover, the reduction in the number of firms does not necessarily reduce the institutional pressures for improvement *within* large organizations,[1] where what is called in other countries 'socialist emulation' can be vigorously encouraged by centralized management-consultancy and organization-and-methods teams. Many of these improvements could no doubt have been achieved without one or the other of the changes that have occurred; e.g. the electricity boards could themselves have standardized the detailed design of switch-gear equipment, provided a productive advisory service, and let three- or four-year contracts to the lowest bidders: but if British business chooses to progress through the traditional method of acquisitions, why should we complain?

Sutherland[2] offers us several reasons, of which the chief ones are these. First – and this is a point made forcefully by Caves in his Brookings study Chapter VII – in terms of pure size most British firms (perhaps not establishments), are already large by world standards. Why should British GEC compare in size with American GE? Are there not many successful electrical firms in other countries far smaller than the new GEC–EE–AEI amalgam? Secondly, 'we find that in about half the cases analysed the acquired company had a rate of return 10 per cent or more *above* that of its acquirer' – acquis-

[1] See the interesting paper by R. M. Cyert and K. D. George, 'Competition, Growth and Efficiency', *Economic Journal*, June 1969.
[2] A. Sutherland, *op. cit.*

itions are a way of maintaining the profitability of sleeping giants, not of speeding up the transfer of the latest techniques from big firms to small ones. Thirdly, the pace of innovation can be restrained, and the profitability of existing capital maintained, by the acquirer 'sitting on' the innovator longer than society, or competition, would optimally choose.

The easy-going attitude of the Board of Trade to mergers is therefore, in this view, the wrong policy. (The deliberate actions of the Industrial Reorganization Corporation may be more acceptable, since they have a clear aim in mind.)[1] One response to this complaint is to consider the example of paragraph 10, and many other examples that could no doubt be found, where progress depends on the spreading of new methods of management and control – spreading the light to the heathen. It may be true that in Britain we have no more than a couple of dozen first-rate management teams, and if their abilities are not to be wasted they should be allowed to reorganize not just one firm, but a whole industry (or at any rate large parts of it). But this response is arguably not consistent with an economist's view of how business works.

VIII. By Way of Conclusion

This leads me to the last of the four policy problems – the provision of management (and workers) of greater skill and ability. I do not offer another sermon on this theme, but ask rather whether 'better management' is a cause or an effect of higher growth. The capacity of managers to perform (or of young university graduates to show management skills – a question so often asked ingenuously by potential employers) is a function of the conditions in which they work as well as of their innate abilities. We have all seen firms, or universities, or departments of State, that contained many able people, but worked far worse than they should or could. Occasionally (perhaps even often) established organizations need a few knocks to push the iron filings of the magnetic field into new patterns. The changes that have been taking place in British industry, by this analogy, provide the opportunity for managers to improve their performance.

A good example of this benign influence of change upon performance is perhaps provided by the impact of the Industrial Reorganization Corporation, not on the firms which it has helped to merge,

---

[1] Although many observers of the recent moves in the ball-bearing industry have wondered what that aim might be.

but on the financial institutions whose peace and calm it has rudely interrupted. Whereas in Germany it has been traditional[1] for merchant banks and insurance companies to take an active interest in the firms in which they hold small equity interest, in British practice 'arms length' dealing has been the rule. Now, under nudging from the IRC, and a loosening of traditional bonds as industrial frontiers change, a more active relationship is developing.

The blurred snap-shot of industrial policy which I have presented is a picture of policy caught in the process of change; and the British economy, hopefully, is in a similar posture. If all goes well, the new structures of ownership and market organization, in the right conjunctural framework and with the right nudging from government planning, will provide the stimulus for managers to improve 'residual efficiency' and allow productive potential to accelerate. But it is impossible at this stage to assess the chances of success.

[1] See the PEP volume, *Economic Planning, op. cit.*; and A. Shonfield, *Modern Capitalism.*

6. Report of the Conference Sessions

by C. A. Blyth

SESSIONS 1 AND 2: THE ROLE OF DEMAND MANAGEMENT

This first session, devoted mainly to the aims and instruments of demand management, started with some clarificatory statements about the aims and conclusions of the Brookings Report. Professor Solow pointed to a possible misunderstanding about the Brookings conclusions which sprang from different uses of the word *stabilization*. In American usage a stabilization policy means more than just ironing out fluctuations at a particular level: instead, the policy is essentially short-run macro-economic policy aimed at such things as a high level of employment, some sort of target for the behaviour of the price level, and in an open economy some attention to the balance of payments as well. By adopting a narrow view of stabilization, Professor Matthews had skirted around what really should be at the centre of any current discussion of stabilization policy, namely, the relation between pressure of demand, the level of real output and employment on one hand, and wage and price behaviour on the other. The balance of payments certainly enters as well into this relationship, although as Worswick emphasized in his paper, it is affected also by the simple compression of incomes, quite independently of the consequent behaviour of the price level.

Consequently, Solow would interpret the Brookings conclusion (and he emphasized that this was their collective opinion) about the performance of demand management in the British economy a little differently from Matthews. When Brookings conclude that the average pressure of demand over the post-war period was just about right, it is in terms of the balance of payments and the price level that they are weighing the consequences of having on the average a little higher or a little lower pressure of demand (Solow doubted, for example, whether Brookings even considered the remote possibility, which Matthews mentions, that higher average pressure might have reduced productivity enough actually to reduce the aggregate level of output). Thus on Solow's interpretation the Brookings conclusion was that the United Kingdom did sacrifice output on behalf of the balance of payments. Nevertheless, Solow interpreted Brookings to

168

mean that a lower or higher average pressure of demand would not have brought an advantage or disadvantage in terms of the balance of payments or price level sufficient to justify having departed from what in fact actually happened.

Caves welcomed the opportunity to point out that the Brookings Report was trying to think in terms of the theory of economic policy in which one has a set of instruments and a set of targets at which they are aimed. In general one does not think in terms of particular associations between the individual instruments and the targets, yet in practice one thinks of demand management as ordinarily oriented towards objectives to do with internal balance. In trying to develop some kind of appraisal of opportunities foregone, the Report was forced to adopt this same procedural assumption.

Clearly a number of changes in demand management in the last fifteen years have been forced on government not by the state of the internal balance but by the balance of payments. The Brookings Report recognized this situation, and it is reflected in the fact that the Report's qualitative appraisal of the execution of aggregate economic policy was largely based on the sort of multiple-regression analysis that the Musgraves used, associating changes in the particular instruments or proxies for those instruments with good or bad proxies for the states of the targets. The team was impressed with the point that multiple-regression analysis does potentially tell something about how regularly fiscal policy has responded to the state of internal balance after the influence of external disturbances has been taken into account. In the statistical sense, multiple-regression analysis does do that, and thus the team tried to slant their calculations in that direction. Caves suspected that he was taking issue with Worswick on this score: taking issue in the sense of invoking that property of multiple-regression analysis. On the other hand, Caves agreed that there have been times when the problem has been a shortage of instruments that would attack targets with a consequent pull in different directions; one can always convert a particular policy problem *ex post* to the problem of a lack of enough significant instruments.

A closely related point is that in appraising the success of the British use of fiscal policy for attaining internal stabilization or balance, i.e. 'pushing the targets in the right direction' – which is as formal a concept as the team had in mind – the Report was not trying to establish a direct correspondence between the mechanical measures of success in pursuing these targets and the probity, ability or any other attribute of the incumbents of Whitehall. It is possible

169

to fail in policy formation for all sorts of reasons – inadequate number of instruments, inability to make short-run forecasts – as well as some lack of ability or diligence on the part of the people in the firing-line. The Brookings Report was not concerned with apportioning blame.

These preliminaries out of the way – and Solow's interpretation of the Brookings use of the broader concept of stabilization still left open what was meant by the concept of destabilization – the discussion centred on the issues of the actual objectives of British policy and the role of the unemployment rate as an indicator and as a target.

The Brookings Report had not based its appraisals on what British governments had been trying to do, but on a set of objective or arbitrarily chosen criteria. One contrast between these two sets of objectives was underlined by the absence of any reference to price stability in Matthews' statements of what the British government was trying to do, and the explicit assumption by the Brookings team that price stability was a desirable objective. Lord Roberthall dealt with this point in a review of the actual objectives of post-war UK policy.

He agreed very much with what Matthews in his paper said about the need, in making judgments about British economic policy in the post-war period, to consider what the objectives actually were and not to measure it against what the critic thinks they ought to have been. Matthews had suggested that the objective was as high a level of activity as was compatible with the balance of payments. This was nearly right, but it would be more accurate to say there was an alternation of objectives. The primary objective was a very high level of employment because this was where the failure had been in the inter-war period. It was found, however, that the maintenance of this led to balance-of-payment, or rather reserve, difficulties, and when these appeared restrictive measures were taken and unemployment allowed to increase. Another objective was the desire to win elections, and this raised the subject of the character of the oscillations, dealt with by Matthews in his paper. The typical cycle started with a period of very high (over-full) employment with stagnating output leading to a balance-of-payments crisis and successive doses of deflation, leading eventually to a growth of unemployment. As unemployment grew, the economy was given a stimulus and this was overdone, largely because it was possible to choose the period of the upswing in output, before prices were much affected, for an election. Unemployment then fell rapidly and there followed a period of

170

pressure on resources, weakening balance of payments, gradual application of deflation, and then a repeat.

Price stability was *not* an object of policy in the sense that anything was done to bring it about. Lip service was paid but the first real attempt to do anything was the Selwyn Lloyd wage freeze started late in 1962, which did not last long. The general policy was successful in that high employment was maintained most of the time and the balance of payments responded to corrective measures.

Lord Roberthall agreed strongly with Matthews when he said that 'no past period in the least resembles 1968–70 from the cyclical point of view'. Although a lot was learned about the techniques of demand management between 1947 and 1968, the operation of policy was fairly simple. During periods of pressure, demand was left too high and ability to control the pressure was not tested, since there is no difficulty in keeping your foot hard down on the accelerator. It was hoped that if enough room was left for exports they would take place. During the 'stop' phase the brakes were put on until unemployment rose, but as soon as it was clearly moving to uncomfortable levels the policy was changed, so that there are hills with sharp peaks rising above a flat plain (of high employment). Since mid-1967, however, the economy has been maintained with some spare capacity and unemployment more or less steady at around 2·3 per cent. This may not be the same as 2·3 per cent before 1967, but judging by the vacancies figures it is certainly well above the 1·2 or 1·3 per cent of previous 'go' periods. This implies a much finer tuning than in previous times and we ought to be able to learn much more about the effect of demand management on economic variables than we have hitherto been able to do.

This final point raised the question, assuming that the British economy became accustomed to being run at a lower level of excess demand with adequate reserves: what would be the response to an exogenous fall in exports? It was pointed out that there would always be a problem of interpreting correctly an exogenous change, e.g. was the export fall a temporary matter due to a slight US recession, or was it a reflection of the fact that devaluation had not worked? Nevertheless, despite the problem of interpretation which after all is a persisting feature of economic forecasting, the important difference between the present situation and the past is that previously the British economy had never been in a position to ride things out: now there was a possibility that a more steady rate of growth of activity could be maintained in the future.

In his introductory remarks Solow referred to the relation of prices

171

and wages to pressure of demand. Matthews had said that the Wilson government had been converted to the Paishite view, but Solow questioned this, asking also why over the past two years the UK had had quite high unemployment with rapidly rising prices. Was it simply an unwinding of prior inflationary positions? The labour market might be tighter than the employment figures suggested, and vacancy statistics and hours of work might show different trends. Was it possible that there had been a change in the demographic, regional or industrial structures of the labour force? A related point raised by Matthews was that there has been a reduction in the last two years in cyclical labour hoarding. This would have had no direct effect on potential output; but Solow pointed out that if unemployment had any disciplinary effect the outcome would be in the direction of greater output for a given standard of price and wage behaviour.

Caves said that one issue that would lurk behind all of the discussion – and one which had troubled the Brookings team – was the extent to which some kind of ineluctable relationship existed, presumably with lags, between the level of aggregate demand – however measured – and some measure of the aggregate price level. In the US there appeared to be a fairly tight relationship of this sort, although with some rather formidable lags, so that having aggregate demand pressure in one period of time, say 1955, was very likely to yield echoing increases in the general price level in 1957 and 1958. If these same powerful but not readily visible relationships exist in the UK, can policy instruments be devised which can use them? Caves expected that this subject would underly much of the subsequent discussion, and he was right in the sense that the issues surrounding the stability of the wage/price/demand-pressure/unemployment relationships were considered in several sessions.

On the question how to interpret recent UK statistics of demand pressure, it was pointed out by the UK forecasters present that unemployment does not measure the pressure of demand in the same way as it used to. Various other indicators – vacancies, overtime, hours, labour turnover statistics, capacity utilization of manufacturing industry – tell different stories, and quite a number of relationships involving unemployment which looked compatible and adequate for forecasting purposes up to 1966 have broken down: for example, the relations between unemployment and vacancies, between unemployment and labour turnover, and between unemployment and wage-rate changes. The fact that voluntary unemployment may have risen as a result of redundancy payments and higher unemployment benefits does not mean that the 'true' unemployment rate can be estimated from the vacancy rate (it has been asserted in some quarters that 2·5 per cent unemployment now equals 1·7 per cent pre-1967) because the latter in theory should also have risen, and in fact it has done so. Unemployment and labour turnover used to move inversely; since 1967, however, high turnover coexists with high unemployment. This and other changes may reflect the structural changes following devaluation: the expansion of exports and manufacturing industry with a consequent shift of labour to exporting firms. As far as the Phillips type of relationship is concerned, what correlation did exist before 1967 between un-employment and wage changes (or price changes) has now – for the time being at least – completely disappeared, although it was reported that the Phillips relationship could still be found if labour turnover was substituted for unemployment, suggesting that wage rates were still responsive to some measures of pressure of demand.

The problem of interpretation of the unemployment statistics is clearly related to the apparent fact, noticed by several participants, that the British public, as well as the TUC, does not appear unduly concerned with the present unemployment figures, very high by post-war standards. There were some dissenters from this view, especially those who pointed out that it was significant that a govern-ment, going into an election for the first time since 1951 without having engineered a boom, had lost the election. But in view of the fact that the price and wage rises now associated with given levels of unemployment (even supposing the present level has to be reduced somewhat to make it comparable with the past) were greater than in the past, (and it was stressed that this was the prevailing real economic problem both in the UK and in the United States), it is important to know whether the public would tolerate a higher level of unemployment now than in the past. In the early 1960s serious thought had gone into choosing 1·7 per cent as a desirable economic norm; with present redundancy payments it would now be some-what higher, but by how much? And how much more would be politically tolerable?

In contrast with this line of thought, which accepts the existence of a Phillips relationship but asserts that it has shifted, was the line developed by Phelps Brown, that the Phillips relationship had been misinterpreted, and in any case had ceased to obtain in recent years. That relationship – the loop rather than the curve – summar-ized the behaviour of wages in the course of the eight-year cycle. The level and direction of change of unemployment served to indicate the phase of the cycle; deviations of pig-iron output from

173

trend did this equally, and it was gratuitous to ascribe the association between unemployment and wages to the movements of wages being governed by the balance of supply and demand, as represented by unemployment, in the labour market. It seems rather that those movements were governed proximately by the expectations of workers and employers, which were linked with the phases of the cycle, themselves viewed as acts of God: it was accepted that when trade was good rises were in order, and when it was bad cuts might have to be made. Under sustained full employment negotiated wage movements have continued to be governed by expectations, but these have become detached from the current level of activity, and latterly even from its direction of change. They depend now rather on what the government allows or what is actually agreed, in some conspicuous examples, which shape a consensus about the prospective general movement, with which it will prove unavoidable to conform. Recent experience shows this consensus as even moving contrary to the course of activity. There could be no question of regarding unemployment as an effective regulator: it was necessary to act on expectations themselves, as national incomes policy had attemped to do.

On the subject of the general performance of the British economy and its management since the Second World War there was some agreement that all the evidence showed that the performance was very good by historical and comparative standards. Unemployment had been very low compared with the past, fluctuations had been considerably reduced (and were smaller than in other countries) while British growth, although slower than that of other countries, was substantially faster than in earlier periods of our history. It was argued that British stabilization policy was distinguished by frequent fiscal-policy changes, and that this probably was the result of having a constitution which permitted such frequent changes. Other countries had had frequent policy changes but these had been concerned with public expenditure and monetary policy. Another distinguishing feature of British cycles since the war pointed out by Matthews has been their regularity and their short duration, in contrast to the situation before 1939 when the economy was characterized by long cycles; although Matthews confessed that he was not clear as to the significance of these distinctions. It was suggested (for example by Lord Roberthall above) that the British cycle was largely the result of political actions, in contrast to those in other countries which were largely due to export and investment fluctuations. But discussion on this point was inconclusive.

174

In conclusion Reddaway made the point that it is probably un-
realistic to use a steady trend as a standard of reference for examining
fluctuations and stabilization policy. Most government activities,
if judged as independent activities, would not show steady trends,
but lumpiness and fluctuations, e.g. electricity investment. Consequently it may be extremely costly to stabilize the economy by,
for example, keeping public expenditure growing at a steady rate.
There are risks in trying to balance the fluctuation in the things
that cannot be controlled by holding back (perhaps indefinitely)
the things that can be controlled; the post-war road programme
provided a good illustration of this. One should be very wary of
aiming at a norm of stability in public expenditure which one does
not really expect private industry to achieve.

In introducing the second session, concerned principally with the
connection between pressure of demand and the rate of growth of
productivity, the Chairman pointed out that on each occasion in the
post-war period when the British economy was given its head it got
into balance-of-payments trouble. At no time was it possible to
conduct the experiment long enough to find out whether a sustained
high pressure of demand would in fact cause productivity to grow
faster. Thus the British historical record is inconclusive, providing
neither proof nor disproof of the hypothesis that the pressure of
demand exerts an influence upon the rate of growth of productivity.
From the theoretical point of view, there is no good reason why the
direction of causation should not be exclusively from the side of
supply except at very low or very high demand pressures.

Both of these matters – theory and empirical knowledge – were
discussed by Caves, who pointed out that the hypothesis that growth
was demand-led had been developed very extensively in Britain
in the early 1960s, associated in particular with the names of Beckerman and Lamfalussy.[1] However, nowhere had the theoretical
rationale of the hypothesis been thoroughly and adequately examined. When the Brookings team considered the matter all the members
were impressed with the problems of empirical inference involved.
The alleged connection between the rate of growth of aggregate
demand and the rate of growth of productivity was one that could
well run in two directions and the team concentrated their efforts
in finding out which direction might be the dominant one, i.e.
whether the rapid growth of demand facing either a whole country

[1] See W. Beckerman and Associates, *The British Economy in 1975* (Cambridge
University Press for the National Institute of Economic and Social Research,
1965, and A. Lamfalussy, *The United Kingdom and the Six* (Macmillan, 1963).

175

or a particular industry could increase productivity, or whether an exogenous increase in productivity would lower the supply curve and cause it to sell more because it lowered its price.

Different forms of price behaviour are implied in these differences, and there were only one or two pieces of evidence found by the Brookings team which bore directly on this. This evidence suggested that supply influences affected the rate of growth of productivity, rather than demand influences. Later evidence confirms this view. First, there is the interconnexion between growth of output, incremental capital-output ratio and rate of capital formation. These three variables are of course linked definitionally, and in order to use the data one needs independent information about the direction of causation. Furthermore, when growth rates differ between countries one can conclude little about productivity differences by comparing gross incremental capital-output ratios. A recent study shows that, when reasonable assumptions are made about rates of depreciation, Britain's *net* capital-output ratio was not necessarily much higher during the 1950s than those of fast-growing countries such as Germany. This suggests that the main puzzle may be not why British capital formation was relatively ineffective, but rather why relatively little of it was undertaken. Similarly, evidence from recent inter-industry studies confirms the view of the Report that exogenous disturbances come from rates of growth of productivity rather than rates of growth of aggregate demand. Consequently Caves was prepared to state dogmatically that the co-called Verdoorn hypothesis that growth of output causes growth of productivity has no significant body of evidence to support it. There still remains, of course, the problem of explaining what determines the growth of productivity.

Denison affirmed that his own view as well as that of the Brookings team as a whole was that neither a higher nor a lower pressure of demand, nor less variation in demand, would have changed the growth rate very much. He pointed out that one of the arguments for believing that demand influences growth concerns the effect on capital accumulation, but this is not a well understood process. In his contribution to the Brookings volume, Denison had found that the level of productive capital per worker was very low in the UK (lower not only than the US but than France and Germany also), and had attempted to relate this to the growth of employment in large-scale industry in an attempt to test Kindelberger's thesis of the role of an elastic labour supply.[1] Matthews in his paper

[1] Brookings Report, p. 273

is critical of some aspects of Denison's capital estimates, but agrees that the UK capital-labour ratio was low at the beginning of the post-war period and has risen more slowly than in Continental countries over the period. In contrast to this picture it was asserted that between the mid 1950s and mid 1960s capital in manufacturing in the UK rose 50 per cent faster than output.

At this point three opposing views emerged. The first was that with this increase in capacity it would have been possible to expand output faster if demand had not been restrained. The second was that the investment in manufacturing was a misallocation of resources due to faulty policies of encouraging investment and that it did not provide the permanent basis to sustain a faster rate of growth. In fact, by depressing profits it might have aggravated the problem of slow growth. As a variant of the latter view it was suggested that if wages had risen faster in manufacturing there would have been a reallocation of labour into manufacturing which would have allowed an expansion of output. The third view was that when due allowance had been made for all the factors in the measurement of output per unit of input – as in Denison's work – there remained in the UK economy some residual sources of inefficiency in comparison with other countries. For instance there might be a persistent tendency to over-man equipment in British industry, and the installation of new equipment would not remove this tendency or its effects. Denison himself concluded that possibly the only way to remove this inefficiency was to operate the economy at a lower pressure of demand so that businessmen would work harder for their profits and workers would give up their inefficient practices. However, Matthews pointed out that while the high pressure of demand was a post-war phenomenon, slow growth and low productivity had existed for many decades before 1939.

MacDougall raised the factual question whether, balance of payments considerations aside, the economy could have continued expanding in its post-war expansionary phases. He suggested that a case could be made that in 1957 and 1961 supply factors were not constraining expansion. Cairncross agreed that, if the economy started from a position of under-employment, expansion of demand would lead to expansion of supply and there might be the extra dividend of rising efficiency – but only up to a point. For instance, both in 1961 and 1965 expansion had reached a point where the rate of increase in wages was alarming. At sufficiently high expected rates of return, investment would be undertaken which would raise productivity, but not sufficiently to yield an expansion of output

M

that would match the expected rates of return unless employment expanded simultaneously. The labour shortages associated with high pressure of demand might induce some productivity-raising investment, but the importance of this would be slight. Industrial investment by itself would not increase productivity sufficiently to be self-justifying. Some of those present remained unconvinced by this argument, but the ensuing discussion showed there was fairly general agreement with it.

MacDougall referred again to the empirical issues, pointing out that the UK experience was so dominated by cycles that it probably provided very little useful evidence as to what would happen if expansion continued for a lengthy period of time. It was pointed out that in the US, after nearly a decade of expansion, the potential growth of productivity now was probably no faster than it had been estimated to be in the late 1950s. In the UK, productivity growth has usually accelerated briefly in the periods when demand growth has been restrained and unemployment has risen. The maximum productivity growth has usually been experienced in the early phase of the expansion period before unemployment has started to fall. However, as MacDougall pointed out, the relevance of this to the policy problem is dubious. (Reference was also made to two international comparative studies which show that there is no association between the rate of inflation and the rate of growth of real output.)[1]

Matthews drew attention to the importance of distinguishing between the experiences of manufacturing and services and agriculture. Comparing post-war and inter-war periods, growth of output per unit of composite input had been slower in manufacturing post-war than inter-war. The situation was quite the reverse in services and agriculture, where productivity growth had been very much more rapid than in the past. Matthews was inclined to ascribe this rapid growth to demand pressure. The technological changes which had occurred in both services and agriculture had probably been largely a response to labour shortages. (Some questions were asked about the meaning of productivity growth in agriculture in view of the size of the subsidy it receives.)

The role of taxation and investment allowances in stimulating or

[1] Tun Wai, 'The Relation between Inflation and Economic Development', *International Monetary Fund Staff Papers*, 7, 2, October 1959. Joint Economic Committee, Congress of the United States, 86th Congress, 1st Session, *Staff Report on Employment, Growth and Price Levels*, December 24, 1959. E. H. Phelps Brown and M. H. Browne, 'Distribution and Productivity under Inflation, 1947–57', *Economic Journal*, 70, December 1960.

depressing manufacturing (and other) investment was briefly considered. One hypothesis put forward was that the significant effect of tax and allowance changes was upon the cash flow rather than on the rate of return. This assumes that internal cash flow is the important determinant of investment outlays. If so, the changed position of company financing during the last two years may have important effects in the future: since 1968 companies have become net borrowers as the public sector has become a net lender. So far, companies' investment behaviour has not been affected, although there is evidence that some companies are reducing investment projects because of inadequate cash flows. In the past, the cash flow position was not regarded by companies as important and it was pointed out that US experience suggested that much investment was undertaken not because profits were high but for essentially defensive reasons: to protect profits. In the UK the evidence collected by the Richardson Committee supports this view.[1] However, in so far as this evidence tended to give a small importance to changes in cash flow, strong views were expressed that tax changes must be important, and that the UK investment allowance must have been a major influence in manufacturing. One middle view was that the allowances had a marked, but small, effect, but that a much larger effect would have been obtained if the allowances had been given directly and indiscriminately as subsidies.

If growth is unaffected by pressure of demand, the implication for policy is clear. But if growth is affected, the implications for policy are not all clear. One view is that the relationship between demand and growth is asymmetrical – at both low and high pressures of demand there are adverse influences upon growth, although for different reasons. The desirable level of demand pressure is probably slightly less than the typical high level of the post-war period. Against this view, Worswick and others stressed our lack of knowledge of the trade-off between the policy goals, and also the fact that the short- and long-run trade-offs probably differ.

In commenting on the discussion at the conclusion, Matthews said it appeared that most of the participants took the neo-classical point of view that the rate of growth of productivity was unaffected by the pressure of demand. Extreme expansionist views were not represented at the conference, and must be held to be unproven. In any case the extreme expansionists would not place the burden entirely on investment, but would make it more general ('if you've got to do it, you can do it'). If we are agnostic on the relationship

[1] *Report of the Committee on Turnover Taxation*, Cmnd. 2300 (HMSO, 1964).

between growth and demand, then running the economy at less than full employment must involve placing an enormously high price on exchange-rate stability.

Solow had chastised the participants for talking about investment as though no one had worked on the subject before. But Matthews asserted that, while this might be true, most of the research into investment, because it is short-period or cyclical analysis, is not necessarily useful for growth theory. Moreover, cross-section analysis of industries and countries is usually very difficult to interpret. Matthews illustrated this point by referring to some of his own results which showed that amongst UK manufacturing industries in the post-war period there is a higher correlation between output growth and employment growth than between the former and capital-stock growth.

SESSIONS 3 AND 4: TRADE AND PAYMENTS

The first session on trade and payments was opened by Cooper, who said that it was an unaccustomed pleasure to talk about the UK balance of payments without having to worry about it, although interpreting what had actually happened remained as fascinating as ever.

The turn-round in the UK balance had surprised both a sceptical public and also foreign officials, but not necessarily economists, many of whom had believed that trade would be quite responsive to changes in relative prices such as those brought about by devaluation. Worswick, however, attributed only about half of the turn-round to the 1967 devaluation and the other half to the spectacular growth in world trade and to the slow-down during the past year in the British economy. Cooper himself was inclined not to place much weight on the slow-down: the link between growth and trade is extraordinarily complex – as demand grows imports grow also – but it is also true that as supply grows the capacity to export or to substitute for imports also grows. There did not appear to have been a cyclical effect to be taken into account during the last two years: the level of utilization of capacity, as measured by the rate of unemployment, was unchanged over the period. How important this is could not be deduced from Worswick's paper because he did not distinguish the effects of growth in the world economy from the slow-down in UK growth.

As Worswick pointed out imports are the real puzzle in the British balance: he imputed a 'zero-plus' price-elasticity of demand to

180

imports and called this barely credible. Cooper pointed out that the rise in import prices in sterling had an important income effect, and that a zero total price-elasticity would imply that imports were inferior goods (that is, a rise in income would induce a fall in demand for imports), with the income effect of devaluation exactly offsetting the substitution effect. This Cooper found difficult to believe. He suggested three possible reasons for the import behaviour and the apparently low import-elasticity, noting that none was fully satisfactory.

First, there may have been shifts in the pattern of demand toward imports that were independent of relative price movements. This was suggested by the sharp rise in the observed marginal propensity to import, from less than one-third in 1965 to over three-fourths in 1967, despite some slackening of aggregate demand during this period that should have resulted in a decline in the propensity. Second, there was a sharp drop in the savings rate in early 1968, linked no doubt to uncertainties concerning the international financial situation, expected increases in taxes, and the possibility of another devaluation. Given the high marginal propensity to import this would have a substantial effect on imports that would perhaps overshadow the effects of devaluation; but this effect should have passed by 1969, when the savings rate rose again. Third, Worswick's analysis, like Cooper's in the Brookings Report, was cast in terms of partial equilibrium. This is inappropriate when the foreign-trade sector is as large as it is in Britain, and perhaps competition for limited resources by increased exports drew in additional imports elsewhere in the economy. This factor, however, should not have been important during a period in which there was as much apparent unemployment and excess capacity as there was in 1968.

Cooper pointed out that Worswick had followed standard UK practice in discussing the balance of payments in terms of pounds. It would be better, since the problem was one of scarce foreign exchange, to put the balance of payments in terms of dollars. After devaluation the picture looked somewhat different if the balance of payments was calculated in dollars; on the import side, Worswick showed a very substantial rise in imports in pounds – about £1,000 million – due of course to the rise in the sterling price of imports. In fact, however, dollar expenditure on UK imports fell by nearly $1 billion, because foreign suppliers cut their prices by 4 per cent. Thus there was an elasticity of import response to devaluation of between 0·25 and 0·3, which happened to take the form of a fall in the foreign-currency price of imports. If the whole balance of pay-

181

ments is done in this way, and Worswick's estimates (above, p. 87) are converted into dollars, the improvement, taking the optimistic estimates, is $1·7 billion, 20 per cent greater than Worswick's net effect converted at the official rate.

Krause did not find the import behaviour of the British economy very surprising: the UK experience was very similar to that of other industrial countries. The explanation probably was that when growth is near to capacity it is normal for the ratio of imports to output to rise as specialization proceeds. (Japan is an exception: the import content of output is declining.) On the export side, the position is different because the UK does not maintain her share. This share loss is inevitable because UK potential growth has been less than the potential growth in her markets (i.e. in other countries). There is also a growth effect which runs the other way: the higher the pressure of demand the less competitive UK exports become.

The statistical evidence that had been referred to suggested to Caves that British preferences for importable goods appeared to be undergoing a shift. If this were so, certain types of reallocation of resources might be expected to be taking place. Some disfavoured import-competing sectors ought to be experiencing slower growth and releasing resources to favoured export sectors. Caves asked if any research was being undertaken in this field to see if the adaptations were slow or fast. If these changes were taking place, they would probably be taking place in engineering, but no results of research in this field had appeared.

MacDougall referred to the problem of the apparent stability of the share of UK output exported. Cairncross had pointed out that UK export prices had risen in relation to other countries' export prices, but MacDougall said that the more relevant ratio here was export prices to home prices, which did not fall in the UK following devaluation, unlike the situation in several other countries. Since 1945 the share of UK output exported had been fairly steady, but if one took a longer view there were striking differences: before 1918 the share was high, in the inter-war years it was low, since 1945 it had been high again. Furthermore, these differences were positively related to the ratios of export to home prices during the periods.

Posner commented that Worswick's results for the post-devaluation experience implied that the transfer problem was both very expensive (with implications for the cost of joining the EEC) and also almost impossible to solve. It is hard to believe that the situation is quite as bad as this. If a devaluation is arranged so that you depreciate against your competitiors but suppliers come with you, favourable movements in import prices will give a more favourable result than Worswick's calculations suggest (as Cooper pointed out), but nevertheless, if a devaluation is to be successful, better responses on both the import and export sides are needed. The need for a speedy reaction to devaluation appears to be much more important than was hitherto thought. There is an early period during which export prices are low *vis-à-vis* foreign prices when there is an opportunity to achieve a once-and-for-all rise in the share of output exported. If the rise is not achieved in this period, home rise costs and the opportunity is lost. If this is true, then there is a case for using frequent small changes in the exchange rate rather than infrequent large changes.

The issue of zero price-elasticity was taken up by Johnson, who started from Cooper's reference to the need to go beyond a partial equilibrium analysis and to consider the income effects of changes in exports and imports, and Krause's comment about differential potential growth rates. This led to the point that capacity is the budget constraint and that the ability to change the balance of payments is a matter of the relation between capacity and the demands that are put upon it: movements of prices are part of the mechanism of adjustment. The concern in devaluation is the effect on the overall balance. If we abandon the notion that exports and import-competing goods are differentiated products, and instead take into account the input-output mix and the high degree of specialization in modern industry, then any number of patterns might emerge from devaluation, each of which would be consistent with the same overall balance effect. There could be increases in both exports and imports, the imports being used as inputs in the export industries or to replace resources diverted from the home market.

If the UK position is looked at from this point of view, there is less reason to think that the import effects are puzzling: we ought not to have expected the effects to be those given by the traditional elasticity model. What is important is the investors' responses to devaluation and the extent to which domestic demand is squeezed after devaluation. This point of view embraced that expressed by Caves regarding shifts in demand preferences, and there was some discussion of the problems posed for empirical research. For instance, a shift of resources into manufacturing following devaluation might be accompanied by a rise in material imports: in fact, after 1967 these imports did not rise. Johnson said that it would be necessary to ask where the resources which made exports possible came from.

183

Are the extra exports found by diverting resources from the home market which is then supplied by imports? A modern highly-specialized and diversified economy is competitive with other economies at different points in its industrial structure, and it is difficult to predict in advance where the substitutions will occur. On the question of material imports, there was no reason why an expansion of exports should require a large increase in basic raw-material imports: the post-devaluation rise in semi-manufactured imports (included in the UK trade statistics with basic materials as 'industrial materials') tends to bear out Johnson's argument about the importance of the input–output mix. Another factor is the degree of competition: substitution might have been expected to be quicker in the home than in the export markets because in the former there is a much greater number of producers engaged in competition with foreign goods.

Cooper agreed with Johnson's stress on the need for an aggregative approach, but did not think it could explain all of the events following devaluation. For instance, the marginal propensity to import was extraordinarily high in the post-devaluation years. If the economy had been operating at capacity, Johnson's hypothesis might hold, but in fact from mid-1966 on there *was* spare capacity to deal with devaluation without pulling in imports. It is difficult thus to argue that imports rose because resources were bid away into exports. Johnson accepted this, but with others stressed the complexity of margins of substitution and also the distinction between short- and long-run effects. What evidence did exist suggested that substitution was very sluggish. Machine tools were cited as an example of very long delays in import substitution – post-devaluation plans to replace imports would not yet have shown up in the statistics.

Duesenberry attempted an eclectic account of the post-devaluation experience. Part of the rise in imports immediately following devaluation was clearly due to expectations of various sorts – buying in expectation of another devaluation, of import controls or of severe tax increases. The other part was due to the phenomenon stressed by Johnson – the export-led improvement in the balance of trade accompanied by rises in imports. There had been some reference to the existence of spare capacity in the economy after 1966 which would not support the Johnson view, but the previous day's discussion had instead stressed the *high* level of activity, as measured by vacancy and turnover statistics, and this made it more likely that the basic forces on imports were the changed competitive position of exports and the pressure of demand.

184

Duesenbery's sceptisism of the spare-capacity hypothesis raised some discussion of the actual state of the UK economy in the post 1966 period. In the first place it was likely that in the crucial six months following devaluation the pressure of demand *was* high. Secondly, while there probably had been some excess capacity in general, a sectoral analysis would show a mixed picture. In parti- cular, manufacturing industry as a whole had probably been operat- ing at high levels of capacity, and although in the engineering indust- ries the position probably had been mixed, the level of operation had by no means been low, despite the appearance of some statistical indicators. For instance, steel output had been inadequate over the period. It was also pointed out that the UK ratio of imports of investment goods to investment in plant and equipment had been rising rapidly, in contrast to the position in consumer goods and in contrast to the position in other countries such as Germany. To form a firm view about the degree of capacity utilization would require a very detailed inquiry.

MacDougall raised the question whether devaluation gives a once-and-for-all boost to exports, or whether it will get exports on to a faster growth path. There was a possibility that exports would get on to a new, permanent growth path if the competitive advantage given by devaluation were large enough and lasted long enough to encourage firms to make significant new investment in overseas selling and servicing facilities, as well as in new capacity to produce. This response to the competitive advantage would be less if exports formed a small proportion of a firm's sales and if extra capacity were not available. Solow asserted that behind the idea that a once-and-for-all increase in selling effort would raise the rate of growth were two assumptions: first, that selling effort was investment and built up a stock of, for example, goodwill; and, second, that there were no diminishing returns to the investment. The second assumption hardly seemed plausible. In the ensuing discussion it was pointed out that there was a learning process involved in exporting which might offset diminishing returns.

The meeting turned to the relationship between exports and growth. Worswick had been sceptical about the relationship, and Posner suggested that it depended on whether the authorities were prepared to allow demand to rise if and when exports happened to grow rapidly, so as to move the economy on to a faster rate of growth of capacity. The Brookings volume took a rather negative approach to the matter and Caves was inclined to carry Worswick's scepticism further: it is not just a problem of two-way causation

185

between exports and growth of productivity – both of these factors are likely to be correlated with several other factors. Only a careful analysis of lags might throw light on this, but the prospect of fruitful applied research in this field appeared slight. Cooper agreed with Posner in his emphasis on the role of the authorities. In so far as the balance of payments is a constraint, policies to protect the balance may adversely affect investment and growth even if investment is not linked directly to export performance.

The remainder of this session was devoted to a discussion of Common Market issues. Heller inquired whether UK economists were now more anti-EEC than they were a few years ago. In answer it was said that although British economists had not indulged in much public debate on the issue, on balance they were probably anti-EEC or neutral, in contrast to industrialists who tended to be pro. But the lack of debate made it difficult to say how opinion had shifted in recent years. Indeed, the absence of public debate between economists was a remarkable phenomenon. Nine years ago, at the time of the first EEC entry negotiations, there was a certain amount of informal polling of economists, and on the whole their views ranged from lukewarm to hostile. This was despite the vagueness of CAP ideas at the time. With the completely different situation in agricultural policy now, a poll of economists would probably show more hostility than nine years ago. Johnson suggested that one of the reasons for the lack of public debate by economists was that the EEC issues straddled both industrial and agricultural economics and there were very few economists competent to speak in both fields.

Krause considered that the White Paper, devoted mainly to balance-of-payments consequences, should have been directed towards welfare consequences. For instance, the supply response of UK agriculture to participation in EEC was likely to be very great, partly because CAP prices are higher than UK farm-gate prices, partly because of the method of price formation. This would reduce the impact on the balance of payments. But this lesser cost in balance-of-payments terms would be at the expense of a substantial misallocation of resources. As far as industry is concerned, much depends on whether UK firms respond favourably to competition. Krause doubted whether this would happen. If industry did not respond favourably *and* Britain gave up the power to vary her exchange rate, then it would be a bad deal indeed. On this point there was general agreement, and it was stressed by several of those present that the gamble involved in accepting the case for entry depended upon a supposed large increase in industrial efficiency.

186

In the agricultural sector, the Chairman pointed out, there would be socially undesirable redistributive effects such as a rise in grain production and a reduction in marginal dairy hill farming. Sir Eric Roll agreed, although he thought that the precise directions of agricultural stimulus could not be known in advance. Also, it was likely that UK farmers could be won over to the CAP system since it resembles the 1939–45 system which the farmers were loath to give up; but they would resist decision-making in Brussels. Within the Community, in view of the farmers' unwillingness to accept price reductions as surpluses increase, there would probably be a move in the US direction of introducing acreage restrictions and other types of quota control, and EEC would also sell in other markets at subsidized prices (as they have started to do already).

Duesenberry brought the discussion back to the issue raised by Krause, namely going into EEC involves a gamble on the efficiency argument, which he pointed out was a form of the export-led growth idea. If the gamble failed there was the danger that the UK would become a depressed region: old England would have to go through the process that New England was going through. This gamble was related to two practical issues. First, was there an advantage in reducing tariffs to a nil rate which would apply indefinitely – was a reduction from 8 per cent to zero more likely to raise efficiency than a reduction from, say, 16 per cent to 8? Would it make cost-reducing investment less risky? Secondly, what are the alternatives? If there is a big risk that either the US or the EEC might become more protectionist in the near future, then joining might be a sensible insurance policy.

Lord Roberthall stressed the importance of the UK being in a position to vary her exchange rate, although he thought that the EEC was a very long way from maintaining a policy for fixed rates. One view expressed was that too much was made of the exchange-rate issue: a country could always vary its rate, and possibly the real danger was that a country in the EEC might try and hold its rate too long. Krause referred to the desirability of changing exchange rates as part of a planned policy rather than as a response to a crisis: one of the problems of the EEC was that policy changes required a crisis to effect them.

The final issue to be taken up in this session was the threat to UK trade of growing protectionism, particularly in the context of the recent substantial redirection of UK trade from the Commonwealth to the EEC. First it was suggested that the real threat is not so much old-fashioned protectionism as new ways of changing comparative advantage through such means as export subsidy and science policy. The American participants, however, were unanimous that old-fashioned protectionism, while not necessarily the greatest threat, was reviving in the US. Labour in the US was now protectionist. Johnson suggested that the danger was not a rapid move to high tariffs but a drift to quotas and new forms of protection, and also the end of the drive to free trade. Also, there was a drift towards various forms of regional trading arrangements (of which the EEC itself is an example).

Others expressed themselves even more pessimistically than Johnson, pointing out the special problem facing the US because of the absence of any balance-of-payments adjustment mechanism. As one participant put it, there is a danger of a critical mass from a combination of circumstances all of which foster protectionism. In some respects it was surprising that more alarm had not been expressed in the US about the growth of restrictionist policies.

SESSIONS 5 AND 6: LABOUR POLICIES

In no session was the discussion so obviously held under the shadow of outside events – a new government and very rapid wage inflation – than in the first session devoted to Phelps Brown's paper. It was proposed to leave the subject of the first part of the paper – slow productivity growth and its causes – to session 6, and to devote this session to incomes policy.

It was generally agreed that, since World War II, the British procedures of determining wages, in conditions of full employment, had led to cost inflation. Not only does industry-wide collective bargaining lead to inflation (as firms agree to wage increases in the expectation that increases over and above rises in productivity will be recouped by price increases without any effect on the market shares of individual firms) but the actions taken by unions to maintain differentials (between different occupations, industries and grades of labour), resulting in the familiar leap-frogging process, also lead to inflation. This process in all probability seriously interferes with the efficient allocation of resources in the economy – although just how quantitatively important is this particular source of misallocation in relation to other sources of misallocation has not been measured.

It does not appear that the incomes policies of the second half of the 1960s have been able to weaken the link between full employment and cost inflation. Before 1939 wage bargains did not lead to

188

persistent cost inflation because while wages rose in good or prosperous times they did not rise – sometimes even fell – in bad times. Whether this phenomenon is to be interpreted essentially as cyclical (as Phelps Brown argued), or whether it is to be interpreted in the terms of the original, simple version of the Phillips relationship – the lower the level of unemployment, the greater the rise in average earnings – the interpretation seems to be irrelevant in explaining the failure of the incomes policies of the 1960s. These policies in the United Kingdom have operated when unemployment has been very low compared with the pre-1939 position. Also, the climate of business and trade-union expectations, as well as generally understood government policy, has been completely different from the situation prevailing before the Second World War. In these circumstances, can any type of policy of income restraint, of either the compulsory or the voluntary type, work in the sense of avoiding a rise in average incomes greater than that in average productivity? Must full employment be dropped if cost inflation is to be avoided?

It would be wrong to say that the conference answered this question. There were unchallenged statements that the government, in operating incomes policy, especially in 1968–69, was not tough enough. On the other hand it was pointed out that incomes policy is an educational activity rather than a device for stopping wage increases. If it is used, as it has been in the past, as a freezing device as well as an educational activity, it inevitably becomes overburdened and the educational function suffers. There was general agreement that an incomes policy needed sanctions. Unemployment was one sort of sanction, although the idea that unions could be left to live with their own mistakes was hardly practicable. For instance, there is the view that an incomes policy can be operated by holding the money supply constant. Wage rises will then lead to reduced employment. The story was told how a version of this was tried out in a government department in 1957, when a salary increase resulted in a deliberate reduction in the staffing of the department to prevent the salary bill from rising. But when it became clear that the work done by the department was declining, the policy had to be altered. Other sanctions such as delaying tactics – cooling-off periods – and special taxes on excess wages, levied both on wages and profits, were mentioned but not discussed at any length.

Duesenberry set out a scheme involving two levels of enforcement. One was the PIB type involving delay, investigation and publicity: essentially this was the educational function. The other level involved a 'filter' for picking out outrageous cases of wage or salary demands

189

(or price rises) and 'knocking them hard with public support'. It was pointed out that to achieve this second level of enforcement the government would require punitive powers and that the prospects – as seen a day or two after the election – that such a tough incomes policy would be publicly accepted seemed poor. (The way in which the SOGAT strike during the election was handled by all parties strongly suggests that neither government nor employers want a 'showdown', although it must be admitted that the timing of the strike – in an election – and the industry concerned – reputedly unprofitable newspaper publishers – make generalization difficult.) The trade unions are clearly opposed to a punitive policy, and as far as the political parties were concerned there was little policy guidance in the election platforms, although the Tory pronouncements suggested a tougher line on public-sector wages.

In his paper, Phelps Brown suggests a way in which the public interest might be injected at the point where pay decisions are taken: members of a public service – such as an expanded PIB – should take part in pay negotiations and make certain that the public interest is understood. In discussion Phelps Brown said that the basis of the idea was the system of compulsory wage-fixing by judicial bodies practised for many years in Australia and New Zealand. (The accidents of history and the peculiar features of the Australian and New Zealand economies of course play a large part in explaining the adoption and acceptance of the Antipodean system, an important feature of which is its centralization.) This was regarded as an important suggestion, although it was obvious that part of the price would be a very large expansion of bureaucracy and extensive policy-making and reporting machinery. The public interest should be clearly stated: one view was that any standard other than zero price rises presents problems, and the government should announce in advance permissible wage increases. But there was always the danger that, faced with an intransigent union, public representatives would back down because the cost of strikes was much greater to the economy and the employer than to the strikers.

In connection with strikes it was asserted that, while price rises are much the same in all industrial countries, in the United Kingdom profit margins have been falling. Possibly the cost of strikes had risen at the same time, although the relationship between this and the supposed attempt by industrialists to restore their eroded profit margins was not clear. These matters were not sorted out satisfactorily in discussion and offer a further opportunity for clear thinking and possibly research.

190

There was also reference to the Swedish labour-market policy which has been in operation since the early 1950s. The idea underlying it is that cost inflation can be avoided without unemployment if the level of demand is not raised high enough to ensure the employment of the workers who are most costly to employ, but these marginal workers are found work by retraining, resettlement grants, and assistance in rehousing. At the same time projections of the demand for labour by occupation and locality should guide training and mobility so as to match supply to demand and avoid scarcities of particular types of worker that will pull up their pay above the general movement. This was regarded as a policy which might be more acceptable to unions than would be many others.

The session concluded in an atmosphere of mixed feelings. The conference listened to an account of President Nixon's proposed wages and prices policy, which was described as a disappointing rejection of the achievements of the Kennedy and Johnson administrations and a refusal to accept political responsibility – despite the President's reputed statement that 'we cannot protect the value of the dollar by passing the buck'. The United States apparently at the present time has no guidance to offer the United Kingdom, where the problem of 1970, it was said, was how to prevent the more rapid wage rises from becoming the norm. Three rays of hope presented themselves. In the first place the special international inflationary conditions of 1968–9, associated with demand pressures, may change during 1970. Secondly, trade-union leaders have always accepted an incomes policy and in 1965 the TUC adopted its own vetting policy: in this sphere new developments could emerge. Finally, as one participant put it, 'we will never know whether an incomes policy works until it is really tried out'.

The second session on labour policies was devoted mainly to their role in growth, but several of the broader growth issues were discussed. Phelps Brown's paper had shown that the relatively slow advance of British industry, in comparison with the United States, Germany and Sweden, goes back at least a hundred years. Since the Second World War, although UK productivity has been rising faster than before, so has that of Germany, the United States and also France. (In this connection it was pointed out by Matthews that the turning-point in manufacturing productivity growth in the UK came before the Second World War: at some time in the inter-war period the level of productivity in manufacturing started to rise rapidly.) Phelps Brown argued that the operation of each of the three factors that comparative studies have found to be positively

191

related to high or rapidly rising productivity – the amount of capital per worker, the relative size of an industry in the whole economy and the rate of growth of total output of industry – is ultimately dependent on human responses and initiatives. The discussion was then led to consider the constraints on British growth arising from managerial and labour practices.

One participant suggested that 'management gets the labour relations it deserves'. The original Brookings Report had described the syndrome known as bloodymindedness of workers, and while it was asserted that unions were still obstructive, restrictive and old-fashioned, it was also argued that these attitudes were encouraged by bad management practices, such as paying excessive overtime and making incentive payments which led to wasteful practices and high costs. Furthermore, restrictive labour practices dissuade management from installing new, more productive equipment. This raised the question referred to by several speakers as to whether British workers really understood the trade-off between real wages and bloodymindedness. Perhaps labour does not understand that it is missing out on growth.

But one can go further than this and ask, as did the Provost, whether we really want growth. It could be – and has been – plausibly argued that the British people are aware that growth has not only economic but also social costs, such as disturbances to old-established, comfortable ways of doing things and the disruption of social relationships, and what we do not want is to incur these costs. Only the top dogs – those insulated from disruptive social changes or likely to benefit materially – wanted growth and were prepared to let society as a whole pay the price. But the answer to these assertions was not to deny them, but to point out, as did several participants, that even if we do not want growth as such we want so many more things like schools and hospitals that without growth we shall not satisfy any of our aspirations.

The conference was entertained by two ideas that in different ways suggested that there was really nothing particular to express about British growth. The first was Solow's hypothesis of convergence of income growth rates. According to him it is implausible to suppose that the income levels of countries like Germany and Britain, with similar characteristics but with different growth rates, will diverge indefinitely; a differential in average income levels may remain, but the growth rates will tend to converge. Thus the faster present German growth rate is to be seen as essentially a catching-up process. This proposition was not generally accepted by those present: it was

192

not easy to understand why growth rates should converge; nor should such an hypothesis disregard the continued and apparently widening gap between Britain and the United States. Another suggestion was that the distribution of the product governs the rate of growth. If in fact British output contained unusually large proportions of services and government activities, then it was unlikely that total output, as conventionally measured by statisticians, would show fast growth. However, these possibilities apparently do not stand up to the empirical test. Denison reported that his work did not show that Britain had an output composition which differed from what can be expected for an economy of the British income level. In other words there was nothing unusual about the British distribution of product.

After the discussion of growth and bloodymindedness there seemed to be an argument for educating workers in the advantages of becoming rational economic (and social) men, but the conference did not seize on that argument and in fact the participants had very little to say about the possibility of directly improving labour relations and altering disruptive and restrictionist attitudes. The absence of new ideas on this subject may have been influenced by the view expressed by some of the Americans present that there is really no basis for concluding that labour relations are now worse in the UK than in the United States.

There was, however, one area which offered some hope for reform. Lord Roberthall pointed out the difficulties caused by the fragmentation of unions and the managerial time taken up in dealing with several unions. In one, not atypical case which he cited, an engineering firm had spent several years trying to negotiate a productivity agreement with the large number of unions included in its labour force, only to have the whole arrangement broken down because one union would not support the agreement – the remainder would not endorse the agreement unless all the unions were in. Possibly there is scope for reform of this situation from within the union movement.

Lord Roberthall also referred to management attitudes. At the end of the Second World War it was believed that all that British industry had to do was to follow American processes. But this belief no longer prevails: it is clear that British industry has a problem of poor quality management. Complacency was emphasized as its characteristic, although there are signs that the complacency is going: business schools and the merger movement may be inculcating new attitudes. The reference to business schools raised issues of management training and these were to be considered later in the light of Posner's paper, but this session was reminded that the British education system – at least until recently – was designed 'to produce imperial proconsuls rather than business tycoons'. (In a later session it was asserted with more practical relevance that the UK produced scientists rather than engineers.) It had been argued frequently in recent years that an improvement in the quality of industrial management depended upon a stream of some of the better university graduates going into industry. On the other hand it was pointed out that in the United States the best graduates do not go into business, but that the motivation of those who do is important.

SESSIONS 7 AND 8: INDUSTRIAL POLICIES AND GROWTH

The first session based on Posner's paper was concerned primarily with the effects of structural industrial change on growth. Caves referred to some of the striking changes that had occurred in UK industrial policy in the last twenty years. The abolition of Resale Price Maintenance (RPM) was comparatively recent, and the consequences were as Caves would have expected: a reduction in some market prices and some mergers in the lines of trade affected. The Brookings study had criticized the wave of horizontal mergers that were occurring in the mid-1960s and the policy of supporting these mergers, and Caves believed that there was now less support for these mergers. One view that was common in the UK at the time of the study was that management is a scarce resource and that firms could be advantageously merged into others where good management was under-utilized. Brookings were sceptical of this, although Caves allowed that here there was more scope for dispute. It was an empirical question. The Board of Trade had been favourable to mergers of all types, and like Posner, Caves thought they should be more selective. The Industrial Reconstruction Corporation (IRC) had operated with wide powers to encourage mergers. The Brookings team had thought that there might be scope for such an institution and suggested vertical mergers as the likely field.

Peck commented on what appeared to him a gap in the original Brookings analysis: emphasis on the role of new entrants in raising industrial efficiency and in the diffusion of new technology. In the US the technically most efficient firms are either the very large (like General Electric) or the originally small but rapidly growing (like Texas Instruments). In the UK the role of the latter group is frequently played by US subsidiaries.

The Chairman said there had been little discussion of the government's attempts to encourage new technology by offering contracts

194

to firms. Posner commented that the size of these contracts was very small, and it was difficult to establish that significant results had emerged.

Krause asked whether the UK tax structure militated against growth and risk-taking by small firms. In reply it was asserted that some small close companies fear that they will be forced to distribute and that this limits their rate of expansion. However, it was pointed out that it was more profitable to start a small company and sell it on the open market than to join a large firm as a salaried official. But despite this – and before 1966 the UK tax rates were lower than they were in the US – there appears to have been nothing comparable in the UK to the growth of small research-based firms in the US. The possibility was raised that the success of these firms was dependent on the size of the US defence effort. Peck did not think the defence effort was exclusively important. He would also stress the propensity to found businesses in the US, the availability of capital, the mobility of middle-aged executives (note the small companies founded by ex-IBM executives) and also the willingness of the US Defense Department to put work out to small and even untried firms.

Posner pointed out that it is extremely difficult to demonstrate that there is a shortage of capital in the UK; rather it appears there is an unwillingness on the part of small firms to borrow venture capital and take on new shareholders. This view was qualified by the opinion that venture capital is not available in the UK to the same extent that it is in the US. Financial institutions are not actively seeking new ventures. The traditional UK institutions are very conservative, and have no feeling that they should try ten ventures in the expectation that one will come off. The exceptions to this are the property companies since the Second World War, and these are very largely associated with enterprising individuals (although one participant facetiously remarked that it was typical of an under-developed country that it should want to put its money into real estate).

It was suggested that this unwillingness to invest in risky ventures might be related to the fact that lenders in the UK usually did not vary their rates to suit the circumstances of the loan and the borrower, and that this reflected a general unwillingness in the UK to use the price-system flexibly. Frequently the prices of industrial products bore no relation to risk, quantities or conditions of sale. Basically this is due to lack of competition: an unwillingness on the part of customers to pay realistic prices and a lack of incentive on the part of producers to charge realistic prices. Someone remarked that in

195

the UK few businessmen would admit that they did anything 'for the money', which prompted one of the American participants to remind his British colleagues that they might not know when they were well off.

In the US, it was pointed out, there was both a willingness on the part of scientists with ideas to go into business (although this may have been a post-World War II phenomenon as far as academics are concerned) and a willingness on the part of underwriters and investors to provide capital. It had been suggested that the provision of this capital depended to a large extent on careful assessment of the borrowers' prospects: but it was strongly asserted that anyone in the US with a scientific idea could get money to launch a new venture – the end-result did not spring from careful assessment but as a random process. In reply to a question whether the contribution of the small firm which was being discussed was very large in the US, Peck said that it would be small overall, but very important in the fast-growth industries. It was pointed out that such industries in the UK would be important for the balance of payments.

The discussion had emphasized that in the US there were close links between academic institutions, government and business which favoured the growth of profitable science-based industries. In the UK, one striking thing is that a large proportion of the officially-sponsored research is done inside government establishments, which contrasts with the position in the US. However, in view of the fact that the problem to be explained has existed for a long time and that government played little role in scientific research before World War II, the important phenomenon is possibly the mobility of people between business, academic life and government which has existed for a long time in America. Possibly this mobility reflects the high degree of mobility within each of the three groups.

Very large universities and university groups in the US acted as a magnet for the location near the campus of research-based business enterprises, and it was pointed out that there were signs that this trend was developing in Britain as well. Government might be unwittingly fostering this through its policy of expanding numbers of students without providing more resources. One way of doing this was by holding down academic salaries and this would force – as it had in America – more academics to look for extra money from business.

Peck raised the problem of the output of scientists and engineers. A British peculiarity was the smallness of the ratio of engineers to scientists, which he suggested was a demand phenomenon rather than

196

one of supply. He matched this with reference to conservative employment policies he had found in UK industry. The view that the low engineer-scientist ratio is due to lack of demand appears to be confirmed by some unpublished research which finds a low rate of return on investment in engineering training. In the US, where there might at first sight appear to be an excess of engineers produced from universities, business employs engineers in all occupations including those of salesmen and general managers.

The question was asked whether the differences observed between the UK and the US would be reproduced in a comparison between the UK and European countries. Worswick replied that the National Institute was engaged in a comparative study of the diffusion of new technologies in the UK and five other countries, and the results from the ten techniques studied so far (ranging from the oxygen process in steel-making to the use of gibberellic acid in brewing) was that the UK was certainly not a laggard in the adoption of these techniques. Other evidence tended to confirm this view.

The second session on industrial policies and growth started by considering the problem of mergers, briefly dealt with in the previous session. Posner pointed out that the so-called conglomerate mergers were not new in the UK – it was possible to find examples of the formation of holding companies with a number of small, disparate subsidiaries a long way back in British industrial history. What the UK had had in recent years was a large number of horizontal plus conglomerate mergers, and very little in the way of vertical integration. The process had been on a large scale in the sense that a large amount of assets had been affected. (As an aside it was said that the fear of these mergers acts in the same way as the threat of bankruptcies: it improves efficiency.) Posner, while accepting Cave's general view that bigness in itself was unlikely to improve efficiency, referred to the difficulty of laying down any general rules to guide public authorities responsible for controlling mergers in the vertical and conglomerate fields.

Caves gave some background from the results of recent US studies which suggest that, despite the publicity given to the conglomerates, vertical mergers are becoming more important, although there is no evidence that such mergers are productive in the economic sense. There is also evidence that a substantial premium (possibly 20 per cent on average) over the market value of the assets is normally paid by acquiring firms, and it is not clear what this premium depends on: it may represent the potential productivity-gain envisaged from the use of larger resources, or it may represent the price the acquirers are prepared to pay for growth for its own sake. Other evidence supports the latter explanation: merger activity appears to be correlated with growth independently of profitabity.

Caves referred also the issue of foreign investment and the idea that US firms in Britain were more efficient than their UK counterparts, and were so because of the size of their parents. Recent research modified this picture: in all countries the foreign subsidiary was the most efficient and this stemmed from the fact that the international company is usually very efficient wherever it is domiciled: presumably it is large partly because it is efficient. Moreover the US stake in international companies does not seem to be disproportionate to the total size of US manufacturing assets.

In connection with Cave's first point about mergers, Posner said that the main merger activity was amongst firms which were already very large (BMC and Leyland). In the cases where a large firm absorbed smaller firms there was some evidence similar to Caves' that growth rather than profitability was the main result or consideration.

Cooper said that Caves' results for direct investment did not necessarily imply that UK direct investment was efficient. In fact other research pointed to US direct investment in third markets being more profitable than UK investment in these markets, while UK direct investment in the US was less profitable than the average of all US manufacturing. Reddaway said that such comparative results were complicated by the problem of measuring the cost of knowledge and know-how. This raised the problem of the variety of measures which could be applied in such international comparisons. For example, it was likely that the physical productivity of US subsidiaries in the UK would be nearer the UK than the US average.

The British aircraft industry was considered as an example of an industry whose poor post-war performance might be explained by small firms. Peck said that, while it was true that UK companies had had smaller runs than the US firms, the product development strategy had been poor. In particular, in the 1950s the UK industry tried to produce a full range of aeroplanes comparable to the US. In Europe there had been more specialization and the firms were correspondingly more profitable. It was also stressed that the UK firms had been too inclined to try to meet the needs of individual clients.

The session next turned its attention to the direct interventions by the British government in industry through the IRC, the PIB and the Ministry of Technology. When the IRC was set up Lord Roberthall had doubted whether it would be effective, not only because there

198

was a danger that it might try to keep some parts of industry which competition might blow away, but also because it was difficult to see how the IRC could get men of such managerial ability that could raise the efficiency of the firms involved. However, Roberthall now believed that the IRC has a considerable 'shaking up' effect upon firms through its investigations and backing of particular managers. Probably the PIB, simply through its inquiries, had had a similar dynamic effect.

Reddaway also believed that the inquiries of the PIB (of which he was a part-time member) had been useful in causing necessary decisions to be taken, partly because industries were placed in the pillory. In this respect the use of consultants had been important. Also, making improvements to productivity as a condition of a wage increase had been very important, the best example of this being the agreement to operate one-man buses. Sir Eric Roll agreed with the views expressed about the PIB, but he was sceptical about the value of the IRC. The original idea was that what was required was a state merchant bank, with powers of persuasion, because while the ordinary city institutions were normally adequate there were cases where some more authoritative action was necessary. However, what had transpired was something different. It was not only an instrument for reconstruction, but also a tribunal for judging whether mergers were required, and here it conflicted with other institutions. Unless it was to become a nuisance it had to be geared into the other institutions of official industrial policy.

The last subject taken up by the meeting was planning and the relationship of the public and private sectors. Caves pointed out that there is no empirical evidence to suggest that investment decisions taken by firms lead to misallocation of resources through failures of co-ordination with the rest of the economy. Such American research as has been done does not suggest that US business is badly astray in its forecasting. Caves allowed that there was a case for official general equilibrium forecasting, taking into account the input–output relationships, but contrasted this with planning in which a required change in output would be allocated to particular firms. This latter activity was likely to encourage conservatism and inefficiency, when actually what was required was a shake-up and a change in behaviour.

MacDougal judged the 'little Neddies' useful; at least people were still prepared to sit on them. It is possible to point to instances where some of them have raised efficiency, and the modern breed of corporate planner found them a useful place to check his forecasts. As far as

199

planning in general is concerned, MacDougal referred to the constraint imposed by the balance of payments, and the difficulty of obtaining the confidence on which the 'confidence trick' aspect of planning depended. But whatever one thought about this aspect of planning, there were sensible practical arguments in favour of periodically listing and analysing the policies which were being or should be followed, and of a public discussion of the government's planning of its own expenditures. In this connection it was obviously necessary that any planning of public expenditures should be examined in the light of forecasts of the growth of productive capacity and the likely demands upon that capacity from the private sector.

Indicative planning, according to Cooper, seems more appropriate for a nearly closed economy like the US than for a very open economy like the UK. He believed that planning in France had become less important as the involvement in the EEC deepened. Peck suggested that, except for the special cases of capital goods with long lead-times, planning at either the 'little Neddy' or the national level would be inefficient because it would become a device for market sharing.

Posner in conclusion pointed out that the economists' contribution to industrial policy is to ensure that the economic structure and incentives will get the best out of management and labour. He thought it inconceivable that the changes of the late 1950s and the 1960s would not produce some measurable benefits in the 1970s.

FINAL SESSION

After a review by the Chairman of the earlier sessions, of which an extended version is included in this volume at pp. 217–36, Duesenberry thought that it would be a mistake to disregard the basic idea that pressure in the labour market is related to wage increases. In the United States there is much macro-economic statistical evidence and micro-economic evidence (from employers and trade unions) to support this view. This led to the policy issue of demand management and the optimim degree of tension in the labour market. Duesenberry referred to the Swedish idea that instead of balancing supply and demand for labour by varying only the demand for labour, it might also be possible to vary the supply by altering the length and other aspects of training programmes. Quite apart from such flexible policies, there was also a need for an incomes policy – we need to dig-in for the long haul – although not too many demands should be made of the policy: it needs demand and exchange-rate policies to work with it. The policy should be designed to prevent an unbearable degree of inflation, but it should not be counted on or operated (as with a freeze) to deal with the whole inflationary problem. This is contrary to the usual strategies which are designed to deal with crises, not with a year-on-year problem which is the issue as Duesenberry saw it.

In the field of growth also, Duesenberry was less sceptical than others that orthodox policies would be helpful. With similar technologies the UK should approach the US productivity level *minus* some 'discount' which represents the intangible inefficiency or the 'residual' in the Denison analysis. If we began with a more labour-intensive technology, investment should raise UK Productivity to the level in the US *less* the discount. Duesenberry believed this was clear from Denison's work: what is required is more investment in both physical and human capital: the intangible factors are much less important. There must be some level of interest rates and tax concessions which would make even inefficient and lazy businessmen invest and manage so as to achieve faster rates of growth.

Denison pointed out that in his comparative study of the UK and Western European countries the significant differences lay in the lower level of capital per worker, and the lower level of output per worker in the non-agricultural sectors, in the UK compared with France or Germany. From this Denison was led to believe that the 'intangibles' – such as labour and management attitudes and practices – were important. Duesenberry commented firstly that the UK position in comparison with Western Europe was very similar to the New England position compared to the rest of the US, and secondly that Denison's results did not disprove the proposition that more incentives would lead to more investment which would raise the growth rate. The difficulty of knowing how much investment was necessary to adopt new techniques and best practices was referred to by Posner, who pointed out that the early post-war Productivity Teams and subsequent industrial studies of firms had said that many new techniques could be adopted without much investment, although of course this sort of improvement was not limitless.

There was some argument over the price to be paid for the extra investment suggested by Duesenberry. Some thought it paradoxical that an economy with a low rate of return to capital should be asked to reduce consumption (temporarily) further. Others pointed out that if the restraints on high productivity were both too many tea-breaks and not enough incentives for managers and investors, it might be easier to increase the incentives than to abolish the tea-

201

breaks. Against this it was said that an increase in income tax to provide more investment allowances might cause tea-breaks to become longer, whereupon Goode pointed out that the solution might be tax reductions, particularly selective reductions. Redda-way to some extent countered many of these suggestions by pointing out that investment in UK manufacturing had been subsidized for twenty years, and had, indeed, been quite high.

Worswick shifted the discussion back to Duesenberry's first point, the Phillips curve, where, he said, the Phelps Brown paper and other recent UK research had clearly disproved the existence of the rela-tionship – at any rate in its original form. In the ensuing discussion it was clear that on the whole the US participants believed in the exis-tence of the relationship while the UK participants did not. A re-conciliation was suggested by Ulman, who pointed out that if the rate of change in wages depended on both the level *and* rate of change of unemployment, the peculiar shapes and shifts of the curve relating wage-change and unemployment level might be due to the influence of the change in unemployment.

Ulman took up Duesenberry's reference to the Swedish idea of varying the supply of labour, and pointed out that this idea was a response to the belief that a high pressure of demand prevented an incomes policy from working satisfactorily. Possibly if the UK is becoming more Paishite – in the sense of tolerating a higher level of unemployment – then there may be scope for adopting the 'ideal' Swedish type of manpower policy. Ulman also observed that in-comes policy attempts to take advantage of centralization in the labour market, but with high excess demand this centralization breaks down as power tends to devolve on to the shop floor. Another aspect of this is that incomes policy now turns out in many countries to have been costly: unions demand an assurance of real gains which must be greater than those recorded in the period immediately preceding the imposition of policy. In addition, new thinking on the subject may have to take account of productivity bargaining, profit sharing, and demands for a greater share in decision-making within the enterprise.

Johnson pointed out that incomes policy was being discussed as if the UK was a closed economy; in fact Britain has to live with the American price level. Since 1967 two things have influenced the UK price level: the first was devaluation and the second was inflation in the US, and we could not talk about British prices as if there was a continuity between pre-1967 and post-1967. First, following devalua-tion there had to be a corresponding inflation in the UK price level.

Secondly, this price level tended to be forced up by the amount of the American inflation. It followed that it was impossible to keep the old cost curves by operating an incomes policy and that such a policy must be considered in an international inflationary context. Needless to say this made an incomes policy very difficult to operate. It might be difficult to judge what price rise was inescapable, but it would be quite wrong to disregard the inflationary consequences of devaluation and the American developments.

In subsequent discussion Johnson made it clear that his argument depended on the assumption that the devaluation became necessary because of high-employment policies, and that political pressures would be such as to cause high-employment policies to be re-adopted after devaluation. In order to avoid a return to over-valuation it would be necessary either to adopt a higher level of unemployment than before, or – after the price level had settled down – an effective incomes policy. On the other hand, it was a moot point what degree of control an open economy like Britain's has over its internal wage and price levels. The marginal products of the export industries are set by world prices and eventually these must work through into the rest of the economy.

7. Second Thoughts on Britain's Economic Prospects*

by R. E. Caves

Subject to the limits of time and resources, the authors of the Brookings study of *Britain's Economic Prospects* tried to accomplish a number of objectives:

(i) To set forth the evidence on how the British economy operates and responds to the instruments of economic policy.

(ii) To indicate the gaps in this evidence and to make starts at filling some of them.

(iii) To weigh the system's performance and attempt some judgment on the conduct of economic policy.

The papers prepared for the Ditchley conference, held two years after publication of the Brookings volume, provide an opportunity for reconsidering some of its conclusions against the background of subsequent informed discussion in the United Kingdom, recently published scholarly research, and the lessons of further experience with policy formation.

ECONOMIC MANAGEMENT IN THE SHORT RUN

Our somewhat critical view of the success with which Britain's macro-economic affairs have been managed has drawn various demurrals, including those contained in the papers by Professor Matthews and Mr Worswick. As background for considering their comments, it may prove helpful to restate our general diagnostic viewpoint. Maintaining equilibrium in both aggregate demand and the balance of payments requires separate policy instruments of adequate strength and flexibility, and more instruments are needed if separable aspects of aggregate activity (prices, growth rate) are to be controlled. A country can fall short of perfection in attaining its policy goals for various reasons. The number and flexibility of policy instruments may be inadequate relative to the number of indepen-

---

* Although suggestions received from members of the Brookings team have been gratefully incorporated, responsibility for the views advanced in this paper should be considered as personal.

dent objectives. Information may be inadequate, either concerning the prospective short-run movements of the system or its response when the levers of policy are pulled. The skill with which the instruments of policy are used may be insufficient, or the political constraints on their timely use too great.

The main conclusion reached by the Musgraves (pp. 34–45) and Kareken (pp. 69–83), as well as by Professor Matthews, was that the need to adapt fiscal and monetary policy to cope with recurrent crises in the balance of payments rendered them relatively ineffective as stabilizers of the (fairly minor) fluctuations of the domestic policy targets. The Musgraves' statistical analysis also suggested that tax changes, although by-and-large correct in direction of response to both domestic and external targets, did not succeed in carrying through their effect to the net fiscal impact of the total UK public sector. One can say either that sufficient policy instruments were not at hand, or that they were not used with sufficient force or analytical insight. Just where in the process of government or the perversity of nature the blame for a less-than-ideal policy situation lies we did not attempt to settle.

Worswick's attack on our diagnosis is aimed not at these principal conclusions but at an exploratory statistical analysis undertaken by the Musgraves and reported separately as a mimeographed appendix to their chapter. While this material was presented (p. 44) as support for a qualitative analysis rather than a definitive judgment on policy execution in Britain, Worswick's criticisms of it strike me as inappropriate:

1. If stabilization policy were completely successful, there would be no correlation between movements of the target and the policy instrument that attains it. The answer to this is simple: as the charts on p. 36 of the Brookings study show, the targets were not continuously attained, so that the question of whether policy succeeded in steering toward them can indeed be asked after the event.

2. A 'correct' sign indicates that policy pulled upward on a variable when it was too low; but a perverse sign might mean either that it pulled down when the variable was too low, or that it pushed too hard and turned an *ex-ante* too-high value into too low a one *ex-post*. Agreed, but in the first instance perversity is perversity, whatever its cause; and I am surprised that one with Worswick's knowledge of recent British policy-making should consider the latter alternative equally likely.

205

3. The multiple-regression technique is inappropriate if disturbances calling for conflicting corrective measures regularly coincided. In fact such conflicts frequently have posed dilemmas for fiscal and monetary policy in the UK. However, their effect would be to invalidate the Musgraves' statistical technique only if collinearity among the targets is significant; none was significant at the 5-per cent level.

4. If some target variables are unique and invariant functions of other target variables, then policy cannot operate on them independently. As a logical statement, this is of course true. We argued that employment depends on, among other things, lagged levels of aggregate demand, and Worswick's chart suggests that prices (both retail and GDP deflator) depend with lags on these variables. But care must be taken in weighing the consequences of this interdependence. First, functional interdependence between targets is one thing, *unique and invariant* dependence is another; the main point of the modern theory of economic policy, which assumes the former type of interdependence, is that enough independent instruments must be found if all targets are to be satisfied at once. Second, the objective of the Musgrave's statistical exercise was to determine how policy instruments had in fact been used, not to suggest that each policy variable could have been shifted regularly in a direction that was correct for all policy targets.

It is easy, especially if one is under no obligation to produce this pudding for the eating, to agree with both Matthews and Worswick that only an elaborate simulation exercise can show the full consequences of alternative versus actual policies. But does this judgment render retrospective attempts to uncover decision-rules that have been used in policy formation irrelevant?

Professor Matthews' concern seems to lie with the tactics of policy management in a world where the number of instruments is generally inadequate to cope with all competing targets. Perhaps a good deal of contention can be avoided by agreeing with him that every policy situation then becomes unique and no recipe universally applicable. For instance, if aggregate demand must be destabilized to attain external balance, should consumption (especially of durables) always bear the brunt? Not necessarily, but occasionally frustrating the plans of consumers may have less adverse consequences than frustrating those of business investors. (In this context, we regret giving Professor Matthews the impression that the broad approval we expressed of the average level of domestic demand sought in the mid-1960s was contingent on averaging in the restrictive episodes forced by the state of the balance of payments.)

Matthews suggests that the climate of operation of short-run policies has improved significantly for Britain since the 1967 devaluation, and that seems clearly the case. In line with our own plea for more quantitative information, I would also note the accretion of new research on the operation of the British economy and its policy instruments, expecially monetary policy. The responsiveness of advances to change in Bank Rate seems to be established, and recent research on bank portfolio behaviour has suggested that changes in the gilt-edged rate and limitations on advances are effective regulatory instruments but Special Deposits are not.[1] Likewise, recent research on income policy has complemented Smith's findings in the Brookings volume by employing a more elaborate procedure for detecting the effects of freeze and pause, securing similarly negative results. Indeed, there is danger that incomes policy may have perverse effects when pressure on the economy is only moderately heavy, in that a maximum norm for wage increases can easily become a minimum as well.[2] (Professor Phelps Brown's paper mentions the alternative of warning sectors striking inflationary bargains that the government will decline to finance the result and will force them to live with the consequences of their actions. I agree with him that, even if this threat were credible, it is hard to see how it could be brought to bear on particular sectors or industries.)

If one must live in an imperfect world, it is good to know how to minimize imperfection. Thus Matthews usefully raises the question of policy costs extracted by the historic level and fluctuation of aggregate demand in the form of foregone output and real growth. We shared his view about the relation between aggregate demand pressure and growth; slightly high and slightly low levels of demand pressure in the neighbourhood of full employment both have various advantages, all subject to diminishing returns; an optimum thus exists in principle, most difficult to measure but not obviously different from the target level that British policy apparently has sought.

Matthews registers scepticism that labour hoarding in the business cycle could impair growth. What is at issue in the first instance is efficiency: if labour was hoarded during the last recession, the chan-

---

[1] A. A. Walters, 'The Radcliffe Report – Ten Years After: A Survey of Empirical Evidence', in *Money in Britain, 1959–69*, ed. by D. R. Croome and H. G. Johnson (London, Oxford University Press, 1970).

[2] R. G. Lipsey and M. Parkin, 'Incomes Policy: An Appraisal', *Economica*, 36 (May 1970), pp. 115–38.

ces are reduced that in the current expansion workers will be most efficiently distributed among sectors of the economy. The effective capital-output ratio would thus be reduced. Whether this effect is important is an empirical question, and Matthews mentions interesting (negative) evidence that the standard deviation of employment growth rates across industries has not fallen in the high-employment post-war years.

Whether or not the level of aggregate demand has been such as to maximize the level of productivity is perhaps an interesting question, but one that the Brookings study did not weigh closely. Whether fluctuations in demand, creating uncertainty for the firm about future output levels, extract serious consequences for the growth rate is hard to determine without knowledge of their impact on the choice of technique. I would add two qualifications to Matthews' judgment on the minor significance of this effect on growth: (a) the answer depends on the width of the range of options in the choice of technique that is available and, as Posner suggests, this is not necessarily small; (b) perusal of Denison's figures suggests that elements of discretion in varying the rate of growth by more than a handful of hundredths of a percentage point are not easy to come by.

The hypothesis that allowing aggregate demand to proceed full steam ahead for a period would cause a significant increase in the rate of real growth per head enjoyed great vogue during the 1960s. Analytically this proposition is closely related to the hypothesis that the rapid growth of exports will prove favourable to productivity growth. This is because a necessity for both arguments is a mechanism for stimulating productivity growth by high or growing levels of demand. (The mechanism is not sufficient, however, for making faster growth compatible with financial balance.) Both Professor Matthews and Mr Posner make the point that the case against demand-led growth as a viable means of raising productivity advance remains unproved. This is true in at least two senses: (a) the social experiment has not been performed straight on (unless one counts runaway inflations in some developing nations); and (b) no statistical test has succeeded in isolating the causal link running from the growth of aggregate output (or exports, in the case of export-led growth) to the growth of output per unit of input from the link running the opposite direction. The Brookings study resisted the temptation to a lengthy detour through the relevant theoretical and empirical evidence, but we did feel that this evidence weighs quite heavily against the hypothesis.[1]

[1] I have considered it at greater length in 'Export-led Growth: the Short Run',

Given this dearth of hard quantitative evidence, Worswick's report of tests run by the NIESR on the export-led hypothesis holds considerable interest. Broadly speaking, they show the expected correlations between the growth of total output and output per head but very little connection between exports and output per head. Unfortunately no procedure is employed for distinguishing between the two hypotheses that predict positive correlations between these pairs of variables: demand-led or export-led growth, on the one hand, and the neo-classical hypothesis that rapid exogenous productivity growth will tend to cause the rapid expansion of output or exports. (Discrimination is possible either by inserting time lags or by taking the movement of prices into account.) Lacking this distinction, one would say that 'output-led growth' remains a possibility, but the NIESR's data seem inconsistent with the hypothesis of special virtue in the growth of exports.

FOREIGN TRADE AND THE BALANCE OF PAYMENTS

Mr. Worswick's chapter on 'Trade and Payments' presents some highly useful statistical research on questions of the foreign sector other than the export-led growth hypothesis – a happy response after he was taken aback by certain bold quantifications in Cooper's and Krause's chapters in *Britain's Economic Prospects*.

A factual question underlying most issues of external balance for Britain is: What really happened to her share of trade and the distribution of consumption and production between the domestic and international sectors? Our study concentrated on merchandise trade, especially manufactures; Worswick provides data for trade in goods and services. One wants to examine both sets of figures, but this enlargement is not without its own ambiguities. Services include net receipts of interest and dividends, largely the result of past capital flows. Furthermore, constant-value figures for the services sector are notably subject to hazard.

One proposition given stress in the Brookings study was that the slow growth of productive capacity (or potential output) in Britain must be considered as a factor explaining her declining share of world exports of manufactures. Worswick's analysis of short-period changes in the British trade share since 1950, while adding useful judgments about the shifting balance of forces, reveals scepticism

---

Growth, Induction, Trade: Essays in Honour of Sir Roy Harrod (Oxford, Clarendon Press, 1971).

about the significance of this factor except as a constraint on export 'availability' in times of high domestic demand. But we feel that the significance of slow growth in the nation's productive capacity is broader than this. One can, in a rough sense, view a country's share of manufactured exports as dependent on the position of the rest-of-world demand for exports and the level of the country's incremental costs. These costs will certainly be affected by the rate of domestic cost inflation, as Worswick stresses. But they will also be affected by the rates of growth of total and sectoral capacity. This is not just a matter of constrained availability during brief booms. Slow overall growth will fail to constrain the growth of export capacity and restrict the country's share of world exports only if special conditions are satisfied: 'tradables' and domestic goods in the UK would have to be perfect (long-run) substitutes in both production and consumption; or special combinations of the income-elasticities of home demand for imports and exportables and relative productivity growth rates in exportables and domestic goods would have to prevail.

One could certainly make use of supplementary tests to assess the effect of slow growth on export shares; e.g. the prices of exports should not be falling relative to home goods at times when this force is supposedly significant. But Worswick's tests of the export-led growth hypothesis do not directly illuminate this issue, which is one of the growth of capacity rather than the growth of demand. Krause's arguments might be taken to predict a negative association across industries between changes in domestic sales and changes in exports, but not between exports and total output.

This leaves for review the behaviour of imports, which present the same kind of puzzle in many different contexts. If slow growth constrains exports supply, it ought (via reciprocal demand) to constrain import demand as well. Why have imports grown relatively fast over such a long period? Why does the NIESR's import equation chronically underestimate them? Why is the one really puzzling feature of the British foreign-trade sector since the 1967 devaluation the failure of imports to show any significant price elasticity? One can appeal to a high income-elasticity of import demand, but this provides us with a definition rather than an answer. The market for UK imports clearly deserves more attention than it has received. The behaviour of imports of other than finished manufactures needs investigation in relation to the growth in the British economy's raw-material capacity, although the growth of manufactured imports since devaluation is even more puzzling. One helpful hint for explaining the behaviour of imports lies in the suggestion of some British observers that the unemployment rate today overstates the true level of unemployment, as compared with measured levels of a few years ago. If this is so, the relatively unchanged measured level for the period since 1967 corresponds to increased pressure of demand, and might account for bulging imports.

As Worswick's recapitulation of the British experience since devaluation shows, the devaluation and, on balance, other developments since 1967 have greatly relieved the balance-of-payments constraint on short-term financial policy. (This would appear more clearly if his calculations were in terms of foreign currency, appropriate for assessing the changing health of the balance of payments itself.) Britain's major policy problem of international economics is currently that of membership in the European Economic Community. Although a façade of political unity has been maintained in pressing the application for membership, it became clear during the 1970 General Election that the cracks in the façade are rather deep. The Brookings authors did not seek to reach a collective net judgment on the case for membership in the EEC; significant economic arguments exist both for and against it, and political questions weigh heavily. So far as the question for Britain is one of real welfare gains from lowering her own tariffs, EEC membership is (as Worswick notes) not the only approach. Other political routes exist for lowering both British and foreign tariffs, and one is surprised that alternatives such as a North Atlantic Free Trade Area have received so little official attention.

The recent White Paper[1] summarized by Worswick quantifies some of the costs of membership in the EEC. Although the White Paper unfortunately concentrates on implications for the UK's balance of payments rather than economic welfare, its data suggests that the welfare cost of the Common Agricultural Policy would be quite high when one totals the opportunity cost of the excess factors of production that would be sustained in the British agricultural sector and the expected net transfer payments to the Agricultural Fund. Also, a net loss of surplus to British consumers due to higher food prices would have to be set against the gain in consumers' surplus associated with the general elimination of tariffs between Britain and the EEC countries. As Worswick indicates, the size of the potential dynamic benefits – or costs – remains as uncertain as ever.

It is worth remembering that the effect of market enlargement on the

[1] *Britain and the European Communities: An Economic Assessment*, Cmnd. 4289 (London, HMSO, 1970).

costs and potential revenues of various groups of UK exporters are qualitatively similar to those resulting from the 1967 devaluation: devaluation raises potential unit net revenues for both exporters and import-competing producers; a customs union raises them for selected exporters and reduces them for selected import-competing producers. It becomes hard to believe that any golden opportunity for industrial salvation lies in tariff-free access to Continental markets or the threat of tariff-free competition by the Continent in the UK home market.

GROWTH AND EFFICIENCY

Certain central conclusions of the Brookings study might be summarized by saying that the potential gains in real growth from changes in demand management have been overestimated and the extent to which the attainable growth rate has been constrained by inefficiency underestimated. We ascribed revelatory force to neither proposition, but felt ourselves at some variance with the 'average opinion' that we detected in the past decade's discussion of economic policy in Britain. 'High-level opinion' reflected in the preceding papers, however, seems to be in agreement.

That the growth of the British economy might be seriously constrained by the efficiency of some of its principal sectors was a conclusion that we drew mainly from Denison's evidence on the particular sources of Britain's comparatively low level of efficiency and by qualitative inference from the types of inefficiency that seem most marked in British managerial and labour organization. The preceding papers elaborate on this point in several ways.

As Professor Matthews suggests, if a low rate of investment were due to a constraint on the supply of savings, rather than to the slow growth of other factors or to inefficiency in the planning and use of capital equipment, it ought to be reflected in a high rate of return. I am somewhat puzzled by Mr Posner's reference to investment incentives, the effectiveness of which was questioned by the Musgraves. Posner seems to say that any reduction in investment inducements would slow the rate of growth; this may be true, but the question is whether or not these incentives are set at the right level, and whether they are the most efficient instrument for the job. In this context I might note recent evidence suggesting a high interest-elasticity of investment in British manufacturing.[1] I do not see any inconsistency between the following propositions:

[1] A. G. Hines and G. Catephores, 'Investment in UK Manufacturing Industry

(a) Compared to other European industrial countries, the British capital stock after the war was relatively small and dominated by relatively old buildings and equipment (a hypothesis, this, not a firm conclusion):

(b) among British industries, those with relatively large initial capital stocks (again, of relatively old equipment) were subsequently the slower in raising capital per worker.

It may be true, as Matthews suggests, that our industry sample supporting this second conclusion was inappropriately dominated by water and electricity so that the conclusion falls on statistical grounds. But the calculation still seems a reasonable one in principle; even if the inter-industry variation in capital intensity at any one time predominantly reflects technical differences, this would seem to predict a zero rather than a negative correlation between initial levels and subsequent changes.

We are deeply indebted to Professor Phelps Brown for putting our conclusions about growth and efficiency into the perspective of a century's social and economic change, showing that retardation in Britain's relative growth of labour productivity appears to extend back nearly that far.[1] He also reminds us that some of the social patterns associated with slow growth are of long standing. These insights lead to important lessons for appraising policies to further economic growth, such as the relevance of the Swedish and German experience and the limitations on that of the United States. I would add, however, that their warning against simple 'economism' cannot be blown up into an *a priori* argument against policies that might undercut socially-based inefficiencies in the system.

Professor Phelps Brown's diagnosis concentrates on the social bases of two features of Britain's economy, the rate of capital formation and the organization and utilization of the labour force. His conclusion that capital intensity is as much the effect as the cause of high levels of efficiency and productivity, matches our own and conveys a powerful warning to proponents of policies that seek

---

1965–1967', prepared for Conference on Econometric Models of the UK Economy, Southampton University, April 1969.

[1] His paper is nicely complemented by Professor Matthews' long-run statistical investigation of the sources of British growth, 'Some Aspects of Post-War Growth in the British Economy in Relation to Historical Experience', reprinted in *Economic Growth in 20th Century Britain*, ed. by D. H. Aldcroft and P. Fearon (London, Macmillan & Co., 1969), pp. 80–100.

faster growth solely from incentives for capital-deepening (and neglect the complementarity of efficiency and the attainable rate of growth). I would only add two relatively technical qualifications to his discussion:

1. The consequences of a slight reduction of the observed marginal capital-output ratio are easy to underestimate unless one keeps in mind its nature as a ratio of the change in net output to the change in *one* input. Unless a full general equilibrium adjustment of all other input prices accompanies a slight fall in the ICOR, it can correspond to a large windfall increase in the rate of return on capital and hence to an increase in the induced rate of capital formation and thereby the level of net output per head.
2. Professor Phelps Brown's argument at several points depends disturbingly on the implicit assumption of a closed economy. Consider, for instance, the effect of a payroll tax on the relative prices of (physical) capital and labour. In an open economy changes in the prices of goods, and perhaps factors of production, are constrained by the linking of international commodity markets, and the force of a payroll tax may be channelled into changes in outputs and the redistribution of income, rather than to changes in the prices of capital goods and other commodities.

The ill effects of two-tier collective bargaining, trade-union fragmentation and a lack of enforceability in labour-management contracts are related both to their historic antecedents and to recent developments, notably the report of the Donovan Commission and the past year's outburst of wage inflation. He notes that union fragmentation, though diminishing, continues to provoke minor stoppages aimed at increasing or restoring skill or similar wage differentials. This problem is worsened by a sustained high level of aggregate demand, as are the dysfunctional consequences of federation bargaining. A recent investigation by Steuer and Gennard elaborates on our own findings about the efforts of US international corporations to avoid the more inefficient aspects of British industrial relations and the productivity of the heavier commitment by these firms of managerial talent to industrial relations.[1] Tending to eschew federation bargaining and apparently offering relatively firm resistance to trade-union restrictive practices, they nonetheless

[1] M. D. Steuer and John Gennard, 'Industrial Relations and Labour Utilization of Foreign Owned Firms in the United Kingdom', *The Multinational Enterprise* (London, George Allen and Unwin Ltd., 1971).

manage to incur smaller numbers of labour disputes, especially the disruptive minor stoppages that plague much of British industry.

Questions of efficiency and growth in the industrial and public sectors are taken up by Mr Posner. He seems to share with the Brookings study satisfaction with the main lines of recent UK industrial policy and doubts about potential gains from increasing seller concentration in British industrial markets. The recent wave of mergers in Britain has continued to reflect the enthusiasm that we criticized for selective increases in concentration; casual empiricism reveals little if any of the efficiency gains hoped from such amalgamations. (In parallel to the United States experience, many recent mergers comprise 'defensive' expansions into profitable or fast-growing markets by firms sited in industries lacking these virtues. Although the welfare significance of conglomerate expansion is not a settled question, it seems unlikely to prove large in any direction.)

The Brookings study noted some deficiencies in the allocation of research and development resources affecting both the private and public sectors. The inadequate use of engineers and applied scientists, we felt, reflected both an inappropriately low demand by British industry and a misallocation of resources within the educational sector. Posner echoes our pessimism over any further unscrambling of these factors. However, research in progress that has been reported to me[1] suggests that the rate of return to investment in the training of engineers in Britain is relatively low – a fact that would throw the emphasis toward the former explanation. I join Posner in welcoming recent moves to increase the market orientation of research and development in the UK public sector.

Posner's comments concerning our judgments on the allocation of resources in Britain's public sector pose some problems of interpretation. He provides a restatement, largely uncontroversial, of the principles that should govern public-expenditure decisions. He then notes that any misallocation would have involved violation of one or more of these principles, and concludes that major allocations in the public sector are about right. We found that some of them do not look right, on the basis of evidence cited concerning current and prospective opportunity costs, and this is not challenged explicitly. Again, as with our criticisms of macro-economic policy, it may be appropriate to stress that *ex post* failing of policy may be ascribed to many causes other than the incompetence of policy-making officials, and we have not pretended to provide an unique identification of their source.

[1] By Mr R. Layard, London School of Economics.

215

The Brookings study gave relatively little attention to the possibility of gains in growth or efficiency for the British economy through the greater use of planning. We had no desire to tangle with the ideological issues involved, and felt that the empirical evidence on its use in industrial democracies fails to point clearly one way or the other. As Posner indicates, there is no denying the case for 'indicative' planning, at least at an aggregative level, to make sure that micro decisions are based on the best available evidence on the general growth of the economy. On the other hand, if indicative planning is pressed in detail to the industry level, it raises specific threats in context of our general diagnosis of the ills of the British economy. Co-ordinated planning of the rate of expansion within an industry seems likely to encourage some of British industry's well-known undesirable traits: a tendency to favour the 'orderly' sharing of a market and a propensity to continue doing in the future what has been done in the past.

On the other hand, there is more to be said for other types of indicative intervention at the level of the individual industry. The Brookings study took an agnostic view of what could be accomplished by mutual problem-solving through the EDCs ('little Neddies') and free management-consultant services offered through the inquiries into efficiency and productivity undertaken by the National Board for Prices and Incomes. Casual evidence appearing since then suggests that a more favourable view might be in order. Likewise, a positive nod is deserved by Posner's suggestion of public attention to 'bottleneck' sectors that seem to reveal technical inefficiency or (neo-classical) increasing costs to an unreasonable degree.

8. Concluding Reflections

by Sir Alec Cairncross,
Chairman of the Conference

I

The Brookings Report covered a wider canvas than was appropriate to a short conference. It was necessary, therefore, to select the topics for discussion and narrow the focus so as to throw light on a single primary issue – the rate of growth of the British economy – to the neglect of other aspects of performance and policy. The discussion itself was too wide-ranging for any summary or concluding reflections to do justice to it; and all that I shall attempt is to single out some strands of thought that seemed worth emphasizing or pursuing.

It would be fair to say at the outset that no very novel ideas emerged either by way of explanation or recommendation: anyone seeking clear leads for action by an incoming government would have needed considerable ingenuity to detect them. What the discussion did do was to make it possible to take stock of the different aspects of policies aiming at faster growth.

The point of departure was the slower rate of growth in Britain than in other industrial countries, taking growth to refer to the efficiency with which given resources are employed, not to GNP or the volume of output, since this is affected by swings in the employment of resources or by variations in the rate at which the stock of resources happens to be increasing. But the difference between Britain and other countries, as Professor Phelps Brown insisted, is of long standing and is not peculiar to the post-war period. Industrial productivity has in fact grown faster in Britain over the past twenty years than in any previous period of comparable length and there is also some evidence of acceleration since the late 'fifties. What needs explanation is not just the continuing lag in British growth but a number of distinct phenomena.

1. First of all, there is the margin of difference between the United Kingdom and other countries, as measured over a span of years by the movement of indices of industrial productivity (net annual real product per operative, employee or occupied person). Over the past twenty years, industrial productivity in the United Kingdom has

217

improved by about 3 per cent per annum. This is close to the American rate over the same period but well below the rate in France and Germany (around 5 per cent) or even in Sweden (about 4 per cent).

2. There is also the degree of acceleration in comparison with earlier periods. If we start from the inter-war period, for example (or more precisely the years 1925–38), there appears to have been a slight *deceleration* in Sweden, a perceptible acceleration in the United Kingdom, a much more pronounced acceleration from the very low inter-war rate in the United States, and a still more marked acceleration in Germany from an almost negligible growth rate before the war. If we start from the 1950s and make comparisons with the 1960s there seems to have been a general acceleration over time in which the United Kingdom shared.

3. We have to look also at the comparative *levels* of industrial productivity, since differences in level may not only reflect ante-cedent differences in rate of growth but may react back on growth rates in a variety of ways (and not uniformly in one direction). The best available estimates suggest that industrial productivity is at least two and a half times as high in the United States as in the United Kingdom and that it is substantially higher in Sweden and somewhat higher in Germany. In absolute terms the margin of difference between the United Kingdom and the United States has continued to widen but without much change in the ratio of two and a half to one. In comparison with Sweden the ratio has become less favourable since the war and the post-war margin of advantage over Germany has progressively disappeared.

4. We also need to look at these comparisons in terms of the whole economy and not just industry. This tends to make British performance look worse in so far as there is now less scope for transfers within the economy out of agriculture and other sectors with a low output per head. On the other hand, as Professor Matthews reminded us, the British record seems to have been less satisfactory in industry in the post-war years than in, say, distribution and agriculture where productivity has risen comparatively steeply.

What we make of British performance depends, therefore, on the basis of comparison. It would be helpful if more comparisons could be undertaken, for different periods, and sector by sector, with the leading industrial countries on the Continent. It is unlikely that this would take away from the general impression of greater sluggish-ness in the British economy. But it might pin-point specific diver-

218

gences from the common trend and direct attention to the standards reached in countries not obviously better placed than Britain.

In looking for an explanation of slower growth we need to keep constantly in mind the limitations of the statistics. Some economists (e.g. Morgenstern) have been so impressed by the deficiencies of economic data that they have challenged our ability to measure with any accuracy the changes in productivity from year to year. Others, observing the symptoms of affluence in Britain, find it hard to reconcile the statistical data with the evidence of the naked eye. There are in any circumstances technical difficulties in making international comparisons or in making corrections over time for changes in the value of money, in capacity utilization, in the amount of overtime worked, and so on. But there seems no reason to question the broad picture that is now generally accepted of slow growth in Britain in comparison with most other industrial countries. The defects of any single set of figures are less striking than the self-consistency of the data. The trade statistics, for example, confirm all too plainly the shortcomings of British industry in comparison with its Continental competitors.

On the other hand, the differences are not so enormous that they are at once apparent to the most casual observer. If this were so, the explanation would probably also be obvious. But in fact most explanations follow lines that might be equally valid if applied to other countries. Suppose that the conference had met in Italy and had addressed itself (in the absence of statistics) to the question why economic growth in Italy was so disappointing. It is easy to imagine the ingenuity with which explanations would have been found in governmental mismanagement, inappropriate social attitudes, class differences, inadequate educational systems, and the rest of the catechism of British backwardness. There are few features of British economic life that could not be paralleled elsewhere, whether the factors are judged healthy or unhealthy from the limited point of view of economic growth. What is different is the mixture. Presumably the things that make against growth are more heavily concentrated here or the things that make for it have become more diluted.

It is, of course, possible to pick on some one economic variable that rises more slowly in Britain than elsewhere and represent it as the laggard element, *the* bottleneck in growth. This happens most commonly with investment. The British press still treats investment as if it were the moving force in the economy, when it fits the facts just as well to treat investment as a reflection of the behaviour of output. Indeed this is an understatement if investment is narrowed

219

(as often happens in comment on the British economy) to manufacturing investment. The gross stock of manufacturing capital increased half as fast again as the volume of manufacturing output between 1954 and 1969. The significant feature of the situation is not that investment grew slowly but that output grew still more slowly. The fact is that the whole economy is permeated by the comparative sluggishness reflected in the statistics of productivity. All the figures seem to move up more slowly in Britain: productivity, production, consumption, exports, imports, investment and any other significant aggregates. It is the totality that needs explanation, not some individual feature of it.

II

There were two distinct questions before the conference. What in the working of the British economy accounts for its sluggishness? And what can or should be done about it? If these questions proved to be unanswerable, the second was more unanswerable than the first. The conference was long on analysis but short on policy.

What was clear from the analytical part of the discussion is that we do not know for sure how the economy works and that it certainly does not work in the same way for long. The short-run relationships in the light of which stabilization policy takes shape are variable and imperfectly understood. The long-run relationships that should form the basis of growth policy seem to rest on social and political values at least as heavily as on economic variables. There is, moreover, no agreed theory of growth composing those relationships and providing the agenda for action aimed at accelerating growth. There are few historical examples in advanced industrial countries, as Mr McMahon pointed out, of acceleration under government auspices, as distinct from a sustained higher rate of growth. This is not to dispute that acceleration occurs, particularly in the early stages of industrialization, or that a change of gear may take place in special circumstances, as after a war. But few industrial countries would claim that they know the recipe and could devise policies to add one or two percentage points to their rate of growth. Any that do make such a claim might be asked to study the history of the National Plan.

The limitations of policy are not simply a reflection of ignorance or of the ineffectiveness of government action. They derive also from the way in which policy takes shape and the pressures that it reflects. At one stage in our discussions the Provost asked whether the British public really wanted growth very much and what price they would pay to get it. One answer to this is that they have returned governments that have promised faster growth or that have taken risks in the hope of promoting it. But this tells us very little about the state of mind of the public. All it tells us is that governments are over-confident and make large promises. They have their own reasons for wanting faster growth since it yields them a dividend in taxation and helps them to avoid embarrassing economies. Indeed, their eagerness is apt to overreach itself and oblige the economy to grow more slowly in the end.

What the government does in adopting expansionist policies has little or nothing to do with the strength of the public's desire for material growth *measured in terms of what it will give up in order to achieve it*. If the public is unaware that growth has its price and still more if it is led to believe that the government has a duty to use some magic wand for increasing GNP, it may only too readily unload responsibility for growth on the government. It can then have the double satisfaction of obstructing every kind of action calculated to produce growth and encouraging every act of policy which lack of growth must inevitably frustrate.

Similarly it is no answer to the Provost's question that individuals ask for higher wages or enter into productivity agreements: the exertion of bargaining strength is no measure of the urge towards material advancement. Nor is it an answer that in their corporate capacity people want more public expenditure on education, health, etc., and that this in turn must rest on faster growth. The fact that people dislike higher taxation may oblige them to grasp the other horn of the dilemma and acknowledge the need to make real incomes grow. But the grasp may be intellectual and half-hearted, and they may desist from the personal exertions and sacrifices that would be necessary in order to bring about such growth. The question is not whether people would like to have more income if it could be had for nothing but what they are prepared to put up with to get it.

III

We started by discussing the management of the economy in the short term, recognizing that the contribution that could be made by better management to long-term growth was a limited one. The relationship between demand management and growth is necessarily asymmetric, in the sense that while there may be little to be gained by increasing the pressure at or near full employment, it may be very wasteful to reduce pressure when there are already idle resources of all kinds. It is conceivable that if the pressure is sufficiently intense there may be an actual fall in output because productivity suffers (as has happened under conditions of hyper-inflation); but if the pressure is very weak this benefits neither output nor productivity.

Since the war there has never been a prolonged period of industrial stagnation in Britain nor one involving unemployment on any considerable scale. The economy ran close – some would say too close – to its economic potential throughout, and even the fluctuations associated with stop–go look no greater in retrospect than the fluctuations in other countries where growth was conspicuously faster. It was argued, therefore, that not a great deal could have been forfeited by errors of demand management. This view might have been challenged by out-and-out expansionists, hopeful that growth would respond favourably to an increase in pressure, but no exponent of their views was present. It was enough for the conference that efforts to add to output beyond a certain point, or even to maintain a steadier rate of expansion, are bound to come into collision with other objectives of policy and cannot be pursued regardless of the state of the balance of payments, inflation of incomes and prices, and so on. Economic management cannot give vent to a single-minded concentration on growth to the exclusion of all other considerations.

Even if it could, this would not necessarily involve operating continuously at the highest possible pressure. There are advantages as well as disadvantages in moderate fluctuations: a little uncertainty may help to keep inflation in check, for example. There are also advantages as well as disadvantages in operating with some margin of spare capacity. We simply do not know enough to say what fluctuations and what margin of spare capacity is best. What we do know is that stepping up the pressure of demand at or near full employment means *ipso facto* stepping up inflationary pressure, and that this can only be disregarded at the risk of having to effect an abrupt reduction in pressure if the inflation shows signs of getting out of hand or generating unsustainable tensions.

There are also technical obstacles to an improvement in demand management. A good deal of emphasis was laid on the fallibility of the available indices: the difficulty of reconciling one with another, the changing significance of a given figure for, say, unemployment, the revisions made after the uncorrected figures had formed the basis of policy decisions.

Two special problems were singled out. First there was the problem of disentangling the cycle and the trend. The recurrence of the cycle may look in retrospect inevitable, but at any point along the way no one can be sure whether in the absence of changes in policy the cyclical forces will assert themselves sufficiently strongly to arrest a strong expansionary or contractionary trend. Then there are the shifts or apparent shifts in relationships over time. How tightly do the key relationships in forecasting models fit together? If they were rigid, it would be sufficient to operate on any one variable and so affect all the others in a fixed and predictable way. But the jointing is loose and the relationships themselves never stay put (although it sometimes turns out that, after a few observations have suggested a major shift, later observations conform to the earlier relationship and the alarm proves – perhaps too late – to have been unnecessary).

These two problems are to some extent interconnected. If it is an object of policy to get rid of the cycle, the relationships that have to be established should be those likely to obtain in the absence of a cycle. But if all the available observations are themselves cyclical, this is no easy matter. We may investigate the behaviour of investment, for example, and observe how it responds to short-term cyclical changes in demand, interest rates, and so on. But this tells us very little about long-term influences on investment in a world free from cycles in activity. Similarly, we may think that we have discovered – in the form of Phillips curves – the relationship between demand pressures and wage changes. But if all that we have are observations over the cycle we may draw quite wrong conclusions about the way in which wages would behave at a sustained pressure involving a steady (or steadily rising) level of employment. The danger of basing policy on such wrong conclusions was frequently emphasized during the conference.

The technical problems are real enough. But they may be thought less than adequate to explain the prolonged ritual dance of the British economy around what David Worswick called 'the eccentric ellipse'. Why does this continue so long? The reason often given is the coincidence (which Lord Roberthall suggested was no coincidence) between the election cycle and the economic cycle. Governments have found it hard to check a boom, or useful to foster one, in an election year. Perhaps this does less than justice to the obscurities of the economic situation in such years: the picture that we have now of 1959 and 1964, for example, is very different from the picture that was current when the budgets of those years took shape. We must allow for the volatility of judgment on economic prospects when so little margin was allowed for error on either side of the unemployment/balance-of-payments equation. We must allow also for the influence of public opinion and the press, which were often remarkably unsophisticated in their assessment of the situation, and either impatient for expansionary action when unemployment was rising or complacent in the face of increasing pressure when concealed by lags in unemployment or the balance of payments. Above all, there was an underlying optimism that, next time round, expansion would not be allowed to proceed so fast or so far, and the competitive position would be gradually redressed without either a sustained reduction in pressure or a change in the external parity.

Looking forward, the conference recognized that one dilemma had given way to another. The problem of combining full employment with a satisfactory balance of payments was less acute; but the problem of reconciling full employment with reasonable price stability was more intractable. Demand pressures seemed to have remained relatively steady for a remarkably long time: there had been no marked change for three years if the unemployment figures were any guide. Cost pressures on the other hand had mounted, at first reflecting the forces released by devaluation and subsequently by world-wide inflationary influences and an escalation of wage claims that originated partly in these influences and partly in the domestic situation. If these years were anything to go by, there was no necessary gain, either in greater price stability or in a higher level of investment, from holding the pressure of demand at a constant level. But perhaps these years were not a fair test: the outcome would certainly have been different in the absence of devaluation and a world boom. Perhaps also the greater steadiness was deceptive, given the major shifts taking place within the total level of activity, e.g. between manufacturing and other elements in output. Pressure on the engineering industry, which occupied an important strategic position in the economy, had increased progressively and other industries had been affected indirectly by this pressure.

The question was asked, what was the pressure of demand at which the authorities should aim? It was not answered, partly because when there is a complex of objectives no single value need be given to any one of them. The nearest we got to an answer was Professor Matthews' suggestion that if the rate of growth in productivity was little affected by demand pressure it would be natural to move to the upper end of the spectrum of sustainable pressures. Why throw away output and acquiesce in more unemployment for no good long-term reason? But there are nearly always good short-term reasons on the other side: in present circumstances, the volume of external debt still outstanding, the signs of deterioration in the balance of trade, the explosive situation in the labour market. No doubt it was for these reasons that no strong view emerged that an immediate increase in pressure was desirable.

IV

When the conference turned briefly to long-term influences on growth, a number of theories were discussed, but none of them seemed to be strongly supported.

There were no takers for the doctrine of export-led growth. It was recognized that there is usually a close association between output and exports and that successful exporting countries tend to enjoy rapid long-term growth; but the line of causation would seem to run from output to exports rather than the other way round. It is not expanding exports so much as growing productivity that engenders confidence and gives rise to investment. In the British case the failure of exports to grow very much was quite consistent with the use of a fairly steady proportion of industrial capacity in supplying export markets because industrial output was also slow in growing. Had British exports held their share of world markets, the result in the absence of higher industrial productivity would have been the absorption of an impossible proportion of capacity on export work.

These arguments were qualified by recognition of the damping influence of an adverse trade balance. The issue was whether, independently of the protection afforded to an expansionary policy by a rise in exports sufficient to preserve external balance, a boom in exports did more for growth than a boom in any other element in demand. The general view was that it did not. This was true both of the expectations version of the theory and of the version attributing some special virtue to manufacturing. But an exception was made by Professor Cooper to cover less developed countries that were able to exploit some natural asset through exports and could develop more rapidly the faster these exports grew.

A second theory ran in terms of investment-led growth. Here, too, there was a good deal of scepticism. The theory is usually couched in terms of industrial investment although manufacturing industry accounts for not more than about a quarter of total investment. But in Britain, contrary to what is constantly said, manufacturing investment has not lagged behind output. It can also be shown that if all that happens is a general increase in investment the return

P

225

on that investment would have to be very high to produce the kind of increase in GNP necessary in order to make it worth while. For example, if we put industrial investment at 10 per cent of GNP, and the return on it at 20 per cent, a doubling of industrial investment would increase the rate of growth of GNP from, say, 3 per cent to 3.06 per cent and this could not conceivably expand the market enought to provide an *ex post* justification for the higher level of investment to those responsible for making it.

It is also difficult to treat a higher level of industrial investment as the key to higher productivity in Britain when the country is littered with expensive equipment of the most modern type that is simply not used at all: in the docks, in printing establishments, and in many other industries. The question that needs to be asked is not 'How could more investment be encouraged', but 'Why is it that more investment is not worth while?'

It is true that the analysis Mr Denison included in his study[1] indicated that 'per person employed, the United Kingdom had less enterprise capital in the form of structures and equipment than any of the other countries except Italy'. But this conclusion seems open to criticism since it is based on the view that 'old assets have little value and are therefore counted as little capital'. This view may be true of equipment but it is not true of structures, which in some important instances form the bulk of fixed capital. In Britain the volume of industrial capital that survived the war, much of it built in the war, was high relatively to most other European countries: so that a comparison which largely disregards survivals from the years before 1946 seems to call for further investigation.

A third line of thought ran in terms of enlargement of the market. This came up in consideration of the advantages likely to flow from membership of the Common Market. Most people would agree that since 'division of labour is limited by the size of the market' there would be some gains from greater specialization if Britain enjoyed the benefits of membership. But it would still be reasonable to doubt whether American levels of productivity would follow the creation of a European market as big as the American one. Not only would free trade confer benefits only to the extent that trade was genuinely freer but these benefits would not be spread evenly over the market. The dispersion of economic activity between different countries would certainly change and the forces making for concentration in the United Kingdom might be weakened rather than strengthened. The gains would not necessarily accrue to Britain.

[1] *Britain's Economic Prospects*, p. 272.

Professor Solow at one point threw out a convergence theory of growth implying that the neighbouring countries in Western Europe might expect to maintain broadly similar standards of living. This might be so under conditions of high mobility between them but it is not obvious, whatever static theory may say of the consequences of free trade, that we can rely on trade to bring about such a convergence in the world as we know it. It is still a little early to dismiss national policies and preferences as irrelevant to the standard of living attained in one industrial country compared with another; and the starting-point of the conference – the divergence in growth rates – is not easy to reconcile with a conclusion suggesting the inevitability of convergence.

V

This brings us to the sessions on trade. What was peculiar about the experience of the United Kingdom? How important in the record of economic growth are trade and the balance of payments? How has devaluation worked out?

Everybody agrees that Britain lost ground in foreign markets from the early 1950s onwards. But this did not throw the balance of payments into increasing deficit: the deficit on trade account, for example, was larger in proportion to GNP in 1948–9 than in 1967–8. David Worswick's charts hardly bear out the view that the trade balance was becoming progressively weaker all the time, unless the emphasis is put on volumes rather than values. In the 1950s the terms of trade improved just sufficiently to offset the divergence in volumes, but this ceased to be true in the 1960s, when the improvement in the terms of trade came to an end (a circumstance rarely emphasized). No doubt it can be argued that the really significant trend was the rise in the ratio of imports of manufactures to GNP, especially after 1958: a rise which, although paralleled in other countries, was not accompanied in Britain as it was elsewhere by an increasing ratio of exports of manufactures to GNP. It is also true that, particularly in the mid-1960s, the rises in costs and in the ratio of domestic to export prices were unmistakable indications of a weakening of competitive power. Nevertheless the behaviour of the trade balance as such was perhaps less significant than two other circumstances: the deterioration in the rest of the balance of payments (e.g. government expenditure abroad) and the failure to add to international reserves over the entire period when this ought to have been a prime aim of policy.

P* 227

Much of the discussion concentrated on the 'mystery' of some of the relationships governing trade: both the influence of price on volume, especially after devaluation, and the influence of income on demand, especially for imports. It is perhaps surprising to find British trade expanding year by year in such a close relationship with GNP when the competitive position was obviously changing and price elasticities are usually thought to be fairly high. One might reasonably expect a more sensitive response, in exports at least. There is also evidence of a remarkable insensitivity after devaluation in the demand for imports: in 1968 the volume of imports rose by 9 per cent in spite of a sharp rise in their price. This is not a change that could have been predicted on the basis of normal econometric equations for the relationship between imports, GNP and prices, Yet if one looks at the surplus of £500 million per annum in the balance on current account in the second half of 1969, and sees how closely it accords with forecasts at the time of devaluation, one is bound to reflect that the elasticities may be less important than the changes in demand and output which weigh both on exports and on imports and may have a more predictable effect on the balance between the two than on either taken separately.

Perhaps also economists are apt to misjudge the speed with which the economy reacts to devaluation. If so, this could be a serious matter. For the effect of devaluation is to pull apart domestic and foreign costs in order to allow adjustments in the allocation of resources. It is not easy to hold them apart for long, as is becoming only too apparent, so that there is a limited time in which to make the adjustments. The more slowly they occur the greater the danger of a fresh devaluation, a further boost to price inflation and an aggravation of the trade deficit. A sluggish economy may find devaluation making matters worse, while an economy with quicker responses but similar elasticities may have no need for anxiety.

When the discussion turned to the Common Market it was not possible to detect any strong note of confidence that if Britain were to join, this would have large and continuing advantages in the form of productivity gains. It is of course true, as Professor Duesenberry pointed out, that there is a deceptive simplicity about the agricultural arithmetic which makes the industrial arithmetic seem correspondingly speculative. Figures can be set down for the prospective addition to the cost of living because of higher food prices, but it is much harder to work out how particular industries, or industry as a whole, would stand to gain or lose.

The fact remains that the agricultural score shows a large debit

228

and there can be no certainty that industry would show a credit. Moreover the debit, however it may be limited during the transition period, could be very large at the end of it; and while British agriculture would undoubtedly expand, the expansion would be highly uneven – probably concentrated on wheat and beef – and would intensify the misallocation of resources by restricting still further the market for low-cost farm produce from sources outside the Common Market. Yet it is not easy to see what concessions the Community can make, except over the transition period, without revamping the Common Agricultural Policy. Probably, in due course, they will be obliged to undertake this in any event before the total financial burden becomes insupportable. In these circumstances, is it better to gamble on changes that are in the logic of the situation or wait for the logic to work through to the policy?

There was also a general disposition to wariness on the grounds that entry means an eventual surrender of freedom to manage the British economy. On this point, however, Lord Roberthall took the view that it was chimerical to expect a common monetary unit in Europe within the next decade, or any similar changes requiring a much closer integration than is yet in sight.

The main interest of the discussion was in the feeling expressed that the US might be on the verge of a major change of commercial policy. The flouting of GATT by various regional groupings, the lack of support offered by other countries to the US in her efforts to create a mechanism of adjustment in her balance of payments, and the increasing scale of competitive imports into the US, were all influences generating what Walter Heller called a 'critical mass' that might push her away from her previous liberal policies. In the circumstances the United Kingdom might want to take shelter in a more exposed and less expansionary world by joining the nearest regional group.

VI

Incomes policy occupied us much of the time, chiefly as a means of dealing with cost inflation. But although there were plenty of suggestions about ways in which we might proceed, they usually turned out to be ways along which the country had already proceeded and from which it was in the process of turning back.

The idea of using an agency like the National Board for Prices and Incomes as an educative instrument was not new, nor was the idea

229

of using it to certificate what Professor Duesenberry called 'outrages': unjustifiable increases in prices and incomes. No agency of this kind can function successfully when inflationary pressure is too high, nor when public opinion does not lend firm support, nor when the groups whose exercise of economic power is under scrutiny are impervious to public pressure. This does not mean that such an agency cannot be of any use. But it does mean that when most is expected of it, it is least likely to deliver the goods.

If cost inflation were no more than demand inflation in disguise there would be a simple means of controlling it. This is the view underlying an approach through Phillips curves with its implied trade-offs between more unemployment and greater price stability. If on the other hand cost inflation represented a quite arbitrary exercise of bargaining strength it might yield to persuasion and sweet reason, or if it did not it would probably be amenable to nothing less than compulsory arbitration or equally drastic changes in labour legislation. But there are other possibilities. Cost inflation is an almost inevitable concomitant of devaluation, of a wide gap between British and foreign costs, and of a rising level of costs in other industrial countries. If this is what we are suffering from, then perhaps we must grin and bear it until it has run its course. Again, if Professor Phelps Brown is right in laying emphasis on a consensus among employers that if a rise in wages is conceded prices can safely be allowed to rise because others will raise their prices too, we may ask whether the consensus is indestructible or would yield to some mild uncertainty about full employment.

Most of the discussion on cost inflation did not seem to be specifically about the United Kingdom. No one asked, for example, whether there is any greater proneness to cost inflation in the United Kingdom than elsewhere; but the answer would seem to be pretty certainly in the negative. Has unionization gone further in the United Kingdom? or public acceptance of inflation as a fact of life under conditions of full employment? We are still a long way short of South American conditions, although Lord Roberthall thought that we were heading rapidly in that direction.

In the past the sanctions by which wage claims were resisted were exercised by private employers. But these sanctions have become less effective and more costly. Men will be more willing to strike when they have built up reserves and can count on being supported out of public funds; on the other hand, employers are exposed to a heavier burden if they have to close down because of the increasing importance of overheads. Can the old sanctions be revived and strengthened

230

and can other sanctions be devised and made to stick? No one seemed very hopeful.

The situation originates, not so much in the greater strength of the unions as in the greater scarcity of labour, organized or unorganized. That scarcity is an objective of deliberate government policy, and the expectations of employers and employees alike are shaped by the knowledge that this is so. Only the government, it would seem, can exert the necessary pressure to offset the bargaining advantage that scarcity confers. But if it is to do so it may well have to take wider powers than it now possesses. What form those powers might take was not discussed, apart from Professor Phelps Brown's suggestion that a government representative might sit in on the bargaining process.

VII

When we moved on to labour and industrial policies it was natural to begin by asking whether slower growth in Britain could be more readily explained in micro-economic than in macro-economic terms. Are British industrial relations worse than in other countries, trade unions more fragmented, restrictive practices more prevalent, business managers less adequately trained? Nobody can say, because in spite of the vast literature on these subjects few international comparisons have been made and it is not easy to devise reliable tests. Many of those who took part in the discussion apologized for intervening at the level of the anecdote. Perhaps this is inevitable. But if it were possible to formulate hypotheses sufficiently sharply there ought to be scope for quantitative investigation.

It stands to reason that labour relations and industrial efficiency cannot be disentangled from the whole structure of the society in which work is done. A factory or office cannot be isolated from its social context. Relationships and attitudes in ordinary life are necessarily carried over into what goes on in industry. It may well be true, for example, that in the more relaxed atmosphere of Britain there is an attitude of live and let live in labour relations: more willingness to rest content with existing practice than there would be in other industrial countries, more complacency and unwillingness to have a row. If so, it would help to explain why there should be less of a head-of-steam behind industrial change.

There is of course no reason why, if the main explanation lies in this area, the difference in performance should yield to government policy. The social climate is not, as a rule, of the government's

231

making but something which in a democratic country conditions both the powers and the policies of government. Even when the government is in a position to decide on the industrial framework it has no control over the response to opportunities within the framework: for example, industry may be organized on a competitive footing, but this does not ensure that businesses will compete vigorously with one another.

There was some tendency to blame the British social system for slow economic growth. Managements were insufficiently professional, out of touch with modern science, drawn too exclusively from the ranks of 'practical men'. It was 'not done' to talk shop over lunch. Too small a proportion of the brightest and ablest young men were attracted to a business career, and, of those who were, too few were engineers. Workers, on the other hand, were 'bloodyminded' because they saw no prospect of advancement out of their class, and had no respect for the management. There was too little mobility in the system, whether industrial mobility or social.

It is difficult to put these sociological generalizations to the test. In some respects at least the British social climate seems as propitious as that in neighbouring countries such as France and Italy, however the comparison with the United States may look. But it may well be true that there is in Britain a less single-minded pursuit of cash gains or willingness to see contributions to growth highly rewarded.

Most of the points that were made related to one or other of three aspects of the process of growth: investment, learning and displacement.

1. *The investment process*

The social product of new investment is divided between different groups in the community, and the way in which it is divided must affect the incentive to invest. Some of the gain accrues to the consumer in a cheaper or better product; some accrues to the state in additional tax revenue; some is secured by the worker either in higher wages for similar work or in a relaxation of working conditions; and the balance (but only the balance) represents the net return to the investor in dividends and re-invested profits. There is no reason why the share-out should be the same in all countries. It certainly differs widely *within* a country between one form of investment and another. The worker, for example, is less likely to intercept some of the gain from the erection of a new power station than from the supercession within the same factory of old machinery by new. What it would be interesting to establish is how the proportion falling to the investor in a range of investments in Britain compares with the proportion in other countries.

How, for example, do the figures work out when American-type equipment is installed in a British factory? We are often told that it yields a smaller addition to output because of the difference in market conditions and hence in length of run. But is there in addition a drop in the financial return achieved because of the reluctance of workers to accept American manning ratios? Is this reluctance more widespread, or made to prevail over a wider area, in Britain than in other countries?

Investment may also be affected by the way in which managers do their sums. If they are irrational, they may, for example, rely too exclusively on arbitrary pay-off periods in judging whether new investment would be worth while. They may fail, through sloppiness of one kind or another, to discard old assets or entire parts of their business which hold out no genuine prospect of covering their costs, however broadly the return on them is interpreted. Is there any indication that British managers are less competent than others in this respect?

2. *The learning process*

Economic development is largely an educational process; but this does not imply that increased expenditure on formal education will yield dividends in faster growth. The educational system may create an aversion for business pursuits or it may encourage business propensities and skills. It is frequently alleged that the British educational system is not adapted to the requirements of a modern industrial state and that it divorces the learning process too sharply from subsequent career possibilities. Whether it is the educational system or the social climate that accounts for it, there has been in the past less willingness to contemplate a business career and less systematic preparation for one than in other countries. It would be a mistake to think that all this has changed because of the creation of two small Business Schools, but their creation is symptomatic of a change of attitude that may have large cumulative effects.

There remains a difference, not at the top level, but further down the line between the educational background of junior staff and foremen in this country and in the United States; and it is arguable that it is in its more broadly-based management team that American industry scores. If so, the cumulative effect of doubling the univer-

233

sity population in Britain by 1980 may be considerable, provided it is accepted from the start that it means a percolation of university graduates to a range of industrial work which they have so far spurned. When one man in four is a graduate it will no longer be possible to equate graduate employment with the professions and senior business appointments.

One cardinal weakness of British industry is the status of the engineer. As Professor Peck pointed out, the output of university-trained scientists in Britain is far higher than that of engineers, while in America the reverse is true. This must to some extent reflect undergraduate choice: in both countries many who take a degree in engineering do not enter industry or embark on an engineering career. But there is evidence also of an inadequate valuation in British industry of the services of fully-trained engineers. If design engineers were better paid, more young men would opt for an engineering training.

Another aspect of the learning process is the speed with which new technology is absorbed. This is perhaps the main determinant of the rate of growth and it is almost certainly slower in Britain than elsewhere. Work done by the National Institute on the diffusion of new processes, however, suggests that the British record is comparable with that of other countries. There is a paradox here that needs further investigation. It may be that what is true of a few major innovations is not true of the innumerable small improvements in technique that are far more representative of technological progress.

3. *The displacement process*

With given resources, progress can be made only by enhancing their productivity. This is likely to mean shifts in employment between industries and between firms. The most striking example of an industrial shift of this kind is the rundown of agriculture, with each industry sucking in manpower from a common pool. In Britain, however, this process is practically at an end. Inter-firm displacement requires some employers to surrender resources to other more efficient or more up-to-date employers. This was the process on which the nineteenth century relied in exalting competition as a desirable social force. But if one is thinking today of the diffusion of newer techniques, one has to look at factors other than competition influencing the alacrity with which firms take advantage of new knowledge and introduce new methods or products. In a world of big business and few bankruptcies, how does displacement take place today?

234

One answer that was given was by way of take-over or threat of take-over. In principle at least – but less commonly in practice – a take-over or merger can bring under more thrusting and successful management a wider range of assets and employ them to better advantage. Lord Roberthall pointed out that the fear of being taken over may have just as galvanic an effect as the fear of bankruptcy and may induce a management to tighten organisational slack and lend an ear to suggestions from the planning department that previously went unheard. But the cumulative effect of take-overs is very different from the cumulative effect of competition, which tends to dissolve, not create, large units.

This alone might make one ask whether the whole process of industrial change will become increasingly subject to central control and direction. There is already in Britain an increasing involvement of the state in the process, not just by way of general policy but in dealings with individual firms.

VIII

One last reflection. Mr Posner emphasized the virtues of open discussion and the need to find the best way of organizing debate before policy decisions are taken. There has been no lack of discussion in Britain of economic growth. Since the war we have had the Cripps working parties and Anglo–American productivity teams, NEDC, the 'little Neddies', NBPI, and innumerable attempts to organize discussion on the problems of productivity and economic growth. If the labour theory of value could be applied to this input of intellectual energy there would be nothing to complain of in the rate of growth. But it would seem instead that the volume of discussion is inversely proportionate to the resulting improvement. In the countries where growth is rapid there is no similar public debate on how it might be accelerated. Those who can apparently do, while those who cannot talk about it.

It seems to be characteristic of discussion in this country that it should be intermittent, lacking in follow-through, and not based on continuing professional enquiry. A debate starts up, work is done in various places and in various ways, and then the whole matter is allowed to drop. Professor Caves asked early in our discussion whether anything could be said about the favourable trends to which the Brookings Report drew attention. But, typically enough, there has been no study following up the Report.

From this point of view it would be reasonable to draw from our

235

discussions at the conference the conclusion that we badly need some way of sustaining discussion more systematically and at greater depth. It is impressive to compare the resources available in the United States – most conspicuously in the Brookings Institution – for continuous and comprehensive analysis of longer-term economic and social problems with the meagre resources available for this purpose in Britain. What resources are available are widely diffused and the few centres of research such as the National Institute do not compare in the range and calibre of their staff with Brookings. If we want to organize debate in Britain in a more satisfactory way we might well begin by seeking to build up an institution of comparable standing.

Appendix

Membership of the Conference

Chairman:

Sir Douglas Allen   Permanent Secretary, H.M. Treasury.
Oxford; Economic Adviser to H.M. Government (1961–4); Head of Government Economic Service (1964–9).

Provost of Ditchley:

H. V. Hodson   Formerly Editor of *The Sunday Times*, and sometime Fellow of All Souls College, Oxford.

Sir Douglas Allen   Permanent Secretary, H.M. Treasury.
C. A. Blyth   Deputy Director. National Institute of Economic and Social Research; Conference Rapporteur.
Professor E. H. Phelps Brown, M.B.E.   Professor of Economics of Labour at the University of London (1947–68).
The Hon. W. A. H. Godley   Deputy Director, Economic Section, H.M. Treasury (1967–70); Director designate, Department of Applied Economics, University of Cambridge.
Professor Harry Johnson   Professor of Economics, London School of Economics and University of Chicago.
Sir Donald MacDougall, C.B.E.   Head of Government Economic Service and Chief Economic Adviser to the Treasury.
Professor R. C. O. Matthews   Fellow of All Souls College, and Drummond Professor of Political Economy, Oxford University.
C. W. McMahon   An Adviser to the Governors, Bank of England.
M. V. Posner   Fellow and Director of Studies in Economics, Pembroke College, Cambridge; Economic Adviser to the Treasury (1967–9).
Professor W. B. Reddaway   Fellow of Clare College, and Professor ~~University~~ of Cambridge.
~~rman,~~ J. Henry Schroder, Wagg
~~der~~ Banking Corporation, New

under *Chairman* read :
~~Cairncross,~~ KCMG
~~St. Peters~~ College'

. Economic Adviser to H.M.
~~al,~~ Hertford College, Oxford

237

Britain's Economic Prospects Reconsidered

Sir Eric Roll, K.C.M.G., C.B.   Executive Director, S. G. Warburg
& Co. Ltd.; Director of the Bank of England; Permanent Under-
Secretary of State, Department of Economic Affairs (1964–6).

G. D. N. Worswick   Director, National Institute of Economic
and Social Research.

UNITED STATES

Professor R. E. Caves   Chairman, Department of Economics,
Harvard University.

Professor Richard N. Cooper   Professor of Economics, Yale
University; Deputy Assistant Secretary of State for International
Monetary Affairs (1965–6).

Professor E. F. Denison   The Brookings Institution.

Professor James S. Duesenberry   Professor of Economics, Harvard
University; Member of Council of Economic Advisers (1966–9).

Richard B. Goode   Director, Fiscal Affairs Department, International Monetary Fund.

Professor Walter W. Heller   Regent's Professor of Economics,
University of Minnesota; Chairman, Council of Economic
Advisers (1961–4).

Professor Lawrence B. Krause   The Brookings Institution.

Joseph A. Pechman   Director of Economic Studies, The
Brookings Institution.

Professor Merton J. Peck   Professor of Economics, Yale University and the Brookings Institution.

Walter S. Salant   The Brookings Institution.

Professor Warren L. Smith   Chairman, Department of Economics,
University of Michigan.

Professor Robert M. Solow   Professor of Economics, Massa-
chusetts Institute of Technology.

Professor Lloyd Ulman   Professor of Economics and Industrial
Relations, University of California at Berkeley.

THE DITCHLEY FOUNDATION

Members of the administrative staff:

Captain R. P. S. Grant, D.S.C., R.N.   Chief Administrative
Officer and Secretary.

Lt-Colonel B. C. Mallinson, M.B.E.   Bursar.

Miss Betty Francis   Personal Assistant to the Provost.

Index of Subjects

Agriculture, productivity in, 178
  rundown in, 30, 234
  and EEC, 93–5, 99, 186, 228–9
Aircraft industry, product development in, 198
  technological development in, 160
Amalgamations, see Mergers
Anglo-American Council on Productivity, 111, 235
Arbitration, in labour disputes, 128, 130–1, 230

Balance of payments, 14–18, 35, 45, 56, Ch. 3 *passim*, 138, 168, 170–1, 180 *et seq.*, 186
  see also Devaluation
Bank Rate, 207
Bloodymindedness, 116, 192–3, 232
Board of Trade, and mergers, 194
Brookings Institution, 9, 11, 236
Business schools, 89, 91, 120, 193, 233

Capacity utilization, see Demand, pressure of
Capital, account, in balance of payments, 45, 61, 86–7, 97–8
  output ratios, 25–8, 31 *et seq.*, 176, 208–9, 212–14
  per worker, 108–9, 176
  shortage, 31–2, 195
  stock, 176–7, 180, 213, 226
  see also Investment
Cash flow, influence on investment, 179
CBI, 140
Chicago School, 35
Close companies, 195
Coal, exhaustion of deposits, 113, 122, 161, 181
Collective bargaining, see 4 passim, 188, 214
Comet, 160
Commission for Industrial Relations, 128, 128
Common Agricultural Policy, 186–7, 211, 229

Common Market, 63, 92 *et seq.*, 181, 186–8, 211, 226, 228–9
Commonwealth and EEC, 187
Competition, and technological diffusion, 151, 234
  in home and foreign markets, 184
  see also Mergers
Computers, 150
Concorde, 160
Conglomerates, 197
Consensus, and movements in wages and prices, 174, 230
Consumption, fluctuations in, 17, 18, 54
Consumer durables, 29, 152, 206
Cost inflation, 71, 133 *et seq.*, 172, 177, 188–91, 229–31
Cycles in economic activity, 15, 29, 37, 47, 170, 178, 189

Deflation, 24, 42, 170–1
Demand management, Ch. 1 and 2 *passim*, 152–4, 168 *et seq.*, 200
Demand, pressure of, 19 *et seq.*, 168, 170–2, 175, 182, 184–5
  measures of, 172–3
  see also Growth, Productivity
Demarcation disputes, 123
Devaluation, 112, 137
  effects of after 1967, 60–1, 80 *et seq.*, 171, 173, 180 *et seq.*, 202–3, 210–1, 227–8
  speed of reaction to, 182–3, 228
  and shifts in use of resources, 183–4, 209
Diffusion of new technologies, 197
Discussion, need for more systematic, 236
Donovan Commission, 59 n., 127 *et seq.*, 214

Econometric models, 13, 149
Education, benefits of, 119
EEC, see Common Market
Elections, 9
  influence of, 170, 173, 190, 211, 228

241

Index of Names

244